Ashes to ASHES

Touring the West Indies with the
1991 Australian Cricket Team

Rod Nicholson and Tom Prior

To Dad on Fathers Day.

Adelaide 1st. September 1991.

from
Mike, Sue, Steven & Paul.
x x x x.

ANGUS
& ROBERTSON

An imprint of HarperCollins*Publishers*

Material appearing in italics throughout this publication is quoted from direct speech.

ANGUS & ROBERTSON
An imprint of HarperCollinsPublishers

First published in Australia in 1991 by
CollinsAngus&Robertson Publishers Pty Limited
(ACN 009 913 517)
A division of HarperCollins Publishers (Australia) Pty Limited
Unit 4, Eden Park Estate, 31 Waterloo Road, North Ryde
NSW 2113, Australia

HarperCollinsPublishers (New Zealand) Limited
31 View Road, Glenfield, Auckland 10, New Zealand

HarperCollinsPublishers Limited
77–85 Fulham Palace Road, London W6 8JB, United Kingdom

National Library of Australia
Cataloguing-in-Publication data:

Nicholson, Rod, 1950 –
    Ashes to ashes: touring the West Indies with the 1991
    Australian cricket team.

    ISBN 0 207 17296 X.

    1. Cricket — Tournaments — West Indies. 2. Cricket —
    Tournaments — Australia. 3. Test matches (Cricket). I.
    Prior, Tom, 1927 –   . II. Title.

796.35865

Photography by Gregg Porteous
Cover illustration by John Shakespeare
Printed in Australia by Griffin Press

5   4   3   2   1
95 94 93 92 91

CONTENTS

FOREWORD

A tour of the West Indies always grabs the imagination of cricket lovers who fancy watching two competitive teams in action on tropical islands in the sun, with rum and palm trees, calypso music and crystal waters to ease the pain of any disappointments. But the tour of 1991 promised even more: this was the showdown for the world cricket crown between two of the outstanding teams of recent years.

So my expectations were outrageously high for this trip. I was fully expecting the Australians to win the contest while seeing the islands for the first time, thus completing the world cricket circuit. The opportunity to catch up with friends of a couple of decades in their own environment also was an exciting prospect and will remain the highlight of the trip, having reminisced and shared a drink in convivial surroundings.

But nothing can hide the dismay of one of the nastiest of tours when goodwill and sportsmanship gave way to bitter confrontations and misconduct. This tour of bad blood was as distasteful as any in 20 years of writing the game, culminating in open warfare in Barbados and Antigua with the spice of Viv Richards snubbing his nose at West Indies officials after his unworthy public criticism of Australian coach Bob Simpson.

Cricket entered a danger zone during the tour when misconduct became the norm, virtually accepted by the professional cricketers, at the expense of traditional values. The events of the tour demand stern actions from world authorities. It was bitterly disappointing to leave the islands with a deep concern for the future instead of delight with the experience.

The cricket was excellent throughout the tour, from the one-day internationals to the Tests, with many memorable individual and team highlights, but the fun was noticeably absent. Opposing players rarely mingled, social events were attended only when necessary and the relaxed calypso country was ill at ease during an intense three months.

The greatest disappointment was the lack of incentive or ambition to return to the Caribbean (except to visit friends) when the tour thankfully ended. Maybe hopes were too high for the outcome of the title bout; certainly my dreams of the Caribbean were shattered by unacceptable on-field behaviour and off-field discrimination.

ROD NICHOLSON

INTRODUCTION

The sweet taste of emphatically retaining the Ashes was a tantalising entree to the showdown for the world cricket title against the West Indies ... but it turned to ashes in the mouth.

The 2-1 series loss to the world champions was the end of a dream for the Australians. It was a rude awakening for the supporters who have enjoyed an upsurge in the game in this country since Allan Border and the players made the fairytale trek to England in 1989 and returned with the Ashes with an historic 4-0 triumph.

There are no ticker tape parades for losers. Sport is a cruel leveller when winners stumble or run headlong into a superior opponent on a given day. So it is worth mentioning up front that the cricket season of 1990-91 is one of which the players, and the fans, should be proud. Lest we forget: Australia played ten Tests, won four, lost two and drew four and won 13 one-day internationals while losing only two. They retained the Ashes 3-0, inflicted the first home defeat of the West Indies (4-1) in a one-day series in the Caribbean, and ended the longest and toughest campaign in the game with the first Test defeat of the West Indies at Antigua.

The entire season must be put into perspective for it wasn't long ago when the public would drool at the prospect of Australia winning a Test or a one-day competition, let alone a series. The swiftness and decisiveness of Australia's improvement encouraged everyone to believe that the time was ripe to knock the West Indians off the perch they have claimed their own for the past 15 years.

The Australians were undisputed one-day champions, having won the 1987 World Cup and almost all intervening series, and the transfer of that success to the Test arena in two Ashes campaigns (4-0 and 3-0) left Australia with only one genuine Test ambition: to dethrone the West Indians. That was a tall order by any standard, considering the West Indians had beaten the Australians 3-0 in the Caribbean in 1984 and 3-1 in the two encounters in Australia in 1984-85 and 1988-89.

The recent results of 9-2 in 15 Tests was a reasonable indication of the relative strengths of the combatants during the 1980s. But at the beginning of the 1990s the battle was between the hardened veterans and a vastly improved challenger which had lost only one of 18 Tests, winning nine, since their last clashes.

WEST INDIES 1991 TOUR ITINERARY

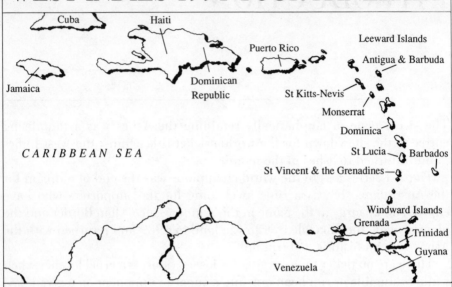

FEBRUARY

16-19	v President's XI	Warner Park, St Kitts
21-24	v Jamaica	Sabina Park
26	First One-day international	Sabina Park

MARCH

1-6	First Test (Jamaica)	Sabina Park
9	Second One-day international	Queens Park Oval
10	Third One-day international	Queens Park Oval
13	Fourth One-day international	Kensington Oval
15-17	v Trinidad & Tobago	Guaracara Park
17	v Trinidad & Tobago	Guaracara Park
20	Fifth One-day international	Bourda
23-28	Second Test (Guyana)	Bourda
30-2 April	v WI Under 23 XI	Arnos Vale, St.Vincent

APRIL

5-10	Third Test (Trinidad)	Queens Park Oval
13-16	v WI Board XI	Kensington Oval
19-24	Fourth Test (Barbados)	Kensington Oval
27-2 May	Fifth Test (Antigua)	Recreation Ground

The West Indians were not to be caught unawares like the 1989 Englishmen, who treated the Australian underdogs with scant respect until it was all too late. The Caribbean champions recently came back from being a Test down to draw the series in Pakistan, an exceptional achievement, and had no intention of surrendering the world title.

Viv Richards, who didn't tour Pakistan because of ill-health, was all too alert to the mounting momentum of the Australians. He was a young batsman fighting for his place in the West Indian team in 1975-76 when he confronted an Australian team led by Greg Chappell with an attack spearheaded by Dennis Lillee and Jeff Thomson. The cocky and aggressive Australians won that series 5-1 and Richards retains bitter memories of that hiding, often recalling it to give himself strength and to inspire his team-mates.

Richards hadn't lost a series since he took over the captaincy from Clive Lloyd in 1985 and he steeled himself for a potential nightmare as traumatic as that at the start of his illustrious career. 'When you have been beaten and beaten badly,' he explained before the series during a flit to St Kitts for the initial selection meeting, 'you do remember.'

It is important to me because I was a youngster and it helped to teach me what I had to do, and what I shouldn't do. You try to instil these things into the younger players who come along, on how hard it was to have a baptism of fire.

The younger players in our side now have been around long enough, and as captain and motivator, you must get it into their heads that losing is not very nice. We have come back against England and against Pakistan and whatever it takes to do these particular acts, the Houdini act, we still seem to have it. We are getting a bit old but this team has one more big punch — I am sure of that.

Smokin' Joe was ready and waiting, even if the team's premier paceman Ian Bishop wasn't. The dynamic speedster sustained a stress fracture of the back during the Pakistan tour and after 53 wickets in only 11 Tests, he was ordered to rest for the entire Caribbean circuit, eventually missing the tour of England to boot.

Equally, the Australians didn't underestimate the challenge, particularly the selectors and officials. The Australian Cricket Board appointed Lawrie Sawle as manager of the team to the West Indies even before a ball was bowled in the Ashes battle, such was the long-term planning for the important series. Sawle, the chairman of the national selection panel, was the esteemed manager for the 1989 English tour. A quietly spoken but forthright man with a passion for cricket, he has a clinical eye for detail and a belief that team commitment and unity is as essential to success as natural talent and toil.

Sawle worked tirelessly to pluck Australian cricket from the quicksand and re-establish it on a solid foundation; he recognised the magnitude of the task ahead as far back as October. His major concern was wear and tear on the players because of the hectic schedule of matches and travel. He pointed out that the Australians would play nine Tests, eight one-day internationals and several tour matches between Boxing Day and 2 May. 'Add to that the travel around Australia, the trip to the West Indies and the island hopping around the Caribbean and that's an awful lot of work. It is a potentially big problem because it may blunt the players' enthusiasm and effectiveness,' he warned.

The selectors kept this in mind during the summer campaign, particularly the one-day international series, and rotated the fast bowlers to allow individuals to rest, with Terry Alderman, Bruce Reid and Carl Rackemann taking turns as drinks waiter while Merv Hughes concentrated on first class matches. But even this friendly treatment couldn't prevent the seemingly inevitable wear and tear. The system cost Rackemann any chance of touring the Caribbean simply because he didn't play enough cricket during the summer. The big, broad-shouldered paceman was the victim of the 12th man blues, being the drinks waiter in the opening two Tests against England and in four of the six limited-over internationals. His lack of match fitness took its toll and he lost his place to Craig McDermott for the final two Tests and any chance of touring the Caribbean.

Because of injury Alderman (groin) and Reid (instep) missed the fourth and fifth Tests respectively. Dean Jones went on tour with a hairline fracture of the right forearm while Allan Border retained a groin complaint which forced him out of the finals of the one-day series against New Zealand.

There is considerable support for Sawle's concern that cricketers can become mentally as well as physically stale, perhaps unwilling victims of too much cricket at the highest level. A case can be made that players, particularly batsmen, suffered a subconscious drain because of the relentless demands of international cricket at Test and limited-over standard during such a hectic period.

David Boon could be a case in point. He collected 530 runs against England and 109 not out in the opening Test in the West Indies to boast 639 runs in 10 Test innings. But he managed only another 157 runs in his next eight Test innings. Geoff Marsh suffered a similar run starvation after scores of 81, 113 and 106 not out in the one-day internationals against the West Indies and 94 in his next Test innings. The dour right-hander mustered all his fighting spirit but managed only 63 runs in his next seven Test innings.

The important issue of programming must be addressed by Australian officials. A tour of the West Indies hot on the heels of an Ashes series is asking too much of even the most enthusiastic, fit and professional of teams. Almost seven months on the road, against their arch-enemy and the world champions, is an assignment seemingly destined to take a downward spiral. It may be coincidental, although I doubt it, that the two players who came into the Test team for the last fortnight of battle against England, Craig McDermott and Mark Waugh, were the two success stories of the West Indies tour. They were fit and fresh, eager and enthusiastic, right to the end of their 14 week assignment while others were feeling the pinch after double that time in the lion's den.

This is the era of the professional cricketer. The players demand to be handsomely paid, and rightly so. They are prepared to play for their pay and cannot argue when administrators add more games and more tours to balance the books. What must be considered, however, is the wellbeing of the players and the game. Too much cricket can be a catalyst for burn-out of the best players and a damning influence on performances and results. The flow-on from that is a lessening of public interest, attendance at matches and financial success.

But not one Australian cricketer worth his salt would have forfeited the opportunity to tour the West Indies for such a high-profile series. The quest for one of the 16 places began in earnest at the start of the Australian summer when the young brigade of batsmen (Tom Moody, Mark Waugh, Darren Lehmann, Jamie Siddons, Stuart Law and Jamie Cox), pacemen Damian Flemming, Paul Reiffel and Wayne Holdsworth, and young leg-spinners Adrian Tucker and Peter McIntyre went on display. They put pressure on the established Test players, along with a couple of veterans (Geoff Lawson, Mike Whitney, Chris Matthews and Trevor Hohns) who wouldn't be talked out of Test retirement despite leading Queensland.

The selectors eventually decided that a tough tour required tough and seasoned cricketers. Thus 16 players were chosen to accompany manager Lawrie Sawle, coach Bob Simpson and physiotherapist Errol Alcott on the Caribbean crusade.

AUSTRALIAN TOURING TEAM — TEST RECORDS

ALLAN BORDER (captain), born 27 July 1955. Played 120 Tests; 8982 runs at 53.14 with 23 centuries and 51 half-centuries. Against WI: 21 Tests, 1479 runs at 42.25.

GEOFF MARSH (vice-captain), born 31 December 1958. Played 41 Tests; 2443 runs at 34.90 with four centuries and 12 half-centuries. Against WI: 5 Tests, 227 runs at 22.70.

MARK TAYLOR, born 27 October 1964. Played 20 Tests; 1831 runs at 53.85 with six centuries and 10 half-centuries. Against WI: 2 Tests, 67 runs at 16.75.

DAVID BOON, born 29 December 1960. Played 53 Tests; 3716 runs at 42.22 with nine centuries and 17 half-centuries. Against WI: 8 Tests, 529 runs at 37.78.

DEAN JONES, born 24 March 1961. Played 39 Tests; 2800 runs at 48.27 with nine centuries and 10 half-centuries. Against WI: 5 Tests, 386 runs at 42.88.

MARK WAUGH, born 2 June 1965. Played two Tests; 187 runs at 62.33 with one century. Against WI: nil.

STEVE WAUGH, born 2 June 1965. Played 42 Tests; 2065 runs at 38.96 with three centuries and 13 half-centuries. Against WI: 5 Tests, 331 runs at 41.37.

IAN HEALY, born 4 April 1964. Played 26 Tests; 704 runs at 20.70 with two half-centuries, 79 catches and two stumpings. Against WI: 5 Tests, 138 runs at 17.25. 12 catches.

MIKE VELETTA, born 30 October 1963. Played eight Tests; 207 runs at 18.82. Against WI: 2 Tests; 71 runs at 17.75.

GREG MATTHEWS, born 15 December 1959. Played 26 Tests; 1384 runs at 41.93 with four centuries and six half-centuries; 46 wickets at 46.28. Against WI: 2 Tests, 21 runs at 5.25, two wickets at 38.50.

PETER TAYLOR, born 22 August 1958. Played 10 Tests; 383 runs with one half-century, 24 wickets at 36.28. Against WI: 2 Tests, 32 runs at 16 and 3 wickets at 71.

TERRY ALDERMAN, born 12 July 1956. Played 40 Tests; 169 wickets at 26.69 with five wickets in an innings 14 times. Against WI: 10 Tests, 25 wickets at 42.24.

MERV HUGHES, born 23 November 1961. Played 27 Tests; 103 wickets at 29.65 with five wickets in an innings five times. Against WI: 4 Tests, 14 wickets at 35.92.

BRUCE REID, born 14 March 1963. Played 22 Tests; 89 wickets at 25.48 with five wickets in an innings twice. Against WI: nil.

CRAIG McDERMOTT, born 14 April 1965. Played 26 Tests; 98 wickets at 31.58 with five wickets in an innings five times. Against WI: 4 Tests, 17 wickets at 30.82.

MIKE WHITNEY, born 24 February 1959. Played four Tests; 18 wickets at 29.55 with five wickets in an innings once. Against WI: 1 Test, 9 wickets at 16.55.

The touring party contained only four players who had ventured previously to the Caribbean — Border, Alderman, Jones and Matthews — and boasted only 76 Tests against the West Indians among the 16 tourists, 31 of those contributed by Border and Alderman with no other player in double figures. Experienced in some areas, yes, but equally naive in others regarding the West Indians and the journey around the Caribbean.

But the troupe set off from Sydney on Tuesday 12 February, the evening after the Benson & Hedges Awards dinner to congratulate them on the achievements of the season. The players collected $203 000 from the sponsorship during the season, with $119 000 coming from the Ashes success and $84 000 from the one-day competition. The evening provided an insight into the genuine mateship among the Australian players when Simon O'Donnell won the International Cricketer of the Year award. O'Donnell had missed selection for the tour despite his brilliant contribution to the one-day successes, and the players were delighted that he received a consolation for his all-round efforts. O'Donnell remained home but added another notch to his belt for the season when he led Victoria to victory in the final of the Sheffield Shield competition.

Spirits and ambitions were high as the players headed to London for an evening en route to the Caribbean. The return to the scene of the triumphs of 1989 jolted happy memories and engendered team spirit. Border and Marsh, the latter a West Australian farmer from Wandering who had never before seen snow, built a snowman in Hanover Square. If only the West Indians would melt so obligingly in their hands. They soon discovered that the Caribbean is fire and brimstone and that cricketers do most of the melting ...

FIRE AND BRIMSTONE:
WELCOME TO THE WINDIES

The initiation to the West Indies was a fiery one for the Australians who attended an unusual barbecue a couple of days after landing in St Kitts. This was not your typical shrimp-on-the-barbie gathering, although the locals of Basseterre could teach Paul Hogan a trick or two. The impromptu reception took place on centre-pitch after a tropical storm at the Warner Oval where the groundsman cum chef, Horatio Versailles, with help from the neighbouring prison inmates, set fire to the pitch!

The players watched in amazement as he poured petrol on the waterlogged batting area at one end of the pitch. This, Horatio said, had nothing to do with the Caribbean quick bowlers they were to encounter during the rest of their stay. The wry grin suggested he thought otherwise. He warned the players to step back as he nonchalantly put a flame to the petrol which instantly set the water-affected area on fire and sent black smoke billowing across the ground.

Drying the pitch, St Kitts style.

Australians are more accustomed to helicopters, super-soppers and modern equipment to dry damp areas, but the constant burning quickly evaporated all the moisture and after minor repairs the opening match of the tour resumed. The exercise was an outstanding success, although it is uncertain how long Horatio would need to grow new grass after setting the area alight on five occasions, narrowly avoiding setting fire to himself several times. Greg Matthews was on hand to take video for the team and the players shook their collective heads in amazement as the repeated burning process converted mud into a hard crust. An unusual beginning indeed to an adventure into the unknown for most of the touring party. As the series unfolded there were to be many more revelations, but none more entertaining than the fiery initiation to the Caribbean.

The opening week of any tour is important for many reasons but this time was vital for the Australians for psychological as well as form and fitness considerations. Border and Simpson, the two leaders and motivators, quickly set about dictating the positive attitude and approach which would be required to survive, let alone succeed, in this unforgiving campaign.

Viv Richards drops in to Basseterre for the selection meeting, and his first look at the Aussies.

The pre-match philosophies of both are worth recording to establish the policies they took with them on this venture. Border's emphasis was on the need for his charges to stand their ground against the West Indians in the psychological and physical warfare ahead. He wouldn't hear of talk of the 'superhuman' brigade which had dominated world cricket since he first played against them in 1978 and didn't want his players to be intimidated by reputations.

'The West Indians are a very good cricket team, but so are we. We are worthy challengers and we won't be overawed as many teams have been in the past,' he said as the team prepared for action at St Kitts. 'We know what to expect: plenty of short-pitched bowling and probably 12 overs an hour. But our attitude is that we mustn't let those things

11

worry us. We will just play our own game and they can play theirs and just maybe we can come out on top.'

Border deliberately concentrated on the abilities of the Australians and played down the reputation of the West Indians. Personal experience warned him that worrying too much about the opposition and their reputed superiority did nothing but undermine the confidence of his own players while providing the West Indians with an excellent psychological advantage. Border explained:

I remember when I came up against them in 1979-80 after the establishment and World Series united. They were considered superhuman: we dwelled on how quick the bowlers were, how good they were in the field and how quickly they could smash you around the park. I listened to that from the blokes who had played them for two years and even if half the time they were joking about it, you ended up going into a match not in the right frame of mind, really thinking they were superior, and it was just a matter of time before they got the better of you. When you got blitzed yourself you started to believe everything you heard about them was true. They played up this awesome respect and used it very well.

But Border wouldn't permit such thoughts within this team.

Look, this is still an awesome line-up and we still talk about their quality as individuals and as a team. But there is not the same aura that was there when I first started. We now believe that we can challenge them because we are positive and feel we have the talents to match them. This Australian side has been together and successful for a couple of years now and everyone has played against the West Indians. We feel we are ready and able to tackle them. We no longer are overawed. We have battled and scraped for a couple of years and then fought on to be successful and we are proud that we have reached this stage of being recognised as worthy challengers. We are ready and maybe it is time they started wondering about us instead of it being the other way.

The bottom line is that we are in the West Indies to win and we expect to acquit ourselves extremely well. The players appreciate that this is a real contest and they know that they have to lift because they might have been cruising throughout last summer. I expect them to respond to this challenge in a positive manner. We respect the West Indians but we won't be treating them as superhuman. We believe we can combat them.

Simpson took a similar tack at a team meeting only hours after the team arrived in the Caribbean and was delighted that the party wanted to adopt the same aggressive attitude against the West Indians as they did against England in 1989. He commented:

We appreciate that this is a tough tour and we have talked about the difficulties and the best way to overcome them. The players have been told to give total concentration to the games and not be distracted by the inconveniences. There are plenty of them because you must play in six different nations which means island hopping and going through Customs every time, hold-ups at airports and all sorts of other frustrating little things which can begin to bottle up inside. We have talked about that and the volatile crowds and all sorts of things and have steeled ourselves not to be sidetracked. And we have talked generally about the way we want to play the game. We must be positive and use the same approach as we did in England in 1989 when we made things happen to our advantage. We greatly respect the West Indians but we won't be overawed by them. We know we will have four fast bowlers coming at us all the time but that is the way it is here so we talked about the mental toughness required. We just have to maximise our skills, the same skills which got the players into Test cricket and here in the first place. There is a real feeling of unity and commitment among the boys, just as there was in England in 1989. They badly want to win this series and they are prepared to give everything they have to come out on top. You can't ask for more than that.

What the Australians did ask for was an agreement to have 90 overs bowled in a day in the Tests, having conceded that a new ball would be

Warner Oval, St Kitts. The first match of the tour.

available after 75 overs. The new ball tour regulation was logical enough given the torture a ball suffers on the usually tough terrain. Besides, the laws of cricket allowed it instead of the usual 85-over benchmark.

What they received in regard to the 90 overs in a day was too little, too late, and the players suffered throughout the tour because of an agreement which allowed the West Indians to dictate the pace of play to their advantage. The Australian Cricket Board and the West Indian authorities negotiated the agreement but it was not finalised until the Australians were in the Caribbean. The decision meant that only darkness would prevent 90 overs being bowled in a day, which, on the surface, seemed acceptable.

But manager Sawle was left to fine tune the agreement and naturally he had no chance as one voice against many once on West Indies turf. The Australians wanted an amendment to the 90-over rule for the Tests because they felt that the team bowling first could dictate the pace of the game and make the side bowling second pay the penalty for an early slow over rate. This, of course, happened repeatedly throughout the tour and on other occasions the spirit of the agreement was ridiculed with 50 overs being bowled by tea and darkness descending before the bowlers could complete the 40 overs required in the final session, which, inevitably, stretched almost an hour beyond the scheduled stumps time.

The Australian approach was to bowl the 90 overs in a day at a rate resembling 15 overs an hour, but West Indian chairman of selectors Jackie Hendricks and skipper Viv Richards conceded immediately that the West Indians wouldn't bowl many more than 12 overs an hour because of their four-pronged pace attack.

Sawle was disappointed at the time and grew increasingly frustrated as the tour progressed when the spirit of the regulation was ignored. 'We feel it is inequitable that the team bowling second, having done nothing wrong, should make up for the lack of overs bowled by the opposition,' Sawle stated at the outset of the tour.

We feel that if a team is dismissed, the team bowling second should have to bowl only an over every four minutes until stumps. What we would like to see is the 90-over rule, for which we have pushed strongly, with no deductions for drinks breaks and dismissals. That is how we have it in Australia and that is acceptable. But we are concerned that the spirit of the rule won't necessarily be applied and that the Australians will be made to suffer for slackness on behalf of the West Indian bowlers. We think that both teams should aim for 15 overs an hour. Not for one team to bowl 12 overs an hour and then the other to have to bowl 21 overs an hour to ensure 90 overs are bowled in a day.

How right he proved to be, unfortunately.

The Australians experienced the difficulties of playing Caribbean-style in the opening match when the President's XI still had 27 overs to bowl in the last hour of the match, despite the heavy workload of leg-spinner Robert Haynes and gentle medium-pacer Phil Simmons, who between them bowled 44 of 79 overs in the day. Prolonged delays throughout much of the day upset Border and century-maker Mark Taylor but no sooner had Australia's victory aspirations abated and the local side's expectations sparked than the over-rate turned to quick-step.

The opening match suggested the 90-over regulation would not be played in the right spirit, only as a tactical manipulation. What made all this doubly distasteful was that there were no financial penalties in the Tests, as there are in Australia, so officials were powerless to react to blatant time wasting.

Time wasting was not possible for the Australians when they rose at 5.00 am on 16 February for a stroll along the beach in front of the Sun 'n' Sand beach village, followed by breakfast and a 20 minute drive through the cane fields of idyllic St Kitts to Warner Oval for the first volleys of the tour. The ground, with the local prison wall providing one side of the boundary, presented a panoramic view over the taller steeples and spires of the capital of Basseterre and beyond to the port and nearby Nevis. A handful of spectators gathered under trees, some ferrying their way from Nevis, while the scent of spicy barbecued chicken wafted enticingly throughout the day. Cricket-starved fans grasped bottles of Carib beer or potent local rum while a steel band beat an irresistible beat. And the sun beat down and cricket in the Caribbean commenced.

The opening match against the President's XI ended in a draw, though not before providing several blessings to counteract the disruptions of illnesses to Simpson and veteran paceman Terry Alderman. Simpson suffered a blood disorder which worsened daily, eventually forcing him to stay at the team hotel with his grossly infected right leg in the air. His absence was a setback although Border took over the training routines with vigorous disciplinary drive, suggesting that one day he could step comfortably from captain to coach. Alderman contracted a virus which likewise sidelined him for several weeks, initially stopping him in his tracks at the start of his tour, which disrupted the team plans. He bowled 17 overs in the first innings and ran back to the team hotel on the second evening to loosen stiffening muscles, only to collapse with fever the following day. He lost considerable weight and spent several weeks as a conspicuous pale-face in the land of sun-bronzed bodies.

Left-arm paceman Mike Whitney seized an unexpected opportunity to play in the opening match — the selectors rested McDermott and Reid — with a haul of 5 for 114 off 32 overs in the first innings of 332. His swing and slant caused all the batsmen considerable concern and his stamina,

15

given the lack of acclimatisation and the hot and humid conditions, was outstanding. Merv Hughes warmed to his task in the absence of Alderman in the second innings to capture 5 for 36 off 11.5 overs to give him 9 for 116 for the match; he and Whitney formed a lively combination, taking 15 of the 20 wickets between them. Whitney's dismissal in both innings of aggressive opener Phil Simmons, who was to be in action in the one-day internationals, was interesting while spinner Peter Taylor also provided food for thought when he bowled Test batting dynamo Richie Richardson in both innings. Richardson, who took 58 minutes to break his duck in the first effort before scoring 14, was out for only 8 in the second innings; he seemed distinctly uncomfortable against the off-spinner.

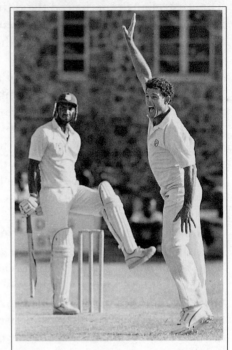

Whitney starts the tour in fine form, with ball and voice.

The Australian batsmen struggled in the first innings against a pace attack of Patrick Patterson, Tony Gray and Ken Benjamin and leg-spin of Robert Haynes. Many of the players were afflicted by a virus — Border batting at number seven because of the complaint — and Boon and Border were victims of questionable decisions, while Mike Veletta was run out while attempting to avoid an umpire. But Steve Waugh batted brilliantly for an unbeaten 96, being stranded shy of a deserved century because Alderman was back at the team hotel, overcome with the virus. The innings was full of merit and his attitude was impressive, leaving no doubt that he wanted to regain a place in the Test team after losing his spot to twin Mark for the final two Tests of the Ashes contest. He looked every bit a veteran of 42 Tests and handled the pace of Patterson and Gray with deliberate aggression and style. His efforts carried the Australians to 233, a deficit of 99, but after Hughes ravaged the President's XI for 147 in the second innings, the Australians needed only 247 for victory off 82 overs.

Mark Taylor's century was the highlight of a final day which ensured that all the Australians quickly discovered the difficulties of playing in the Caribbean. Taylor was stirred into action by constant jibes from the crowd, delays in play and clashes with Richardson. But he showed a grand

Border, run out, signals to the crowd.

temperament to register the first century on tour, even if the tactics frustrated and annoyed him. He received a succession of short-pitched deliveries in gloomy conditions just before lunch; during that time he absorbed a tirade of on-field comments and chants from the small crowd for physical intimidation. The heckles from the crowd annoyed him sufficiently to prompt a verbal reply and he went out of his way to confront Richardson who persisted in belated field placings. When Richardson began moving the fieldsmen when the bowlers were running in, Taylor walked 20 metres to remonstrate and protest.

Border also reacted, giving the crowd a one-finger salute as he left the field after being run out. It was more in friendly rivalry than anger but it showed that Border wasn't prepared to allow West Indian crowds to intimidate him. No doubt he was annoyed for Taylor, who was extremely upset by the tactics and crowd behaviour as he rested in the dressing rooms during the luncheon interval. He eventually faced only 185 deliveries in four hours before being caught, at which point the Australians abandoned the victory chase, eventually finishing at 7 for 204.

The team experienced the rigours of island hopping for the first time when dawn broke the following day. The caravan left the Sun 'n' Sand behind at 5.15 am for a final trek along the narrow winding road through the cane fields to the airport, leaving behind the magnificent views of expansive waters along the coast. Here began the unloading of luggage, security checks, passport collection, payment of departure tax, and seat allocation, followed by the inevitable wait for the 8.45 am flight. Bruce Reid, Merv Hughes and Craig McDermott spread themselves across uncomfortable plastic seats while the rest wiped weary eyes for a final look at the tiny island before heading to the biggest of them all, the mountainous island of Jamaica. The flight diverted via San Juan, Puerto Rico, before arriving in Kingston. The contrast was stark and immediate: from the tiny, scenic and friendly island to the massive, ugly, overcrowded and unwelcome heave of a major city.

Australia's pre-tour stategies were shot down without warning within hours of arriving after the six hour journey. The players booked into what was to prove a pleasant confinement at the Pegasus Hotel on Knutsford Boulevard where the open air dining and bar area beside the pool and tennis courts gave relief from the hustle of the neighbourhood, the road reconstructions and the drab trip past the local high-security prison to the ground.

'Back' is a four-letter word to Bruce Reid and it was the word which set off warning sirens around Sabina Park within half an hour of a training session soon after the team's arrival in Kingston. The beanstalk left-armer, envisaged as the major strike bowler for the tour, complained of stiffness of the lower back in the area where he underwent major surgery in 1988, forcing him out of the game for 18 months. Dismay descended on the Australian camp as swiftly as the setting sun in these parts as Reid, team physiotherapist Errol Alcott and manager Sawle sought help.

They telephoned Perth specialist Phillip Hardcastle for recommendations and eventually concurred that Reid's problems were caused by hours of sitting on cramped planes during the previous fortnight. Alcott strapped Reid's back for the remaining flights of the tour and while the pain subsided, the mental trauma seemingly haunted him for the duration of the trip. Reid, a man of unquestionable courage, explained his mental anguish at the time, declaring he wasn't a wimp who surrendered to the slightest hint of pain. 'I was spooked,' he admitted. 'After all the operations and work to come back, and with the prospect of everything going down the drain, I would have been stupid not to be worried.'

The spasms near the damaged area, where he had two discs fused and a metal plate inserted, forced him to miss the four day match against the poorly performing Jamaica combination. But he showed his determination by bouncing back on several occasions during the series, although never regaining the form which provided him with 27 wickets in four Ashes Tests against England. He seemed dogged by a psychological handicap which prevented him from fully exerting himself; whenever that hurdle was behind him, his rhythm deserted him. To his credit he forced his way through the pain and psychological barriers within a week to play in the opening one-day international. But that first breakdown really was the beginning of the end of Reid and Australia's major hope of skittling the West Indies during the tour.

If Reid's back ailment wasn't enough, the alarm bells were ringing during the match against Jamaica when Craig McDermott was rushed to hospital after being felled during a short-pitched barrage from West Indian paceman Courtney Walsh. McDermott required nine stitches to a deep cut above the right eye, which immediately blackened and closed.

Craig McDermott is helped by Errol Alcott after being hit by a Courtney Walsh bouncer at Sabina Park.

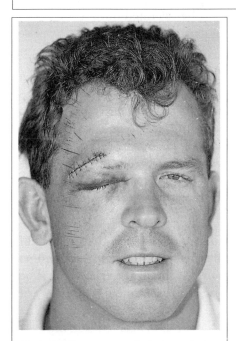

Craig McDermott needed nine stitches above his blackened, closed right eye after encountering a Walsh bouncer.

McDermott attempted to hook a delivery from Walsh and missed the thunderbolt which penetrated the grille of his helmet. He collapsed on the pitch, groggily clasping his face as blood reddened the front and back of his shirt. McDermott showed great courage to return to action for the one-day international and all other major matches, but he never recovered his composure against the short-pitched bowling which incessantly came his way from that moment. The incident was part of an avalanche of bouncers by Walsh, who earlier set his sights unsuccessfully on Dean Jones before striking Mark Waugh on the helmet, forcing him to temporarily retire hurt before returning to score a superb century.

The short-pitched bowling spree earned Walsh an official warning from umpires Anthony Gaynor and Lyndon Bell and a general blast from Border. He reeled off ten bouncers in three overs to Jones and eventually received an official warning for intimidatory bowling when he sent down four bouncers in six deliveries, including the one which felled McDermott. Umpires Gaynor (a police inspector) and Bell (an assistant superintendent) acted competently but unfortunately were not on the Test umpiring panel and did not umpire again.

Border quickly condemned the excessive use of short-pitched bowling which he said 'kills the game and can kill a player', while praising the local umpires. 'I hope it is a sign that repetitive short-pitched bowling won't be tolerated during this series,' he said. Border was critical of Walsh's actions and said he wasn't surprised that Walsh was warned.

'Climbing the step-ladder': Ian Healy evades a bouncer.

> *Craig is a number nine batsman and he was out there for about half an hour and he received about 15 to 17 bouncers. That is a lot to any batsman. I haven't seen anyone warned before and maybe it is a good sign that the umpires are going to be tough on excessive short-pitched bowling. I think the warning was fair enough. I don't mind if he bowls bouncers but he should spread them out, throw some deliveries up and try to get the bloke out. Short-pitched bowling is part of the game and a bit of a concern because you know you are likely to get hit. Craig has joined the ranks of the batsmen who have been pinned.*

Walsh said after the match that he was disappointed with the warning but suggested the Australians could expect little respite from similar treatment during the Test series. As it transpired, the West Indians restricted the short-pitched bowling on unresponsive pitches and performed brilliantly with line-and-length strategy.

The injury to McDermott compounded Australia's problems on the eve of the opening one-day international with Reid (back problems) and Alderman (suffering from a virus) under-prepared; Hughes was struggling with a stomach upset and Steve Waugh was in considerable discomfort with a tooth

Dean Jones in protective gear prepares for the Windies speed attack.

abscess. Simpson also hadn't greatly improved after a week of struggle against the blood disorder and he was unable to attend training or the Jamaica match. The encouraging news however was the form of the players who earned a rest day by thrashing Jamaica in three days by an innings and 137 runs.

The bonuses came thick and fast. First there was Whitney, who was a last minute replacement for the injured Reid. He captured 6 for 42 off 20 overs in the first innings of 158 to add to his haul of 5 for 114 in the first innings at St Kitts. The rewards were deserved for the veteran who came back from two years of bitter disappointments. He captured 7 for 89 and 2 for 60 against the West Indians in Adelaide only to miss selection on the tour of England a fortnight later. The return to favour for this tour gave him special incentive; not even the injury to Reid could dampen his spirits as a return to international honours loomed. Whitney said:

I want to get into the team because of my ability and my performance, not because people are injured. It has been in the back of my mind that in 1981 I was called up in England because Geoff Lawson and Rodney Hogg were injured and that I played against the Kiwis when Merv Hughes and Bruce Reid were injured and against the West Indies in Adelaide when Terry Alderman was hurt. It would be nice to think that this time I've done it on performance if I win a place and not because others are injured.

Whitney's attitude was admirable and his competitiveness exemplary. He would be one of the first chosen as a team-mate and there are few who show as much unbridled joy and satisfaction when representing their country. The effort in the opening two matches, particularly against Jamaica, was timely and encouraging for a team sorely in need of an energetic and fit fast bowler.

Centuries by David Boon (105 off 256 balls) and Mark Waugh (108 off only 148 balls) provided the backbone of an Australian response of 469, a lead of 311. Greg Matthews continued his impressive latter-order batting with an unbeaten 95 while Dean Jones (33) shaped well in his first hit since recovering from a hairline fracture of the right forearm and Border looked confident with 43.

The Australians piled on 326 runs during the second day despite the short-pitched bowling from Walsh, with Boon and Border sharing a 107 run union and Mark Waugh and Matthews adding 159 for the seventh wicket. The going was not easy with Walsh accompanied by an impressive but raw paceman, Rohan Taylor, who is a huge man with a style similar to former Australian paceman Alan 'Froggy' Thompson. The Australians rated him highly for his stamina and relentless speed. Marsh, ever alert, noticed him the moment he went to the crease in the first innings as the last man in. 'I wonder if he is an offie or a leggie?'

Mark Waugh, retired hurt after he too was hit by bouncer, returned to make a century.

he asked Taylor and Boon. There is no doubting the fast bowlers in the Caribbean: they are all giants with the notable exception of Malcolm Marshall.

The Australians skittled the locals for 174 in the second innings with Matthews completing a fine all-round display. He captured 4 for 57 off 20 overs to add to his unbeaten 95, continuing his spree of the Ashes series when he scored 353 runs at an average of 70.60. But the bonus was his ability to capture wickets with his off-breaks, his genuine value to the team, having captured only seven wickets in the Ashes contests. Border was happy enough with the performance, although he would have preferred a slightly harder contest with the one-day internationals to follow.

THE ONE-DAY MATCHES: AUSTRALIA'S SWEET SUCCESS

FIRST MATCH

Australia inflicted the West Indies' first home defeat in 17 one-day internationals during the past five years with an inspiring 35 run win at Sabina Park. The victory was typical of the recently irresistible Australian formula: Dean Jones leading the charge in a solid batting display followed by tight, unflappable bowling supported by snappy fielding.

The Australians amassed 4 for 244 with Jones unconquered on 88 off only 98 deliveries. That was enough to upstage the highly fancied West Indians who were dismissed for 209 with 25 deliveries remaining.

The former world champions retained a chance of victory when Gus Logie (65) and Richie Richardson (64) shared a 95 run fourth wicket partnership in only 15 overs, and despite chasing eight runs an over for the final 13, the pair had Australia on the defensive. But the experienced bowlers struck back to capture the last six wickets for only 19 runs off 25 deliveries to curtail any potential heroics. The Australians kept their cool while the West Indians appeared to panic, with batsmen lashing out indiscriminately.

The Australians, with eight of nine limited-over victories to their credit during the domestic season, won the toss and batted first as is their preference. They fashioned a defensible total in typically unflustered style. Jones and Mark Waugh produced the explosive batting in a fourth wicket partnership of 136 in 78 minutes. Waugh, fresh from his century against Jamaica, blasted 67 off only 61 deliveries during the third highest partnership by Australians against the West Indies. The union was not as productive but no less exciting than the 150 by Border and Kim Hughes at St Lucia in 1984 and the unfinished 147 between Hughes and Bruce Laird at the SCG in 1981.

Jones and Waugh capitalised on the steady foundation of 59 laid by Boon (34) and Marsh (26) and methodically increased the tempo after the demise of Border for 8 with only 93 runs on the board. They clobbered 77

Man of the match Dean Jones straight drives Australia to their first win.

runs off the final ten overs to boost the run rate to an imposing 4.88. Jones was not as ruthless as in many of his assaults, striking only six boundaries but keeping the score ticking over by scurrying between wickets to frustrate the bowlers and the fieldsmen. He didn't become flustered even when his eighth century obviously would elude him but he satisfied himself with a return to a limited-over international average in excess of 50, the highest in the world. The relentless running between wickets exhausted him under the blazing sun; he later chomped on bananas while fielding when he required sustenance to correct blurred vision.

Mark Waugh was calm and calculating and in charge of proceedings from the moment he took block. His driving was a feature and he collected seven of the 19 boundaries in the Australian innings. He had one escape when, at 23, he recklessly lofted an on-drive off Carl Hooper to Malcolm Marshall. The veteran dropped the chance and the West Indians paid dearly until an Ambrose full-toss clipped the top of the stumps as the batsman stepped back to cut. That was little consolation for Ambrose, whose last four overs cost 32 runs, or for Gray whose final five overs cost 40 runs. Jones remained unbeaten at the end of 129 minutes of action, much to the appreciation of the near capacity crowd which acknowledged his gift and flair against a pace attack of quality.

The Australians batted sensibly throughout the innings. Boon and Marsh were intent on providing a solid start and did so, despite a slice of luck for Marsh when he was only one, losing his middle stump to a scorching yorker from Ambrose off a no-ball. Marsh's effort came to an end when he was run out for 26 when beaten by a direct hit from Hooper running in from cover. Boon was beaten by the irregular bounce of the pitch. He attempted a cut but lost his off stump after looking in control during his 34 off 70 deliveries. Border was simply beaten by the spin of Hooper and was bowled for 8 as he failed to commit himself forward or back to a seemingly harmless delivery. Hooper and Richards bowled 18 of the allocated overs as the Australians increased the tempo. After only 28 runs came off the opening ten overs, the rate improved to 40, 40, 45 and then 77 during the other ten over brackets.

The challenge of 4.9 runs an over for victory was not beyond the experienced and potentially devastating West Indian batting line-up, particularly against an Australian attack which included irregular limited-over pacemen McDermott and Whitney and an under-worked Reid. But the bowling was as professional as the batting, and left-arm pace pair Reid and Whitney applied the pressure from the outset. Whitney conceded only three scoring shots in five overs, including an edged boundary, and his opening spell of seven overs allowed only 16 runs; Reid also was a handful, conceding only 12 runs in five overs. McDermott made the initial break when Haynes fended at a delivery and wicketkeeper Ian Healy held a low

Gordon Greenidge loses patience, and two stumps.

catch to dispose of the team's most prolific run-scorer of recent times for only 17.

Steve Waugh then gave the tourists the upper hand with the scalps of Gordon Greenidge (19) and Carl Hooper (6) within three overs. Greenidge, frustrated by containment, shuffled down the pitch as the ball skittled his stumps and Hooper was trapped lbw. But the major blow was Peter Taylor's delivery which spun past Richards' attempted swipe to leg and bowled the captain. Richards looked dangerous with 18 runs off as many deliveries and his wicket fell immediately after Richie Richardson hooked a six into the scoreboard off Steve Waugh's bowling. At 4 for 95 in the 27th over the Australians looked comfortably set, but Richardson and Logie then took control with sensible aggression in a 50 partnership off only 61 deliveries. With 13 overs remaining the West Indies needed almost eight runs an over but the acceleration began in earnest. The pair took 13 runs from Reid's sixth over and another eight off his next; 20 000 fans whistled and cheered when 73 runs off the last 10 overs seemed a reasonable challenge.

Logie was in brilliant form, reaching his half-century off only 57 deliveries and then clubbing two boundaries off Taylor, while Richardson played a supportive role before reaching his half-century off only 59 deliveries.

The union reached 95 off 15 overs before Logie's innings of strength and power (belying his diminutive frame) ended at 65 off only 67 deliveries. The Waugh twins combined, Steve holding the catch at deep square leg from Mark's bowling, to leave 55 runs to win from eight overs. The scene was set for an exciting finish but instead the West Indians collapsed in dramatic fashion, losing their last six wickets for only 19 runs off 25 deliveries. McDermott was instrumental and inspiring, dismissing Richardson and Jeff Dujon with consecutive deliveries to put the result beyond doubt. He ignored sweat dripping over his patched right eyelid and forced Richardson to mishit to Jones at deep point after a dazzling 64 off 66 deliveries, then enticed Dujon to clip a catch to Border at mid-wicket. McDermott finished with 4 for 34 off 8.5 overs and the Australians accepted the US$500 for victory and the same amount for Jones' man-of-the-match award and prepared for a low-key celebration. Even Simpson, his infected leg supported by a pillow during the game, was suitably impressed by the manner of victory and mustered a rare smile after a week in bed.

The outcome merely whetted the appetite for the remainder of the series, particularly as the West Indians were smarting after such a rare defeat. A steely-eyed Richards quickly informed the press:

I hope they do realise it doesn't finish here. The Australians drew first blood and it should give them confidence. We knew the Australians were

Healy was airborn with joy when Richards was bowled by Peter Taylor.

an improving side ... they beat us in the Nehru Trophy in India and are reigning World Cup champions so we cannot lament their improvement. I congratulate them on their win but this is only the start of the series.

Border shot back: 'We are here to win, we are fair dinkum in our approach and we believe we are a force to be reckoned with. We showed that in this game. We wanted to start this series well and although winning wasn't an obsession, we wanted to show we are here and mean business. Winning was a bonus.'

Indeed it was in more ways than one. Just playing in front of such a large and parochial crowd was an experience which the players needed to endure. Border confessed that everyone was a bit on edge before the game and that there wasn't the usual chit-chat or jovial atmosphere among the troupe because of apprehension about the crowd. Border spoke to the players about the crowd reaction — 'if one of our blokes gets 50 there is hardly a ripple, but if one of their batsmen hits a boundary the place erupts with whistling and can bashing and shouting' — and warned the players not to let the pressure get to them if the West Indians made a charge. 'The experience of it all, and especially having come out winners, will be invaluable,' he said as he savoured a long awaited victory on Caribbean soil and set his sights on even bigger booty.

SECOND MATCH

The Australians clinched one of their best one-day international victories in modern times to retaliate to an abysmally manipulated over rate from the Caribbean champions in this controversial match. The West Indians bowled only 34 overs, eight less than the quota of 42 set at the commencement of a rain-delayed start, enabling them to dictate the pace of play to their own advantage with scant respect for the spirit of the game.

The Australian victory by 45 runs with 17 deliveries in hand was the ideal response in what Simpson described as 'one of the top ten wins in my time as coach and certainly up there with the World Cup performances'.

The West Indian ploy backfired when Jones led a batting assault to score 64 off 76 deliveries to provide Australia with 9 for 172. The bowlers then dismissed the cream of the Caribbean for 127 with only Haynes (45), Richards (27) and Simmons (13) reaching double figures.

The overs issue took the gloss off an exceptional performance by the Australians, who were furious with the West Indian tactics. At one stage, Jones asked umpire Lloyd Barker if indeed this was a 42-over innings; the reply was 'maybe, but the innings will close at two o'clock'. So after laying the foundation with 3 for 87 off the opening 20 overs, the Australians quickly reassessed the situation to club 3 for 74 off the next ten overs before the tail-enders had to survive to ensure the team wasn't dismissed.

Supporters provide a fitting background to the victorious Aussies.

That would have given the West Indians 42 overs to score the runs instead of 34.

Border said the team was 'filthy' with the West Indian disregard for the spirit of the game, and went out to prove they could win despite the enormous disadavantage. Richards explained the slow over rate by saying 'we tried our best in the wet conditions'.

Perhaps the only man on the ground happier than the Australian players was match referee Lance Murray, a former Trinidadian spinner. 'I am pleased that the Australians won because it avoids any controversy. I am sure it won't happen again when a side can bowl eight overs less than the required number — I will be speaking to both sides about this — but there is little we can do about it,' he said. Murray met with both team leaders and management before the match but said the issue of bowling the full quota of overs hadn't been raised 'because there is a gentleman's agreement established before this series that this would be the case. The big problem is that there is little we as referees can do. In most places you can deduct prize money in the form of fines but the prize money here is so small that it would be meaningless,' he said of the winner's purse of US$500.

'You can't take away runs or take any other measures in disciplinary action because that makes the game a mockery. It is up to the people concerned to play the game in the right spirit and that unfortunately didn't happen here,' he conceded.

Border expressed similar disappointment.

The West Indians don't have any trouble bowling the full quota in Australia where they are fined $600 for the first over short and then $1200 for every other over. It is imperative that the game is played in the right spirit. If they bowled one or two overs short it wouldn't have been so bad but eight is absolutely silly.

The Australians took the cynical, and possibly correct, view that the West Indians never intended to bowl the 42 overs because they lacked a quality fifth bowler. The statistics suggest as much. Spinner Hooper bowled three overs for 18 runs, Simmons two overs for 15 runs and Richards one over for four runs before Richards reverted to his mainline bowling power of Ambrose, Gray, Marshall and Moseley. Once the speedsters were back in action there was never a possibility that the quota would be reached. Manager Sawle was outraged. 'They bowled 20 per cent fewer overs than the target and that is totally unacceptable considering there were no injury delays, no rain interruptions and no exceptional circumstances. Almost five minutes an over was preposterous.'

The bubbling anger within the Australian team was the impetus which inspired the victory, as Border explained.

We have played some good games recently but that was as well as we have played for a very long time. I am thrilled. We were really annoyed and we felt the best way to prove the point was to win the match to show them that these sort of tactics won't faze us. There was a really grim determination to nail them and we showed the spirit and skill to fix them up.

Terry Alderman, sitting in the players' viewing area, commented to Simpson that the West Indians would get the runs in a hurry or wouldn't get them at all. How right he was. The carefree batsmen, seemingly impervious to the attitude of the Australians, lashed out thinking that the target of 173 off 34 overs with ten wickets in hand would be a cakewalk. They started with a blaze but lost the last seven wickets for only 49 runs as the asking rate climbed past seven to nine as the Australians bowled tightly and fielded brilliantly. Richards was steaming after the match, realising the potential loss of an impeccable home series record and the fact that the Australians had totally outplayed his men. 'This series is not finished yet. Regardless of being 2-0 down Viv is confident,' he boomed with more bravado than conviction. When queried about the apparent lack of discipline in the batting, Richards suggested that 'maybe we have set too high a standard'. More to the point was that the Australians are

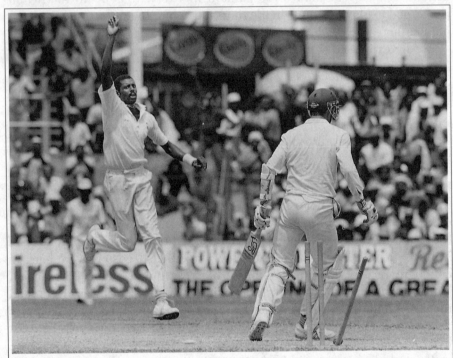

Local hero Tony Gray was successful on his home ground at Trinidad.

A jubilant Dean Jones hugs David Boon, while Allan Border, Craig McDermott and Geoff Marsh look on.

superior one-day players now, having learned so much from the West Indian teams which dominated with bat and ball and in the field during the '70s and '80s.

The Australian innings was full of merit, particularly when the batsmen realised they would be deprived of so many overs after pacing themselves. Jones was outstanding again. His 64 off 76 deliveries included nine boundaries and he was bowled by Gray only when he attempted to lash out in the knowledge that only six instead of the scheduled 14 overs remained. Mark Waugh also sacrificed his wicket for 16 off 17 deliveries with a six and a boundary; Steve Waugh played brilliantly for 26 off 30 deliveries under similar strain. Giant local paceman Gray was awarded the man-of-the-match for his career best analysis of 6 for 50 off nine overs, eclipsing his 4 for 36 against Pakistan at Multan in 1986. The award, judged by a local official, was a final insult to the Australians. Jones, who scored more than half the entire West Indian score to set up victory, was easily the outstanding player of the day. Gray's bowling was expensive and all his victims apart from Border, who gloved a first-ball leg side delivery, were out 'slogging'.

The impressive part of the Australian bowling was the nagging accuracy which claimed the top order with genuinely good deliveries and which prevented any batsman from dictating terms. McDermott was the pick of the bowlers with 3 for 29 off seven overs and his victims were vital — Richardson for five, Dujon for seven and Marshall for five. Whitney continued his excellent one-day form with 3 for 41 off nine overs, chipping away to remove Haynes, Hooper and Richards. Steve Waugh bowled superbly, tightening the screws in the middle of the innings to force up the run rate; he deserved a better analysis than 0 for 24 off eight overs. Mark Waugh came on at the death to collect 2 for 6 off two overs but by then the result was inevitable.

Haynes was the best of the West Indian batsmen with 45 off 62 deliveries with seven boundaries and he looked the only batsman likely to dominate. When he eventually edged a catch to wicketkeeper Healy off Whitney, the fast bowler and the batsman engaged in a verbal departure scene of little consequence except that two competitive cricketers under pressure refused to give an inch.

The Australians had amazing vocal support from the crowd of about 30 000. When Richards was caught on the deep mid-wicket boundary by Marsh off Whitney to virtually clinch the contest, the great batsman received derisive jeers and considerable booing as he walked to the pavilion — an extraordinary scene in his own country. Apparently Richards is not popular in Port of Spain, and even less so after blatantly running out Logie for seven and then surviving a run-out himself. He seemed even less popular when Australia took a 2-0 lead in the series.

THIRD MATCH

The disquiet hadn't abated over the manipulation of overs before another issue developed the following day at Queens Park Oval. The West Indies clawed back to 2-1 in the series when they won on a superior run rate in a rain-affected match, leaving the Australians to ponder the discrepancies of worldwide one-day international match regulations.

The Australians batted superbly to amass 7 for 245 off 49 overs at an average of five runs an over before rain reduced the West Indian innings to 36 overs. The formula in the Caribbean for the victory target is to multiply the average number of runs for the earlier innings by the number of overs available: in this case, 5 x 36 + 1 = 181 to win.

The Australian formula requires the team batting second to score one run more than the equivalent number of highest-scoring overs from the first innings. In this case the Australian version of the target was 220 (the highest-scoring 36 overs adding up to 219 + 1 to win).

The difference of 39 runs is considerable at more than an extra run an over and the Australian system doesn't give too great an advantage to the team batting second, which, with 10 wickets in hand, has an enormous advantage in a reduced-over match. The touring team was aware of the West Indian rule before this tournament, and wasn't making excuses for their first loss of the series, being acutely aware that one-day cricket is, after all, a manufactured contest at the best of times.

But the episode afforded Simpson the opportunity to raise the matter in a continuation of his long-standing belief that one-day games should have uniform rules. He noted that another rule difference in the Caribbean is a delivery which bounces over the batsman's head is called a wide, not a no-ball as in Australia, and therefore a batsman can be caught out off what is accepted as an 'illegal' delivery. The former Test skipper suggested the International Cricket Council should formulate standardised match regulations for limited-over internationals to prevent irregularities in one-day internationals from one country to another. He suggested the Australians are so far ahead of the rest of the world in framing rules for this sort of 50-over competition, because they play so much of it, that maybe world authorities should study them and be decisive in regulations. Simpson pointed out that one-day cricket is assuming considerable status in world cricket with vital financial off-shoots, so that to have varying regulations from one country to another, and from one competition to another, was irrational.

The match provided ample highlights despite the rain interruptions, particularly for Marsh, who compiled 81 off 107 deliveries in his 100th appearance in limited-over internationals. The team vice-captain, who was a hero in the World Cup triumph in 1988, joined Allan Border (222),

Dean Jones (113), Steve Waugh (109) and David Boon (104) in the 'century club' in the most experienced limited-over international team in cricket.

Jones (36 off 49 balls with four boundaries and a six) was brilliant again. He and Marsh added 69 off 15 overs after Mark Taylor, replacing Boon who had a stomach upset, fell in the third over for only three. The middle order contributed methodically with Mark Waugh (16 off 23 balls), Border (22 off 33 balls) and Steve Waugh (23 off 30 balls) keeping the run rate steady at five an over. Healy put the icing on the cake with an unbeaten 33 off only 23 deliveries. The West Indians, who failed by eight overs to complete their reduced target the previous day, managed 49 overs before a last-minute rain interruption.

Ambrose was again the superior paceman with 3 for 37 off his ten overs and his pace, relentless accuracy and unwavering length was the only steadying influence in the attack. Patterson and Gray conceded 111 runs between them in 19 overs and while they shared three wickets, they were expensive considering that Simmons and Hooper bowled 20 overs for only 85 runs.

The rain tumbled down during the luncheon interval and delayed the resumption, eventually reducing the overs to 36 and the West Indian target to 181. The Australians faced a difficult challenge, especially as the West Indians had included

Marsh cools off during his long haul in Trinidad in Australia's only losing one-day international.

Greenidge to bolster the batting depth to Richards at number seven. Reid dismissed Simmons for a third ball duck but Richardson played magnificently and never gave the tourists another sniff of victory. He blasted his way to 50 off only 59 deliveries to always have the team within striking reach and he finished ten runs shy of a deserved century after facing only 94 deliveries with 14 boundaries. His exit was a surprise when he pulled a Mark Waugh delivery high to Border at mid-wicket, but at 3 for 132 in the 28th over he had already assured the West Indians of victory even with 53 runs required off the final ten overs. Greenidge (batting at number four) and the popular and inspiring Logie wiped off the deficit with 15 deliveries remaining. Greenidge chimed in with 40 off only 50 deliveries after a slow start, while Logie sent the 25 000 fans into raptures with five boundaries in 24 off only 21 deliveries. The Australians ran out of ammunition in the end because McDermott, having bowled five overs in his initial spell, was forced into the dressing rooms with a severe stomach upset and associated respiratory difficulties.

Richards, who wasn't required to bat or bowl, was delighted with the result.

It was a do-or-die situation and we were confident we could win. But we didn't feel we had done too well in the field and the Australians made too many runs for my liking. But once we batted we were always going to win. We took a leaf out of the Australians' book with our running between the wickets and the need for one man to get in and stay in for a big score. Richardson did that superbly. We know we can beat the Australians in one-day games and we want to kick on from here to win the series 3-2.

'You little beauty', or the equivalent in Trinidadian patois — the Windies win the third one-day international.

Border and the Australians were equally determined to wrap up the series in Barbados and paid scant notice to this result. 'We played well enough to win it under ordinary circumstances so there is no need to fret,' Border enthused. 'Our batting has their attack under control and we figure we can score enough runs and defend them in almost any situation, so we're heading to Barbados to make history ...'

And head to Barbados they did ... rising at 4.00 am for the five hour

37

transfer to the Rockley Resort where swimming, golf, shopping or sleep preceded an official function before training the following day. The activity off the field was as hectic as the action on it and the pace was taking a heavy toll. The most popular man in the touring party was physiotherapist Errol Alcott, the man with a cure for almost everything from a virus or gout to hamstrings or back ailments. So many unexpected ailments had hit the touring party within the opening month of the campaign that the Australian management had exhausted medical supplies and requested a new batch from Australia. Alcott had been unable to keep up with the demands of the team, which had been afflicted with flu and two distinctly different viruses. 'It has been worse than anything we have encountered on four trips,' Alcott lamented.

I brought enough supplies so that if everyone got the flu I had it covered. But the supply is like Old Mother Hubbard's cupboard: it is bare. The problem is that everyone has had a bout of flu or the virus and then suffered another bout. It is fairly natural for the bugs to spread swiftly throughout a team which travels, trains, eats and plays together, but this is exceptional.

Alcott decided, like in India and Pakistan, that the team would drink bottled water in Trinidad and Guyana, believing that the basic cause of the depressing sequence of illnesses was local water on the various islands. 'This is the unluckiest run I have known since I joined the team in 1984 for the West Indies tour,' he said. 'I always expected the guys to get hit a lot on this tour and I came prepared for blood around the face and for throat balls. I am amply covered to treat fractures or cuts but not the medical problems which have hit us so hard.' The Australian contingent was a physically and mentally tough combination, and certainly wasn't spoiled by the physiotherapist, but the list of woes made you wonder how enough fit players managed to take the field in some games.

The list was staggering, with coach Simpson, Hughes, Alderman, Boon, Healy, McDermott, Steve Waugh, Peter Taylor and Whitney suffering worse than most from a virus which caused vomiting and diarrhoea, or another which sparked headaches, weakness and joint aches. No sooner did one of the troupe stop tapping on Alcott's door than another rang the alarm bell.

Alcott also had problems with Reid's back, Hughes' lower spine bruise he suffered in Perth, Simpson's infected right leg, Boon's cut chin and hurt big toe (suffered in the nets and preventing him playing in the next one-day international), McDermott's nine stitches over the right eye after being hit, Mark Taylor and Mark Waugh's minor head blows, Healy's bruised hand, Dean Jones' slow recovery from a hairline fracture of the right forearm, and Marsh's bout of asthma. Not to mention a few visits from journalists complaining of gout, exhaustion and blurred vision, all natural side-effects of the rigours of the job!

Alcott didn't mind the workload as his only consideration was to put a fit and competitive team on the field. He neither asked nor gave any favours. This experienced traveller knows the players' strengths and weaknesses probably more than they appreciate and he has their total trust, and vice versa.

We have a good relationship and that has been deliberately formed. I don't rush out with the spray can, for instance. That is baby stuff, I reckon. If you run out every five minutes to treat a player it breeds something psychological. I think it leads to a way out and we have toughened up on that. The players are not expected to come running to me at the drop of a hat if they are not feeling well. They tend not to ring me straight away ... usually they won't tell me for 24 hours that they have been off-colour. They know I am not their nurse and they only see me when they are really off-colour. When they knock on my door I know they need help. There are no massages; there is no special pampering. The guys know I am a waste of time as far as that is concerned. That can breed an attitude where the guys just sit around. These blokes are mentally very tough, far more so than they were in the past, and physically I think they are all very good.

Alcott is a physiotherapist but he can turn his hand to most medical matters if necessary. He is a genuinely vital member of the team. The players respect and trust him and appreciate that he has their health and the team welfare as his first priority. But occasionally he tells them exactly what they don't want to hear: they shouldn't play.

The major problem most of the time is that the boys want to keep playing and exerting themselves, even when some bug has got a hold on them. They are professional cricketers with a heavy workload and a real desire to perform, so sometimes it is a matter of telling them to take a breather. I don't get in over my head when it comes to their health. I prescribe what you would expect from a doctor to keep them up and running but if they don't respond as well as they should I call in expert medical advice. I leave the stitching of cuts to the doctors and really it would be only in the far reaches of the Amazon that I would have to give an injection. I can stitch wounds or give injections but there is no real need in most parts of the world. We have contact with doctors in almost every place we play and it would need to be an emergency for me to react to something I can leave to the experts.

Alcott prefers to be unnoticed on tour but there are a number of small yet important chores he undertakes to help with medical safety. 'Monday is malaria day' is a long standing catch-cry for the Australian players on tours to India, Pakistan, the West Indies and Sharjah, and all members of the touring party begin the course of tablets on a Monday so that nobody forgets the dose. So it was without fuss or favour that Alcott walked around the airport lounge in the very early hours of Monday when the team arrived in Barbados to distribute the tablets with information that orange juice was available in the far corner of the room. He was handing out hangover pills a couple of days later.

FOURTH MATCH

Australia confirmed itself the undisputed champion of one-day international cricket by becoming the first team to defeat the West Indies in a limited-over series in the Caribbean. And they did it in style, taking a 3-1 lead in the best-of-five campaign with a record score and a winning margin of 37 runs with 18 deliveries remaining!

The batsmen, magnificently led by Marsh's century, compiled 6 for 283 to force the West Indians to chase 5.68 runs per over for victory, a challenge eventually beyond them after a recklessly aggressive start, a middle-order slump and then a belated burst. This was an exciting and absorbing match between a methodically professional Australian team pitted against the unbridled flamboyance of the West Indian players.

Marsh, voted man of the match by Sir Garfield Sobers for his 113 off 140 deliveries, laid the foundation with tremendous support from Allan Border (79) and Mark Waugh (49); they were the only three batsmen to make more than 40 in the match, despite the small arena and the best batting strip of the tournament. The Australians batted more consistently throughout the series, bowled better and held the edge in the fielding. All those aspects surfaced in this match when the West Indians had so much to prove to stay in the series. The discipline in the Australian team shone through in the batting with the players working together as part of a team while the West Indian batsmen apparently wanted to win the match off their own bat with scant regard for the overall situation.

Border declared immediately that the Australians were the best one-day team in the world. 'I really think the way we have played we can lay a claim to the number one team in one-day games and we deserve it. This series win rates highly on my list, because of the historic importance, and after the World Cup win it is a major consideration in assessing the best limited-over team in the world. We are it,' an elated Border enthused. Richards agreed and congratulated the Australians 'as the better team in the series and really deserving of the title. They definitely are the best one-day team, the champions. We all know that.' The chairman of the West

Indies Cricket Board, former champion batsman Clyde Walcott, also praised the Australians for the series win and congratulated the team on this victory. 'The Australians played better cricket in the one-day games than the West Indians and they deserve the spoils,' he said.

The Australians were jubilant after the match as the players laid to rest one of the giant hoodoos of limited-over cricket — beating the West Indies in the Caribbean. The players celebrated the series win at a nightclub that evening and could reflect on several major achievements in the series which included the first defeat of a West Indian team in a one-dayer at Jamaica; the first home series defeat by any team against the West Indians and, in this match, the West Indies first defeat at Barbados since 1935, during which time they have played nine Tests and four one-day internationals.

The man who led the way for the Australians was Marsh, the 32-year-old vice-captain who helped rewrite the record books during his innings of 113. This was his eighth century in limited-over matches, one more than Dean Jones and the most by an Australian in this style of game. He also became the first Australian to score a century against the West Indians in the Caribbean, and joined Allan Border (127 not out in Sydney in 1984-85), Bruce Laird (117 not out in Sydney in 1981-82) and Graeme Wood (104 not out in Adelaide in 1984-85) as the only Australian batsmen to score a century against the men of speed.

Marsh's innings came off only 140 deliveries with eight boundaries and three sixes. He was always in control, defending grimly against early short-pitched deliveries which umpires David Archer and Lloyd Barker liberally deemed legitimate, and then consolidating after losing Mark Taylor (5) and Dean Jones (7) with only 27 runs on the board after ten overs. He didn't panic — does he ever? — and decided after 15 overs

Geoff Marsh on his way to a match-winning century in Barbados.

to take the initiative by plundering the bowling to reach his half-century off only 68 deliveries. Marsh and Border shared a record 146 run third wicket union, with the veteran skipper contributing a punishing 79 off only 87 balls with seven boundaries and two sixes. Lasting only 95 minutes, the partnership was vintage batting by both Marsh and Border and passed the previous third wicket record of 119 shared by Border and Kepler Wessels in Perth in 1983-84. The team leaders showed the way and laid the foundation for Australia's highest total against the West Indians of 6 for 283 off 50 overs, eclipsing the 274 off 58.4 overs in the final of the inaugural World Cup at Lord's in 1975.

Marsh's powerful striking was a highlight and he wanted to see the television replay of his six off Marshall when his on-drive sailed over the grandstand. 'I don't know how I did it but it sounded sweet and it certainly went a long way,' he chortled. Border wasn't so surprised by the effortless shot: 'He is a big, strong farmer and he can hit the ball a long way. He certainly sent that one into orbit!' Marsh said the adrenalin really began pumping when the crowd began to 'sing for blood'. 'That really gets you going, especially when the ball is whizzing around your earhole and when the West Indian players are joining in with the drumming and the whistling.'

Border was positive from the start, reaching his first half-century in limited-over cricket since his 55 against New Zealand in Adelaide on 2 December, with his 50 coming off only 63 deliveries. He pulled and cut powerfully to rekindle memories of his heyday and was eventually caught at fine leg when he top-edged a pull. Marsh continued to pile on the runs and his century came off 130 deliveries to appreciative whistling from the crowd which earlier ignored his 50 milestone.

Mark Waugh played a cameo innings of the highest quality. He contributed 49 off 31 deliveries which included only one boundary, but struck the ball into the gaps crisply to rattle on an 87 run fourth wicket stand in only 11 overs. The erect right-hander unluckily missed a deserved half-century when he headed for a single and his 50 and couldn't retrieve his ground before Ambrose threw down the stumps on his follow-through.

The Australian score presented the West Indians with a formidable chase of 5.68 runs per over, a target the parochial and vocal crowd obviously expected to be achieved. The volume of noise intensified as music, singing, drums, whistles, cymbals and radios whipped the crowd, and perhaps the West Indian batsmen, into a frenzy.

The pursuit began at fever pitch with Haynes and Simmons clouting 39 runs in eight overs but the Australians refused to buckle under the early onslaught and associated crowd delirium. McDermott bowled Simmons for 23 off 24 balls and Reid accounted for Haynes (22 off 25 balls) in similar fashion. After 8.1 overs the innings reached an amazing 2 for 50.

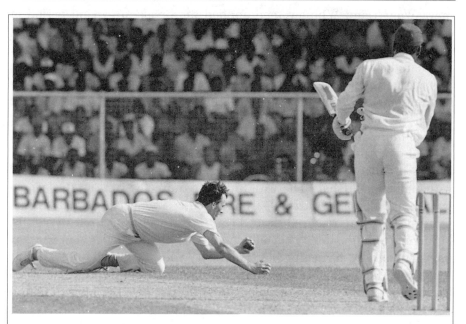

Steve Waugh's brilliant return catch in Barbados to dismiss Viv Richards for his 100th one-day international wicket.

David Boon leads the victory chorus in the Australian dressing shed.

Steve Waugh and Whitney then applied the breaks in a vital period of consolidation. Steve Waugh's varied deliveries, with regular use of the slower ball, confused and frustrated and eventually deceived the batsmen. He snared the important wickets of Greenidge (17) and Richards (20), boasting Richards' return catch as his 100th in limited-over internationals. Whitney also stemmed the run flow and chimed in with the wicket of potential match-winner Richardson (25 off 23 balls) and after 24 overs the Australians had the match in hand at 5 for 118.

But Logie and Dujon refused to concede. Logie collected 37 off 51 balls and then Dujon (top-scorer with 39 off 41 balls) shared a 49 run stand with Malcolm Marshall. The West Indians required 85 runs off the last ten overs but Dujon and Marshall strung together a sequence of five overs at that rate to excite renewed drum-beating and whistling from the locals. McDermott put the match beyond doubt with his 100th victim in one-day internationals by dismissing Marshall for 19 with the total 8 for 226 in the 44th over. Mark Waugh completed an excellent all-round effort to wrap up the innings with the scalps of Dujon and Ambrose. He finished with figures of 3 for 34 off seven overs, a catch and 49 runs.

FINAL MATCH

Australia wrapped up the series 4-1 with a crushing six wicket victory in a match full of controversy at the Bourda ground. The Australians confirmed their superiority and Marsh his individual dominance with his second successive century to win back-to-back man-of-the-match awards.

The Australians, chasing a victory target for the first time in this series, cruised to 4 for 252 with nine deliveries remaining after dismissing the West Indians for 251, an innings which included a remarkable collapse of 6 for 35 off the final ten overs.

The match was the most volatile of the series. Border exchanged words with Haynes and then Richards; the crowd twice hurled bottles towards West Indian players. Border struck a 'free hit' for six and Jones was run out in bizarre fashion as the day provided an avalanche of runs and one amazing collapse by the West Indians.

The highlight was Marsh's unbeaten 106 which took his series aggregate to 349 runs at an average of 87.25, easily the best in both categories on either side. His last three innings of 81, 113 and 106 not out emphasised his importance to the Australians, his stamina and concentration and his underestimated ability to retain momentum to benefit the team. The innings provided a couple of unusual asides for Marsh — he received an unexpected kiss from a delighted male admirer who ran onto the ground to celebrate the century, which came only minutes after Patterson nearly decapitated Marsh on 97 with a 'beamer'.

Geoff Marsh with Guyanan admirer after his second successive century in one-day internationals, which won him the Man-of-the-Series award.

The incidents were commonplace by then. Border exchanged words with Haynes when the opening batsman waited an inordinate length of time before leaving the crease when he was out lbw to spinner Taylor for 58. But the major debate took place when Border took advantage of a delivery which slipped from Simmons' hand and pitched as a half-volley just off the strip. Border pulled it for six, much to the annoyance of Richards. Border didn't back away from the incidents:

Des Haynes and I had an altercation about his dismissal because I didn't like the way he lingered when given out lbw. I had a few verbals over that, and later Viv and I had a bit of a go. Viv said he didn't think it was right that I hit the ball which slipped out of Simmons' hand and

Allan Border swipes a 'free hit' from Phil Simmons over the fence at the Bourda.

I just asked 'why not?' It was a bad ball and if someone bowls a long hop I try to hit it. This is a tough game and we got the better of it in this match. If I hit the ball to a fieldsman and was caught they would have been laughing and claimed the wicket. Just because it was a six they were moaning that it wasn't in the ethics of the game. And what about that hand-to-head delivery from Patterson to Marsh when he was 97. If 'Swampy' gloved it and was caught I bet they would have claimed his wicket even though it was a beamer. I am not going to take a backward step against them. They are used to winning and being on top so maybe they are finding it hard to accept things at the moment. But there is no reason for us to be apologetic.

Richards played down the day's incidents, including the words on the field. 'Everyone has a few things to say when they are competing but I am not going to comment on what was said on the field. We are disappointed with this result and the series result and we can't hide that.'

Border rated the win as one of the best half-dozen fighting efforts, as distinct from massacres, he has seen. 'After 40 overs when they were 4 for 216 we were dead ducks. But McDermott and Hughes pulled something special out of the bag and kept us in the game,' he said, referring to the three wickets apiece which wrapped up the innings for 251 with 6 for 35 off the final ten overs. 'Then Geoff Marsh played another big innings — he is a fair dinkum champ — and the win really was a terrific effort,' Border enthused.

How accurate that assessment was. The West Indians decided to make the Australians chase for the first time in the series and Simmons and Haynes immediately took control with an 85 run partnership in 17 overs. Spinner Taylor eventually broke the ice when he dismissed both batsmen, Simmons for 34 and Haynes for an aggressive 58 off 69 deliveries which included 11 boundaries. The Australian attack steadied as is the custom and the fielding excelled. Mark Waugh exemplified the brilliance in the field when he swooped on the ball and threw down the stumps from long off to run out a bewildered Greenidge for only six. The talented all-rounder then chimed in with Richards' wicket for only ten. The former master blaster of this style of game attempted to hit Waugh's second delivery into the marketplace a kilometre away but succeeded only in finding the safe hands of Whitney at long off. The West Indians were tottering at 4 for 155 in the 32nd over as the crowd began to cheer the Australians. A large proportion of the crowd was of Indian extraction with seemingly little affection towards the West Indians, and they jeered Richards off the field after his demise and often when he went near the ball while fielding.

But Richardson wasn't about to surrender. He mounted an assault to reach his half-century off only 49 deliveries and increased the tempo in a

Richie Richardson, the Windies' best batsman, slams another drive to the fence at the Bourda.

sparkling innings of 94 off only 88 deliveries, with 11 boundaries and a six off Border. He and Logie regained the initiative with a 62 run union in nine overs and the West Indians looked set for a total in excess of 300.

They forfeited any real chance of victory by collapsing in the lower order batting — similar to the opening match when they lost 6 for 19 and in the second match when they lost 7 for 49 — and they lost the last six wickets for only 35 runs in 9.5 overs. McDermott and Hughes, who replaced Reid in the line-up, crippled the innings. McDermott bowled Logie for 17 and Hughes had Richardson caught at the wicket 20 runs and five overs later to ensure that an obtainable target would be on offer.

McDermott added Hooper and Gray to his haul to finish with 3 for 29 off his ten overs, then Hughes bowled Dujon and Walsh to return impressive figures of 3 for 33 off his 9.5 overs. Spinner Taylor also deserved much credit for dismissing the openers in figures of 2 for 45 off his ten over quota. The Australians required only 5.05 runs an over for victory, a target which took on considerably larger proportions when they lost Boon and Jones within eight overs.

But Marsh and Border quickly asserted their authority, as they did in the previous contest which guaranteed the Australians the series. They followed the 146 run stand at Barbados with a 124 union in 24 overs, having come together with the score on 2 for 37 after Boon and Jones fell cheaply. Boon, on nine, deflected a pull from Patterson on to the stumps while Jones, who contributed only 11 to take his series tally to 206 at an average of 51.50, was dismissed in bizarre fashion. He survived an lbw appeal from Gray and, rejecting thoughts of a run, turned his back on the bowler as he ambled back towards the crease. Gray swooped on the ball and threw down the stumps before Jones made good his ground.

Marsh and Border then paced themselves for a half-century off ten overs and a century stand in 20 overs, with both batsmen playing aggressively to seize the initiative. The Australian captain continued his punishing pulls and an occasional hook, with two boundaries in an over from Courtney Walsh and a memorable hooked six in the next over. He reached his half-century off only 52 deliveries with four boundaries and two sixes, the second coming from the 'free hit' off Simmons. Border appeared to lose his concentration and wicket immediately after a debate with Richards about the 'free hit' and he departed for 60 off only 61 deliveries with Australia needing 91 off the final 18 overs.

Mark Waugh blemished his excellent series batting when he was stumped by Dujon off Hooper for only seven but twin Steve gave Marsh the necessary support as the Australians chased 53 runs off the final ten overs. Steve Waugh played a cameo innings of 26 not out off 38 deliveries in an unfinished partnership of 71. Australian cricket must be in an extremely healthy state when a player of his ability often must wait for an opportunity to bat or bowl in this style of competition, and cannot command a regular place in the Test team. He would waltz into any other Test and one-day international team in the world, including the West Indian line-up.

Marsh relentlessly pursued a century and victory. Both deservedly achieved, Marsh could boast his second successive man-of-the-match award and the right to the player-of-the-series. The West Indians simply capitulated at the end, perhaps pleased to leave the arena and the pro-Australian crowd and certainly delighted this was the end of a humbling series of one-day games. The crowd reaction was unhealthily aggressive at times and Walsh was hit by a bottle while fielding at fine leg, requiring his left hand to be sprayed and strapped, while Haynes also narrowly missed injury when a spectator threw a bottle in his direction when he was fielding a ball near the boundary.

The match ended in a fashion which typified the apparent lack of discipline in the West Indian attack, which throughout the series squandered so many runs with wides and no-balls. They conceded an extra 35 deliveries to the Australians with no-balls and wides in this game, involving 11 wides and 14 no balls, with another 10 no-balls from which the Australians scored. The match ended with a no-ball and then a wide from Patterson.

The teams attended an official function after the match and then the celebrations really began. Tag-team wrestling was the sport in the minibus as it returned the players to the Pegasus Hotel bar, which must have enjoyed a record take as drinks of all sorts crossed the counter in a fair dinkum celebration, the likes of which hadn't been witnessed since the triumphs in England in 1989.

KINGSTON:
FIRE IN THE BELLY

21 February 1991, about 3 o'clock in the afternoon, in Old Kingston Market: that was the day, the time and the place in the West Indies I began to realise, not for the first time, that maybe Australia wasn't such a bad place after all.

A young Jamaican, smaller but vastly fitter than I, ran straight at me, spinning me around with a blow on the shoulder. I shouted something like 'hey, watch where you're going' and was bumped from the other side, by another youth. Fortunately, I kept my feet.

A plump old Jamaican lady with a wide apron covering her floor-length skirt, grabbed Alison, my wife, by the arm and pulled her into a nearby clothing stall. 'Here,' she shouted to me. 'Here; they cut you to pieces.' A young girl ran from the stall. I just stood there, alarmed, but still more or less wondering what was going on. The old lady pulled me into the stall and explained that gangs of 'bandits' stalked 'whiteys' and other 'rich people' who visited the markets. She had sent her granddaughter for help. There was a squad of special police in the markets which fought the 'bandits'.

I had my doubts, thinking we were less vulnerable in the aisle than hidden away in a stall, more like a large cupboard, with no windows or rear door, crammed with clothing on tables and shelves — shirts, shorts, socks and underwear, with skirts, slacks, scarves, ribbons and blouses hanging from the ceiling. It was only a minute or two, however (although it seemed much longer), before four efficient-looking police ran up to the stall.

Neatly uniformed in crisp, bleached-khaki, open-necked shirts and trousers, with shiny black shoes, black walkie-talkies on their belts, pistol in open holsters, the police were 'cool', super-cool in fact, in complete control. They escorted Alison and me out of the market and called up a taxi. Tight-lipped, obviously exasperated, the officer-in-charge, who would have been about 25 at most, told the driver to take us 'up-town' to our hotel.

'This is no place for white people,' he said to me, quite ignoring Alison. 'They're waiting for you at the corner with knives. You get killed down here. They cut off your hand to get your wrist-watch. They cut your throat for fun. Stay in New Kingston where you belong. Didn't someone tell you?'

Someone did: Tony Cozier, of Barbados, a top cricket writer whose family has lived in the West Indies for generations. I have known Tony, and respected his judgement, since he covered the 1975-76 West Indies Tour of Australia, which Australia won 4-1. He refused my request for some West Indies autographs after the final Test, saying bitterly, 'losing like that, they're not worth it'. Later he promised through gritted teeth, 'next time will be different.' It has been, repeatedly.

Proud of his English heritage ('There's a Cozier in Shakespeare, a cobbler'), Tony is equally proud of the West Indies and, particularly, West Indies cricket. He doesn't like visitors being hurt, unless they are on-field in the Test series, facing the Windies fast bowlers.

'I wouldn't go downtown if I were you,' he said. 'And if I did, I'd stay in the car. I wouldn't wander around on foot, and I certainly wouldn't go down there at night. There are plenty of nice places in New Kingston, some fine restaurants in the hills, and they are secure.'

Armed guards, some equipped with two guns and a baton, outnumber customers in many of the stores, otherwise we could have been in Toorak, or on Sydney's North Shore, instead of New Kingston. Except, I suppose, that outside we were more likely to be run over by a Cadillac or a Mercedes than a Rolls Royce, and New Kingston businessmen tended to bustle right through you, rather than pausing and confidently waiting for you to step aside.

Also, quite often, somewhere behind you was the sibilant hiss 'whitey' or, less frequently, the derogatory Americanism 'honkie'. As it happened, February was 'Black History Month' on American TV, and practically every night Jamaican TV featured a blood-curdling historical piece on slavery, a replay of 'Roots', or a learned discussion on African influences on western civilization.

Fair enough: the undoubted horrors and injustices of slavery, like the Holocaust, are hard to forgive, let alone forget, even after nearly 150 years, but there appears to be no balance, simply strong emotion and sometimes prejudice, when you discuss race in Kingston, or to a lesser extent, in Port of Spain in Trinidad. And it is practically impossible for race not to be involved in the discussion when you are in mixed company!

If I was asked once early in the tour why there weren't any Aborigines in the Australian party, I was asked a dozen times. Rather than become involved in long, complex discussions regarding lack of cricket opportunities for anyone in northern Australia, where most Aborigines live, or natural talents and inclinations, I'd usually say something to the effect that 'if it was a football team, we'd have Aborigines here, you can be sure of that'.

Invariably, someone would ask whether Aborigines were not 'considered good enough to play cricket for Australia'. It was pointless saying that an Aboriginal team toured England a couple of years ago and that, in fact, the first truly Australian cricket team to tour England was Aboriginal. That, of course, was 'tokenism', 'paternalism', 'patronising colonialism' or whatever the current buzz word happened to be on 'progressive' American campuses or relayed American TV shows.

The few times I asked why there weren't any whites in the West Indies teams, or more pointedly, why there weren't any Indians, I was accused of a) trying to provoke arguments, or b) bad manners. Anyone who provokes arguments with people who look bigger and fitter than Mike Tyson is a fool and, in the Caribbean, it sometimes seems that visitors are like children: to be polite, they should be seen and not heard, while they give a needed injection of hard currency to the local economy.

Jamaicans are a remarkably handsome people, or blend of people, the men mostly fit and athletic, the women, often beautiful, poised, and seemingly always well groomed. Confident, capable, aggressive, that's your typical 'Jake', particularly aggressive, when it comes to an Australian cricketer. Uproar results. Surely it was no coincidence that, right from the start, Queensland's Craig McDermott, who proved the most successful bowler in the series, was the subject of the most sustained, and vicious, physical and verbal attacks from the West Indian cricketers and crowds.

Hit by a bouncer from Courtney Walsh which necessitated nine stitches above his right eye in the four day match against Jamaica, preceding the first one day international, McDermott came back strongly to take 5 for 80 in the first innings of the First Test, hitting Windies opener and vice captain, Desmond Haynes, a painful blow on the instep, opener Gordon Greenidge on the shoulder (Greenidge started limping immediately) and gallant little Gus Logie on the cheek, necessitating seven stitches.

From then on, ostensibly because of his less than dashing batting, McDermott was known by most of the West Indians as 'The Wimp', Man-of-the-Series Richie Richardson, Jeff Dujon, Logie and one or two others being honourable exceptions.

On-field, opener Greenidge never greeted Australian wicketkeeper Ian Healy, McDermott's Queensland mate and closest ally, as anything but 'cheat'. Off-field, he didn't talk to Healy at all. In the Fourth Test, in Barbados, Haynes pointed his bat at Healy as though he intended to part his hair with it, and threatened him with off-field mayhem.

One of the better, though probably apocryphal, stories from the tour was occasioned by Haynes in the same match, when he approached David Boon, fielding close to the bat at silly-point, and pulled down the lower lid of one eye for inspection. Clearly Haynes, a little distraught at the time, thought he had something in the eye and was asking the Australian for advice, or help.

'Can you see anything there?' he is said to have asked Boon, notoriously anything but helpful to opponents. 'Yes,' Boon is said to have replied, 'Terror.'

But there was nothing much to laugh about in the closing stages of the series. Called a 'white cockroach' by a West Indian club official at the Recreation Ground in Antigua, an Australian said he hadn't seen many cockroaches until he visited the Caribbean, but all the ones he had seen there were black or brown.

If he had said that in Kingston, I doubt he would have survived to Antigua, or even to Port of Spain, first stop after Jamaica. Fuses are notoriously short in Kingston.

In 1990, there were at least 714 deaths by violence in Jamaica, including 537 which led to murder charges and 147 which were said to involve killings by police. Most of the deaths, which more than doubled the national road toll, happened in or around Kingston.

Put another way there are twice as many murders in Kingston as there are in Sydney and Melbourne combined, although Sydney and Melbourne have more than ten times Kingston's population. Why the bloodbath? What has gone so terribly wrong in the city which boasts it has the largest English-speaking population in the Americas, south of Miami?

Strangely enough, I perceived the first glimmerings of an answer to that question at the cricket, during the first one-day international, at Sabina Park on 26 February, when Malcolm Marshall, the great Barbadian fast bowler and all-rounder, who was to break Dennis Lillee's wicket record in the last Test of the series, was fielding near the press box.

I have never heard such sustained, personal abuse of a sportsman in my life. It went on and on, amusing at first, then coarse and foul. Sure, Marshall dropped an easy catch from Mark Waugh, on the fence, right in front of his attackers, but ten dropped catches in a row wouldn't have merited the bucketing he was getting from the crowd!

'The catch had nothing to do with it,' I was told by a Jamaican. 'We don't like Marshall because he has insulted us. He has made rude gestures.' Such as what? I couldn't imagine anything as rude as the advice Marshall was being given by part of the Kingston crowd every time he went near the ball, anything as insulting as the comments about his person and family. Australians have been known to jump the fence for less.

Later, one of the 40 Australians who live semi-permanently in Kingston explained that, captaining Barbados a year or two back, Marshall cost Jamaica a possible win in a regional match by refusing to declare. That, and the fact that he was a Bajan in the first place, made him the enemy!

'Jamaicans don't like anyone who doesn't live in Jamaica,' the Australian said.

'In New Kingston they prefer people who live in the same suburb as them; in Old Kingston, they feud with people who live a couple of streets away.

People who vote for the People's National Party [PNP] can't stand people who vote for the Jamaica Labor Party [JLP] living, or even working, near them, and that's very much vice versa. People who live in East Kingston, a PNP stronghold, have graffiti saying 'JLP enter at own risk'. West Kingston is a JLP stronghold and the graffiti there says 'PNP enter at own risk'. They're not bluffing. At election time, it's like war zones, or the 'no go' areas in Belfast and other parts of Northern Ireland.

The elections in 1976 were civil wars. Both sides smuggled in guns and other weaponry to arm their members — 'tribes' would be a better word — and there were literally hundreds of murders attributable directly to politics. In 1980 there were more than 800 violent deaths in Jamaica.

Harsh West Indian attitudes to crime and punishment were similarly determined by the area's early slave and pirate history, said my Kingston informant (an influential and knowledgeable member of the community). Without exception, nations in the Caribbean were strongly in favour of capital and corporal punishment. Jamaica recently voted 84 per cent in favour of a resumption of capital punishment, he said.

Maybe that was the spark which lit the seemingly unquenchable fire in the minds of Jamaicans, and the bellies of West Indies cricketers ...

THE FIRST TEST:
THE BATTLE BEGINS

Clive Lloyd sat at the bar of the Pegasus Hotel, pondering the Australian victory in the one-day international at Sabina Park the previous day while waiting for his mate, former Guyanese and Test batsman and now executive secretary of the West Indies Cricket Board of Control, Steve Comacho. National selector David Holford joined them and only the cooling breeze of late evening tempered the heated debate about the future of West Indian cricket and, more to the point, the immediate future of the Test team. West Indians discuss their beloved game as fervently as rival football supporters in pubs around the globe. It took some time to appreciate that the shouting and arm waving was nothing more than an extension of sound and reasoned philosophies being exchanged by knowledgeable and caring cricket lovers. It took less time to discover that the volume increased in proportion to the replenishment of drinks, which came as fast and as unobtrusively as a Michael Holding bouncer. Jamaican rum has a similar effect to a thunderbolt from Whispering Death, and is just as lethal.

Lloyd expounded his theories in the cold light of the following day and foreshadowed the end of a dominant West Indian era if the senior players failed against Australia during this five-Test series. The Godfather of West Indian cricket during the past 15 years, including 11 as skipper and recently as manager of the team, was not being melodramatic. He honestly believed that Gordon Greenidge, Jeff Dujon and Malcolm Marshall were vulnerable, along with skipper Viv Richards, and that this series threatened to be a final fling for the cluster of champions. As Lloyd suggested:

I think this series might be the end of an era. These senior players have set such a high standard and people expect them to maintain it. If they don't in this series I am sure there will be change and I think the selectors are looking carefully at their performances. But it all depends on what happens here. These guys will decide by their deeds if they are still good enough, otherwise the selectors will decide for them. Greenidge will be 40 at the end of this series, Dujon 35, Marshall 33 and Richards 39. They already boast 356 Tests between them before this Sir Frank Worrell Trophy series and obviously it is hard to keep going. I don't think there should be wholesale dropping of guys because they have a lot of experience and are disciplined cricketers. But we have adequate cover and it is a matter of injecting young blokes who can learn from the veterans. When that happens really is up to the form of the senior men. If the West Indian veterans don't succeed they surely will consider their immediate futures.

Lloyd pointed out that the veterans had been carrying the West Indians for a long time but had recently dropped form.

Greenidge didn't make many runs in Pakistan [58 at 9.66 in the three Tests]; Dujon's form has been patchy; Viv didn't tour because of illness and Marshall captured only six wickets. The older players have been doing the job for so long now, especially the batsmen, and we haven't had any young player who has really been outstanding, except Richie Richardson. The blokes like Greenidge, Haynes, Richardson, Richards and Logie make the runs all the time so there hasn't been anyone else getting a chance. That must happen sooner or later, but not until the men who have done the West Indies proud have had their chance to carry on or step aside. They deserve that courtesy.

Lloyd, who retired as a champion left-hand batsman in 1985 with 7515 runs at 46.67 to his credit in 110 Tests, believes the senior players will know when the time has come to give the game away, just as he did.

You know it when the game becomes a chore, when you know when you have had enough. It's when you look at the clock and hope the last hour didn't exist or when you curse another game when you get out of bed in the morning. My situation was different from these guys in that we were winning and I was running out of goals. I realised that I had had enough because I was captain for 11 years and had nothing more to prove. But I think these blokes will have to look at themselves and assess just what they want to achieve and why they are continuing. They must say 'hey, my standards are slipping, I am not doing as well as in the past, and I can't do it that well any more. I am not just in it for the beer.' They may come to that conclusion during this series if things go wrong, or the selectors may decide it for them, but I think generally the thought would be to keep most of the experienced guys around for the tour of England after this and then perhaps to reshape the side for the World Cup.

Not for one moment did Lloyd suggest that the West Indians were over the hill as a combination; talented young players in the Test team were still dynamic, particularly Richardson and speedsters Curtly Ambrose and Patrick Patterson, with premier paceman Ian Bishop waiting to return from a back complaint. He warned:

> *But I think this will be a really difficult time for the West Indians. I am very impressed with the attitude of the Australians, who play to a plan, bowl intelligently, field brilliantly and occupy the crease for long periods. The pressure will be on the West Indians. The public doesn't think about defeat, just about by how much we will win. If the Australians start winning, the players who fail to live up to their own high standards and the public expectations will have tremendous pressure on them.*

And with that, Lloyd provided the perfect preview from the West Indian viewpoint to the first round in the title fight for the world crown.

The Australians appreciated that the West Indian fast bowlers would be a far more dangerous combination in the Test arena than they were in the one-day game, particularly with short-pitched deliveries available to them with fieldsmen in catching positions. The one-day loss left the West Indians smarting and none of the Australians was lulled into a false sense of security by the half-volleys earlier in the week. Certainly not Dean Jones, who was an obvious target for the Caribbean quicks because of his ability to score quickly. Recognised as the premier batsman in limited-over internationals and already a veteran of 39 Tests with 2800 runs at 48.27 to his credit, Jones knew only too well that protection was essential against the West Indians and he wasn't bashful about parading it. Jones, an individual who usually dresses to kill, showed how to dress not to be killed by the fearsome foursome. Several of his team-mates jokingly queried his courage and his cautiousness, but within a couple of hours of action in the series, the attire was virtually compulsory.

The battle-dress consisted of a helmet (with grille), mouth guard, chest pad, arm guard, thick gloves, protector, thigh pad, shin pad, outer pads, and hard boots in case of a rare full-pitched delivery. And, of course, a bat, if only to protect the protected parts. Such highly sophisticated equipment is regulation these days with perhaps a sweatband and headband thrown in.

Jones quickly pointed out that logical precautions demand the 'cover-up' and that the fear factor is a minimal consideration.

> *It is simple insurance and you are no less a man if you wear it. Some of the West Indian guys don't wear all the gear because it is a macho thing to do, but that's up to them. As far as I'm concerned cricket is my game and my job and if I get one ball which hits me in the face because I'm not wearing a helmet, or breaks a rib because I'm not wearing a chest pad, I am risking my livelihood. A lot of people have invested money in me and those sporting companies deserve to have me out on the park as much as possible. If I were injured and missed a Test or a series or*

whatever and another guy took his chance and did well, I would be back to square one as a Test player.

It is particularly important here. If you bat for a long time against these guys you are going to be hit three or four times. You just hope they don't break any bones. Being padded up in such a way that it doesn't hinder your stroke-play or movements is logical insurance. The only psychological fear is getting out. I don't know anyone who likes facing blokes who are hurling missiles at you at a hundred miles an hour but that's the job. The adrenalin pumps and the thing you fear most is getting out, not being hit. I have a lot to prove on this tour and my goal is to score plenty of runs to help Australia win the series. You can't do that in the pavilion so it is a case of fronting up, protecting yourself against the blows and then getting in for your chop.

The Australians were by no means thinking of taking a backward step. In fact the team was in a confident and jovial mood, especially after late night celebrations twice in three days to herald the arrival of first-born babes for wicketkeeper Ian Healy and then his understudy, Mike Veletta. Healy heard news of the birth of Emma Kate from wife Helen in Brisbane and then Veletta handed out the cigars and cracked the champagne when wife Linda delivered Timothy Ross. The pair had to wait nearly two months to hold their children, but News Limited photographer Gregg Porteous helped the proud fathers exchange pictures with their respective wives with newborn to ease the absence.

The frivolity subsided in the camp as minds turned to the task at hand. Australian and West Indian managements met to abate fears of a bouncer war, feared after the short-pitched bowling episode from Courtney Walsh in the Jamaica match, and to rekindle the spirit of competition generated during the 1960s. This was the 25th anniversary of the beginning of the Sir Frank Worrell Trophy for cricket supremacy between the two countries and an appropriate time to suggest a tough, fair and sporting series. Two men in the meeting, Bob Simpson and Lance Gibbs, played a major role in that 1960-61 series which saw hundreds of thousands of fans give the West Indians a ticker tape farewell in the streets of Melbourne. They were joined by Allan Border, Lawrie Sawle and Viv Richards for a general discussion on playing the game in the best possible spirit.

'We agreed that both sides would try to make this a sporting series as well as a competitive one and it was a good start to the series,' Simpson explained.

There is bound to be the odd quick thrust between batsmen and bowlers, but we're trying to set the atmosphere for a good, competitive series with the accent on cricket. We reached a verbal agreement that we would attempt to bowl 90 overs in a day within the time limit and

*that the public would get value for money. It would be great to rekindle
the spirit of the 1960-61 series when Worrell was inspirational and the
cricket fans loved every minute of a hard but good-spirited series.*

The first step was an agreement for the players to share a drink at the end
of each day's play and not merely compete as 'the enemy' in matches. The
good intentions lasted such a short time — even before the opening Test
finished the social drinking was enjoyed only by a handful, forced by a few
others and generally ignored by the younger West Indians, notably the fast
bowlers. And as the series unfolded and on-field backchat and aggression
took over, the pledges of these early days seemed as sincere as vows of
compassion from Saddam Hussein.

Opening Test eve always is a time of excitement, nervous banter and
inner apprehension, but the players were confident and relaxed after a
team meeting. Border insisted the team would not be intimidated by the
West Indians.

*I think they are questioning themselves a little more than they usually
do. They normally go into every series cock-sure and cock-a-hoop but
after the one-day international loss, and the way we have played in
recent times, I think they will be sitting up and taking notice of us. They
have dominated cricket for so long that it is in their nature to be
aggressive and confident: we hope they are over-confident.*

The West Indians had every reason to be confident as they boasted 15
wins, seven draws and only four losses against Australia since 1978.
Richards considered the pace attack of Ambrose, Marshall, Patterson and
Walsh contained the fire-power to win at Sabina Park and that his batting
line-up was experienced and classy enough to score heavily. The
Australians were forced to overlook Reid because of his lack of confidence
after a back ailment, so Whitney came into the Test team for his first
appearance since capturing nine wickets against the West Indians at
Adelaide in early 1989. Alderman couldn't be considered because of a lack
of fitness, and besides the conditions wouldn't have suited. Otherwise the
Australians retained the basis of the line-up which so easily accounted for
England during the domestic season. So on a hot Jamaican Friday
morning and on a pitch glittering with a reflective sheen, the battle began.

FIRST DAY

What a sensational start to such a long-awaited showdown! The opening
day had everything: drama, batting and bowling heroics, and blow and
counter-blow from outstanding players.

The Australians dismissed the West Indians for 264 and were four runs
without loss at stumps on a day which belonged to fast and fearsome pace

Gallant gnome Gus Logie goes down, hit below the eye by McDermott.

pair McDermott and Hughes and the gallant gnome Gus Logie. McDermott captured 5 for 80 and Hughes 4 for 67 as a relentlessly hostile combination which didn't spare the short-pitched ball to unsettle the cream of the West Indian batsmen. McDermott, who took his tally to 23 wickets in three Tests since his recall, completely rattled the top-order batsmen and sent Haynes (toe), Greenidge (shoulder) and Logie to hospital in a dramatic opening 160 minutes of the Test. Logie required seven stitches under the right eye after missing a hook shot; Greenidge was cleared of bone damage to the point of the right shoulder when he too missed a short-pitched delivery attempting to hook, and X-rays cleared Haynes of fractures of the left big toe when hit by a yorker.

The Australians seemed to have a stranglehold on proceedings only 40 minutes after lunch when the West Indians slumped to 6 for 75, but champions that they are, the West Indians fought back courageously. Logie was the hero. He retired hurt with blood streaming from his face when only nine but returned to contribute a fearless and enterprising 77 not out off only 110 deliveries with 12 boundaries. Dujon chimed in with a timely 59, his first half-century in more than two years and 27 Test innings, and the last four wickets added 189 runs to take the gloss off the early rout. But the Australians had to be satisfied with the day's work especially as the West Indies won the toss and batted.

McDermott's third consecutive first innings bag of five or more wickets was an aggressive revenge for a man who needed nine stitches inserted above the right eye when hit by Walsh in the match against Jamaica the previous week. He was exceptionally fast in the middle session when he captured 3 for 20 off seven overs, including his 100th Test scalp in his 27th Test when he held a return catch to remove Greenidge.

Not everything went the Australians' way. The ball which hit Logie rolled into the stumps but didn't dislodge the bails; Mark Taylor missed a slips chance from Logie off Hughes late in the day, and McDermott misjudged a chance at fine leg off Dujon early in his innings. Whitney went off in the final session because he was so squirmish that he felt he might be ill on the field; Hughes struggled to overcome the effects of the flu, Healy had a stomach upset and Marsh also was off colour. But nobody could have felt worse than Logie when the delivery from McDermott thudded against his right eyesocket. Logie's determination to return to the crease after the stitches was inspiring to his team-mates, but to then ravage the bowling in such authoritative fashion was a tribute to his courage, ability and team orientated character. Physiotherapist Dennis Waight was full of praise for the shortest member of the team. 'He was physically drained but when you get badly hit it is like falling off a horse — the best thing you can do is get straight back on. The 77 runs were the best doctor he could have had and the rest of the players are inspired by his courage and endeavour.'

Richards went a step further in his praise of the popular right-hander. He said with genuine admiration:

He was hit on the face, went to hospital, got stitched up and returned. That is a man I will take with me to the front any day. I used to think Desmond Haynes was my number one man in that category but I will have to find a place up there for Gus. It was a remarkable effort, an effort which would make big men weep to see a guy get stuck in like he did.

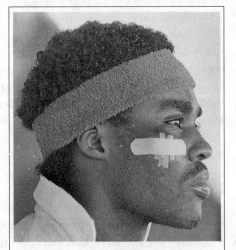

Logie, with seven stitches under his right eye, returns to star in an heroic innings.

With the right side of his face still swollen with seven stitches under the eye, Logie was to suffer a doubly severe blow that evening when he received news of his mother's death. The youngest of six children and a man very close to his mother, Augustina, who christened him Augustine, he immediately gained compassionate leave to fly to Trinidad. But the family delayed the funeral until the end of the Test. Unfortunately the Australian and West Indian cricketers, because of lack of seat availability on the last flight, were unable to attend the funeral to show their respect for a colleague whose courage and devotion is obvious on and off the field.

The day's dramas began in only the fifth over of the Test when McDermott's yorker crushed Haynes' toe, forcing the vice-captain to retire hurt at four with only nine runs on the board. He returned later to add four more runs before McDermott shattered his stumps with a genuinely fast delivery. But Hughes was the man to instigate the early rout with the wickets of Richardson (15) and Hooper (0) in the space of four deliveries. Richardson defensively edged a catch to Healy while Hooper's edged drive resulted in a superb left-handed catch by Marsh in the gully.

Richards strutted to the crease and immediately clubbed two boundaries through the on-side off McDermott, bringing up his 8000th Test run when he reached ten. The champion West Indian skipper became only the seventh player in history to reach the milestone, but the roars of approval of the crowd and his desire to take on the Australian attack contributed to his downfall just one run later. He hooked a McDermott bouncer from outside the off stump and Hughes judged the catch superbly, claiming it high above his head at fine leg. The Australians, having taken 3 for 63 in the opening session, then seized control within 40 minutes after the interval as Greenidge, Haynes and Marshall departed to have the scoreboard attendant in a flap with the total on 6 for 75 and Logie on his way to hospital.

McDermott celebrated his 100th Test dismissal with a return catch to dismiss Greenidge for a stubborn 27 in two and a quarter hours, an appropriate innings in the circumstances while his team-mates were sacrificing their wickets with adventurous shots. Haynes returned to join Logie but within a few minutes Logie missed a hook and retired hurt. McDermott quickly found himself on a hat trick when he bowled Haynes with an express delivery and trapped Marshall lbw. Ambrose denied him the feat and went on to give solid support to Dujon in a 69 run partnership in only 72 minutes. The pair decided attack was the best form of defence in the situation and Ambrose was particularly frustrating to the bowlers by contributing 33 in 72 minutes of hit-or-miss batting. He connected well enough on six occasions to reach the boundary to have more to his credit at that stage than any other batsman. Mark Waugh came into the attack with his medium-pace deliveries and dismissed Ambrose by juggling a return catch, much to the relief of his team-mates. The Australians controlled the session with 4 for 92 to restrict the West Indies to 7 for 155 but nobody figured on the heroic deeds to come from Logie.

McDermott accounted for Walsh for 10 just 20 minutes after tea and Logie re-entered the fray to tumultuous applause from the entire crowd, including a section of Australians who had flown from London and Miami with flags and banners for the occasion. Logie launched into an attack almost immediately, driving and cutting and eventually pulling to scoot to a half-century off only 90 deliveries. Dujon was judiciously selective between attack and defence and he reached an overdue half-century after 156 minutes of intense concentration in a crisis. He and Logie added 68 in 22 overs to boost the score to 234 before Hughes called on all his strength and stamina to produce a rearing delivery which Dujon fended to Marsh in the gully. Dujon's 59 was his first half-century in 27 Test innings in more than two years, but an extremely timely one. Hughes bowled Patterson to wrap up the innings with McDermott taking the honours with 5 for 80 and Hughes proving a fiery accomplice with 4 for 67 while Whitney was economical without success with only 58 runs coming from 21 overs.

McDermott scoffed at any suggestion that the Australians had let the West Indians off the hook: 'If anyone said before play that we would bowl them out for 264 we would have been doing handstands!'

Simpson quickly tempered speculation of a bumper war and considered

Craig McDermott, Australia's aggressive First Test bowling hero.

the Australians hadn't overdone the short-pitched bowling.

It's certainly not the policy of the side; our policy is to bowl them out. If we can use the short ball in a judicious way we probably will. It's a tough sport and we are playing it tough over here. We won't go overboard with bouncers because that would go against our overall policy but we'll certainly keep it up our sleeves.

The West Indians attended a team meeting immediately after play before joining the Australians for a drink and an exchange of medical reports.

SECOND DAY

Australia's bearded wonders of the top order — Marsh, Mark Taylor and Boon — fashioned the Australians a victory platform during an intense second day when they capitalised on the decisive work of the bowlers. They withstood the ferocity of the four-pronged pace attack to provide the bulk of the scoreline of 4 for 296 and a 32 run advantage with six wickets in hand.

The Australian batsmen were as impressively aggressive as the bowlers the previous day with Marsh and Taylor registering their fourth century liaison. Marsh's 69 was outstanding, Taylor barely flinched after being hit on the right jaw by a Marshall bouncer to go on to 58, and Boon's contribution of an unbeaten 71 in four hours completed the trifecta for the men who sprouted stubble for this Test in much the same way as a boxer does for a title fight.

The positive attitude took the West Indians by surprise, but not the courage and determination of Marsh and Taylor which not only blunted the onslaught but took the bowlers to task. Marsh explained: 'It was important that we played positively. Had we gone out there and just tried to blunt their attack it would have been negative and played into their hands. We had to take them on a bit, so if the ball was there to be hit we decided not to hold back.' Taylor, who said he was merely trying to stick around while Marsh 'smashed them', considered the 139 run opening partnership was as much mental steel as positive cricket.

You must be tough against these blokes. You can't afford to give them an inch because they are so good. We had them 6/75 on the opening day and yet they made 264 when most other teams would have been skittled for 120. We knew what we were going to face: we were mentally prepared to face four quicks with plenty of short-pitched deliveries. We expected it and we got it.

The pair revved up to the challenge and the crowd reaction. 'When they bowl short the crowd goes beserk and that really gets you going. The adrenalin pumps and you know it is them and you. The West Indians play it tough and hard but the spirit on the field is good so far,' Marsh said. The century opening partnership, only the fourth by a touring opponent in 37 Tests in the West Indies in the past decade, was a combination of excellent evasive movements, psychological warfare and particularly punishing cutting from Marsh and on-drives from Taylor. The pair totally and deliberately ignored the glares from Ambrose and Patterson if they dodged a short-pitched ball or were beaten by a fine delivery, leaving the bowler mid-pitch without eye contact.

Marsh was particularly ruthless with his cuts off anything short and he skipped to his half-century off only 85 deliveries with seven boundaries. The 50 partnership came in 17 overs and the 100 in 39 overs and the West Indian pacemen began to sag. Ambrose, the giant with the ability to generate pace and bounce from the most docile of pitches, ended Marsh's innings by forcing a defensive edge to Dujon. Taylor reached his half-century, his first against the West Indians after managing only 67 runs in his initial two Tests in 1988-89, after 195 minutes but he departed at 58 to a smart catch in the gully by Hooper off Paterson after spending 42 minutes for his last eight runs when Boon joined him.

The loss of both openers in the space of 20 runs gave the West Indians renewed spirit but Boon and Border weathered the storm and added 68 before Ambrose again produced an excellent delivery to account for Border. The skipper contributed 31 with four boundaries and obviously was keen to maintain the aggressive approach, particularly when he reached the 9000 run career milestone in his 121st Test with his 18th run, leaving him 1109 shy of overhauling Sunil Gavaskar as the highest run-scorer in Test history. But he could do nothing but edge Dujon another catch when Ambrose unleashed another gem with the total on 227.

Jones was the only batsman to fail, gently spooning a return catch to spinner Hooper in much the same manner as he departed for a duck against Phil Tufnell in the third Ashes Test in Sydney. He jumped down the pitch but neither struck the ball firmly nor defensively negated any spin. The indecision resulted in the simplest return catch and the frivolous waste of an innings which again gave the West Indians a renewed interest.

Mark Waugh had a baptism of fire when he entered the fray after the loss of Border and Jones in the space of only one run. He was hit on the back of the shoulder by a short-pitched ball from Ambrose and then popped the next delivery to silly short leg, from where Richards had just moved his catcher. Ambrose and then Patterson, who waited for Waugh to face before taking the second new ball, peppered the right-hander to such an extent that umpire David Archer quietly cautioned Ambrose. But Waugh responded to the challenge and contributed 22 in an unfinished partnership of 76 with Boon.

The West Indians bowled into the gloom of evening to complete the 90 overs in the day, taking an extra hour after scheduled stumps to bowl the final ten overs. They bowled only 48 overs in the first two sessions, leaving themselves 42 overs to bowl in the final session. The Australians capitalised on the tiredness of the pace bowlers despite the deteriorating conditions and the second new ball, but always risked the loss of wickets. The Australians couldn't complain about the late finish because they envisaged a seven hour day as the norm when the West Indians bowled, but it was immediately confirmed that the home team had no intention of bowling the 90 overs within the scheduled hours of play. The overtime made it a long final session of three hours for David Boon, who reached his half-century with six boundaries and barely a blemish in technique or application.

THIRD DAY

The West Indians fought back like the champions they are to spoil a memorable century by Boon in another day of fluctuating fortunes, drama, controversy and exceptional individual feats. Boon provided Australia with a 107 first innings lead with an unconquered 109, but — showing amazing speed with ball and bat — the West Indians converted that into an 80 run lead with eight wickets in hand by stumps.

The speed bowling came from Patterson who claimed a five wicket haul as the West Indians skittled the last five Australian wickets for only 12 runs, and then dashing duo Haynes and Greenidge clouted a 118 run partnership to wipe off the deficit in only 124 minutes off 29.1 overs.

At stumps on the third day the Australians had lost the advantage they so methodically chiselled on the first two days as the West Indians reached 2 for 187. The Australian bowlers had no answer to the assault from Haynes, who reached his half-century off only 71 deliveries with 10 boundaries, and who celebrated his 6000th run in the Test arena just one run before his dismissal. The century partnership, which took only two hours, was the champion pair's 16th in Test cricket and as ruthless as any of their best.

The controversy centred around two crucial decisions by senior umpire David Archer. He gave Matthews out caught behind to trigger the Australian collapse and late in the day he rejected an appeal for a catch at the wicket when Richardson attempted a hook off Mark Waugh. The verdicts changed the course of the game, according to Border, who was matter-of-fact about the appeals. 'Greg Matthews wasn't out and Richie Richardson was,' he said. 'But you must take the good with the bad. A couple of decisions went against us but that will always happen so how important they are will only tell in the final wash-up.' The Australians accepted the decisions without dissent, such was the prevailing early tour spirit, but the incidents came at crucial times. The loss of Matthews for 10 came when the Australians were in command at 5 for 357, a lead of 113, and that rejuvenated the West Indian attack just before lunch. Then when McDermott removed Haynes and Greenidge with a deficit of only 27, the pressure was on the West Indians. The demise of Richardson would have enhanced Australia's victory chances and exposed another batsman late in the day, with the second new ball due within 20 overs.

The controversies couldn't detract from some glorious cricket, however, and the highlights flowed thick and fast in another day of enthralling cricket. Boon displayed skill, patience and courage to record his tenth Test century in his 54th match and his second against the West Indians, adding to his 149 at the SCG in 1988-89. Not even a blow to the jaw from a Patterson delivery at 98 could jolt the nuggety right-hander. He received treatment from physiotherapist Errol Alcott and waited for Dean Jones to add a protective grille to his helmet before reaching his milestone after 343 minutes. The West Indians generously and spontaneously applauded the effort; the Australian players provided a standing ovation as Boon saluted them and the Australian support group chanted 'Boonie, Boonie'.

Boon has played many handsome innings for Australia but few would rival this one because of the place, the pressure and the pace. The unbeaten century continued a purple patch for the nuggety right-hander who came hot off 530 runs against England at an average of 75.71. His past eight Test innings added 593 runs to his career aggregate, coming at the staggering average of 118.6.

Boon is a tough nut, the professional's professional. He was feeling no pain after his innings and rejected a doctor's suggestion of an injection before having a stitch inserted in his chin. Terry Brindle, of the *Australian*, suggested a doctor could have given him a Boag's beer and then amputated the leg of this tough Tasmania tiger. But he accepted the stitch pumped up only on adrenalin and pride, and a place in the history books as only the eleventh Australian to record Test century double figures.

Boon unfortunately ran out of partners far too quickly, the last five wickets tumbling for only 12 runs in 40 minutes and the last six for 42 runs when a demoralising lead was at hand. Patterson, who finished with 5 for 83 off 24 overs, captured 4 for 3 in 19 deliveries to skittle the tail after Boon and Mark Waugh shared a 101 run fifth wicket partnership in only 146 minutes. Mark Waugh contributed 39 during a baptism of fire. He was hit on the back of the left shoulder when he began the previous day and suffered another blow to the left side of the helmet by Marshall when 30, as he was again undecided whether to duck or defend. He eventually was indecisive against a fuller length delivery from Marshall and, playing from the crease, was trapped leg before wicket.

Waugh's obvious discomfort against the short, rising ball raised a question mark about the right-hander's ability to cope against genuinely fast bowlers who concentrated on his technical deficiency. But Simpson, a former champion opening batsman who faced men of speed of the ilk of Wes Hall and Charlie Griffith, immediately quelled any fears. Waugh's courage and natural instincts would determine if he would overcome the biggest, and possibly the last, challenge to his advancement as a superior batsman, Simpson suggested. Being hit on the head by Walsh in the match against Jamaica and then a couple of times in this Test wasn't a reason to panic, Simpson said, pointing to scores of 108 and 39.

Mark has never been confronted with this type of pace before. It takes time to adjust because all the theories don't mean much in practice when a bloke is charging in at you. I have advised him to allow his natural instincts to dictate because as soon as a batsman pre-sets his mind to hook or to duck or whatever, he is in trouble. You must tackle every delivery as you see it and isolate your thoughts on a delivery and forget about theories. It is a huge challenge for Mark, like it is for any player. He has played only two Tests and he has played in English county cricket where the bowling is pretty friendly compared to this. This is probably the last challenge and a really big one. I have no doubt he will cope because he is too naturally good a player not to sort it out. It all comes down to courage and instincts and he has them both.

The coach was proved to be spot on by the end of the tour.

The exit of Waugh was followed by the disputed dismissal of Matthews. This was the start of the major low-order collapse which came all too swiftly. Walsh trapped Ian Healy lbw for a duck and the Australians lost two important wickets in the two overs before lunch. The end was decisive. McDermott took two blows to the body from Patterson then lost his stumps to a yorker and Hughes edged his first delivery to Hooper at second slip. Patterson failed in his hat trick attempt at the start of his next over but uprooted Whitney's middle stump five balls later to claim his fourth haul of five or more wickets in an innings in his 19th Test, his last being against Australia at the MCG in December of 1988 when he won the man-of-the-match award with match figures of 9 for 88.

Patterson proved a handful but Ambrose posed the most problems, repeatedly beating the batsmen and menacing them with short-pitched deliveries from his considerable height. He dismissed Marsh and Border, intimidated Mark Waugh and then didn't have a crack at the tail-enders when wickets tumbled at the whim of the bowler.

The lead of 107 evaporated in an astonishing onslaught from Greenidge and Haynes who belted 70 runs in 78 minutes off 17 overs by tea. If the Australian batsmen had been so successful because they didn't give an inch, the bowlers failed dismally in this undisciplined period by giving the free-stroking batsmen a yard. Haynes suffered two more painful blows to the foot and decided to lash out. He cut and drove the ball with super power to post eight boundaries in 43 by tea while Greenidge, still handicapped by a sore right shoulder, chimed in with another four boundaries in his 22.

They posted their 16th century union in two hours of daredevil batting to remind the world of their era as the devastating opening combination of the past decade. The Australians needed no reminding for this was their sixth century opening liaison against the bowlers from Down Under. They seem to thrive on challenges against Australians and while century partnerships are less frequent these days they remain a menacing pair. Their previous century stand was a West Indian record 298 against England in Antigua in the final Test in 1990, eclipsing their own milestone of 296 against India at the same venue in 1983.

The situation at stumps provided rival skippers Border and Richards with reason to be pleased. 'There is no question that we can match them on what we have shown so far,' Border said while conceding Australia won the opening two days and the West Indies the third. To which Richards responded: 'There is fight in the old dog yet. That was a big comeback.'

FOURTH DAY

This engrossing Test was doomed to a draw because of inadequate protection of the pitch against rain. The entire fourth day was abandoned after heavy overnight rain left a monster damp patch on a good length in direct line between the stumps, and a mud heap around the wicket square and for 10 metres on the bowler's run-up at the northern end. The episode was a disgrace to West Indian cricket and one which local officials tagged as 'embarrassing', 'humiliating' and 'outrageous' and which made a mockery of Test cricket at the famous Sabina Park venue.

The sequence of events was difficult to comprehend. The main cover was put on the practice pitch area and newly purchased reserve covers, being used for the first time, were placed on the pitch. A blackout during the overnight thunderstorm hindered the 20 ground staff when the four grandstand lights didn't work and nobody checked the centre wicket covers during the storm because the groundsmen didn't have raincoats. The groundsmen didn't have raincoats so they refused to venture into the rain to ensure the pitch was safely protected from the elements for this extremely important Test. The abrogation of duty was like water off a duck's back to the groundsmen, who sought out the local media to confirm they didn't fulfil their obligations but, more importantly, to demand that local officials supply them with raincoats. Meanwhile a magnificent Test went down the drain.

The simple fact was that while the groundsmen took shelter in the pavilion, the water swept under the covers at the southern end and penetrated frayed seams on the new covers. The result was a quagmire at the bowler's end, mud heaps around the square, and a pattern of water marks across the block with two major damp spots on the clay pitch. One was harmlessly resting at the side of the pitch but the other was in a dangerous spot in line with the stumps. The clay soil hid the depth of the damage. McDermott stuck his finger in the area and penetrated to the second knuckle without pushing. Jones almost lost a key. The umpires lost hope and the players of both sides lost no time in returning to the hotel even before the scheduled starting time, leaving behind them flooded dressing rooms.

The Test lost all significance as a battle after three fabulous days and obviously neither team was remotely interested in playing in such conditions. The batsmen would have been exposed to a damp spot on the pitch and the bowlers wouldn't have been guaranteed against injury when running in. The West Indies Board, with so much at stake during this series in terms of finances and the regeneration of interest in the game, had to shoulder the blame.

Every precaution must be taken at this highest level of the game to ensure a Test is not ruined by preventable mishaps. A shrug of the shoulders and cry of dismay that rain fell on this Caribbean island just when it wasn't wanted simply wasn't good enough. The lesson should have been learned from the previous year when rain washed out the fourth day of the Test against England. It does rain at odd times in the Caribbean, and every precaution should be taken.

The most annoying aspect was that the sun shone brilliantly all day. Proper protection of the pitch area would have ensured only a minor delay to enable the ground staff to mop up the outfield. As it was, this Test was robbed of four sessions and all its intrigue and potential.

The day at the hotel allowed the Australians ample time to dissect the pattern of play on the opening three days and to evaluate bonuses and deficiencies. The players came to the conclusion that the once respected fast bowlers' union was dead and buried. The Australian fast bowlers came to terms with the reality that they, like the senior batsmen, would be on the receiving end of short-pitched deliveries, and that they needed to retaliate in kind to balance the ledger. 'Our bowlers were surprised by the ferocity of the West Indian attack and the use of the short-pitched delivery. They knocked us over very easily after we had gone a bit soft on them,' Simpson confirmed.

I think our fast bowlers must be more positive. We are not going to get any favours from them as far as our tail-end batsmen are concerned and

I don't think we should issue any in return. It is foreign to our character but at the same time it is the way the game is played here. If those are the rules they play by, so be it. We must adopt the policy that they are batsmen, regardless of what position they bat, just as they did to us in this Test, and be more ruthless with their latter order batsmen referring to the freedom the Australians gave the West Indian tail of four fast bowlers who added 47 runs while the last Australian four was blitzed out for a paultry three runs. There was a fast bowlers' union but apparently that is a thing of the past.

Border suggested that the tail-enders must produce runs 'because it will be no good if we are five out, all out. We have discovered a few things during this Test which we will put into practice in the rest of the series and one of the priorities is to get the tail-end batsmen to contribute runs and for our bowlers to skittle their tail-enders.'

FINAL DAY

Viv Richards and Richie Richardson enjoyed personal milestones in the inevitably drawn Test to allow both teams to walk away from Sabina Park with a sense of achievement and satisfaction. Richards became the highest run-scorer in West Indian Test history and Richardson celebrated his 11th Test century and amazingly his sixth in 16 matches against Australia as the West Indies reached 3 for 334 in a shortened final day.

The champion West Indian skipper overhauled Sir Garfield Sobers' standard of 8032 runs when he reached 32 of his unbeaten 52 at the close. Border, who earlier in the Test passed 9000 runs, was the first to shake his hand. Richards is acknowledged as *the* man in the Caribbean and the brutally powerful right-hander who has devastated bowling attacks around the globe for 15 years reflected on his achievement on the eve of his 39th birthday. He was modest and proud without gloating and he talked emotionally about the young man who emerged from the back blocks of Antigua with dreams of emulating the deeds of the legendary left-handed Sir Garfield Sobers and who finally realised his ambition. The sixth highest accumulator of runs in Test history sipped a beer and declared:

Sir Garfield Sobers was a great player and to eclipse anything he achieved would make any individual feel happy: that's the way I am feeling now. Records come along if you play enough cricket and do well enough and really it would have been better to pass this milestone and to win the Test. But who can complain? I guess I will cherish it a lot more when it sinks in, maybe when I am retired. But I have a few more goals yet, not so much for Viv Richards but for West Indian cricket. We haven't been beaten in a series for a very long time and that's something we want to preserve. That is more important to me now than how many runs I have against my name.

The comparative records of Richards and Sobers are similar. Sobers played 19 fewer Tests but only eight fewer innings for his runs, which included 26 centuries and 30 half-centuries. Richards boasted 24 centuries and 39 half-centuries and both captained the West Indies, both played memorable innings of sheer genius, and both proved compulsive viewing as champions whose mere appearance at the crease emptied bars around the world.

Richardson is the man destined to fill Richards' boots as the batting dynamo of West Indian cricket. He continued his assassination of Australian attacks with his unbeaten 104 in an unfinished 118 partnership with his mentor. The powerful driver and cutter was never in trouble on the final day, reaching his half-century with seven boundaries and adding another eight in a century off 214 deliveries. The only wicket to fall during the day was that of Hooper, bowled by McDermott for 31. The broad-shouldered paceman finished with all three wickets to fall in the innings, while conceding only 48 runs off 24 overs to be the only threatening bowler on display. Richards could afford to smile at stumps although he wasn't happy when umpires David Archer and Steve Bucknor decided against the wishes of both captains to order play to start after lunch.

Richards and Border considered the damaged pitch, with a damp spot on a good length and loose chunks of clay soil dotted in the same area, unsafe for action for their respective batsmen and bowlers. But the umpires, who have the final say and who were under considerable pressure from West Indian and local Jamaican officials to temper the justifiable criticism of conditions, overruled them. Richards was visibly upset and outspoken in his reaction. 'In the process of finding out if it is dangerous do you want somebody to die out here?' he demanded of the umpires. 'I don't want to come out here to find the ball whizzing around my nose.' But a happier man smoothed the waters at stumps: 'We must give the umpires credit for getting the game started when they did. The timing was perfect, even if we didn't think so at the time.'

Both leaders were happy with the respective efforts of their teams although disappointed with the inadequate cover protection which robbed the Test of four sessions. Border lamented: 'Jamaica must make sure this doesn't happen again. Hopefully the right people get a kick up the backside. It is an international sport and it cannot afford to be second rate because you must be professional in everything you do.' Richards added: 'It is up to the administrators to fix this. If it happened again I am sure heads would roll.'

Border insisted the major bonus was that the Australians realised that the Caribbean champions were mere mortals, not invincible superhumans.

The West Indians have had a mystique about them for years and players have always wondered in the back of their minds how they can possibly beat them. No matter how confidently or positively you entered a match that thought always haunted players because of the reputation of the West Indians, their demeanour and aggressive attitude. But if any of the fellows in this Australian team had any qualms about them I can tell you that what they have got out of this draw is the realisation that we can match it with the West Indians. Our fellows would be crazy if they didn't think they could beat these blokes after the way we played on the first two and a third days. We have had a good look at them, seen that they are as vulnerable as any other team under pressure, and must consider that this game only enhances our chances rather than reduces them for the next four Tests.

Richards conceded that both teams 'are well balanced and evenly matched'. But he claimed:

It gave me a feeling of strength and spirit that we came back after Australia was on top for two days and it showed what we can achieve if we get stuck in. We fought back well: our bowlers bent their backs to get rid of the tail-enders and our batsmen hit out like we know they can. The Australians played really well and then we responded. I think we discovered a few things about them and I am sure this will be a really tough and exciting series.

The second Test was three weeks away and between time the Australians pressed on relentlessly to win three of the four one-day internationals, seizing the series 4-1 to be in a confident frame of mind. But both teams played only one-day games between Tests — the Australians' three-day match against Trinidad & Tobago was abandoned after the second day was washed out and a one-dayer substituted — and 17 days after walking out of Sabina Park, they left the dressing rooms at the Bourda ground in Georgetown, Guyana, for the start to the second Test. The time lapse without first-class cricket was the same for both teams, but nonetheless a disconcertingly lengthy period for cricketers involved in such an important Test series. The rain at Guaracara Park was a blow to Steve Waugh who was elevated in the batting order only for the three-day game to be abandoned and replaced with a one-dayer.

The trip to Pointe-à-Pierre was interesting if only to see the massive oil tanks and inhale the smell of money. The hospitality was generous, although the players became tired of eating chicken — 'When I go to the toilet I lay eggs these days' being a typical remark — and the pizza shop across the road from the ground provided locals with a close-up look at the Australian tourists. They headed to the shop like bees to a honeypot when rain tumbled on two of the first three days and hundreds of locals gladly queued behind them or merely peered through the window as the players tucked into giant pizzas. Just how the pizzas affected their cricket didn't concern them, particularly with Guyana ahead!

CHOKE AND ROB:
TO GEORGETOWN AND
BEYOND

Choke and rob: that's the motto, and main occupation, of a million Guyanese, according to some of their fellow West Indians. To say the 'Land of Many Waters', which occupies 210 000 square kilometres of the northeast coast of South America, is not favoured by its Caribbean cousins is an understatement, an attempt, you might say, to gild a smelly swamp lily.

Georgetown, Guyana, is the absolute pits, the bankrupt rear end of nowhere. No-one wants to live there, least of all the unfortunates born there. Georgetown is to be survived, to be endured rather than enjoyed. At least, that's what they say in the Windies.

Early in the Australian cricket team's stay in Georgetown, I would have agreed. Maybe it was cleaning my teeth in dirty water, maybe it was too much rum out of a sticky glass, but I had an ulcer on my bottom lip, the lashes on my left eye were stuck together with dried pus, my left wrist and the big toe on my right foot were swollen and sore with rheumatism (gout?) and I was scared, far too scared and depressed to venture on my own from our heavily guarded hotel.

New South Wales spinner Greg Matthews had a gold chain and wedding ring snatched from his chest while strolling through the near-centre of town, and Sydney photographer Mike Raynor had been 'bailed up' and robbed of a thousand dollars while taking pictures in the crowded Stabroek Market. Happy-go-lucky Mike rejoiced that his dollars had been Guyanese, not American, but all I wanted to do was to lie down, shut my eyes, and maybe have a glass of cold, newly boiled water.

Guyana is commonly regarded as a Third World country, but I'd readily have amended that to Sixth World, to the sorry kind of 'Banana Republic' former Treasurer Paul Keating has warned Australia is in danger of becoming.

Hiding in room 205 at The Pegasus, allegedly Guyana's best and most secure hotel, I began reading *An Unfinished Journey*, the last book written by Shiva Naipaul, the Trinidad-born Indian author, who died in London in 1985. Apart from the fact that Shiva Naipaul is a brilliant and informative writer, a joy to read, he also can be quite inspirational.

Underlining pertinent passages in his thoughts on 'The Illusion of the Third World', I determined to have another crack at Georgetown, and Guyana. Errol Alcott, the Aussie cricket team's physio, gave me some ointment for my lip, some antibiotics for my eye, and some pills for my wrist and big toe. Naipaul's clear thinking and ultimately hopeful attitude to life took care of the irrational fears and forebodings.

On Friday, 22 May, I stiffened my non-ulcerated upper lip and went on a memorable river trip up the Essequibo River into the remote and supposedly dangerous interior of Guyana. On Saturday, 23 May, I walked home alone in the dark from the Bourda to the Pegasus, after the first day's play in the Second Test. It was an average day for Australia (6 for 249 at stumps, with resolute opener Geoff Marsh going in the closing stages) but most of the crowd, the Indians, were supporting us, and I felt like a Boone (Daniel not David), swaggering around the hotel afer I made it home unscathed.

Richie Benaud, the former Australian captain and now Channel Nine commentator, who is polite enough to say we are both 'former police reporters' (he as a youngster with the now defunct Sydney *Sun*), asked me if it was right I had walked back from the ground, and threw his hands in the air when I said I had.

Richie said he always insisted a taxi-driver picked up any purchases he made in Georgetown, and he always cashed all his traveller's cheques at the hotel. Not doing so was simply bravado, he said, and pin-headed bravado at that. As usual, Richie was probably right, but the walk on the wild side did my morale all sorts of good.

Originally I had intended to take a taxi, but all the taxis outside the Members' Entrance were booked, so after checking with a policeman that I was pointed in the right direction, I simply set off. Georgetown thoroughfares are wide, with a grassy walkway between two roads and floodwater drains on either side, so I thought it would be a simple matter to make sure I was on my own, with no-one near me.

The 'choke and rob' technique, I'd taken trouble to check with police, was for a big Guyanese to come up behind you, throw one arm around your neck, tighten the arm, and then go through your pockets with his free hand while you were half-choking. Any struggles and he simply did a proper job with the arm around your throat.

The other technique, the one used against photographer Mike Raynor at Stabroek Market, was for a big Guyanese to walk head-on into you, and then lean hard against you, apologising profusely. While this was going on, you were trying to push him off, his accomplice quickly went through your pockets from behind.

The way I worked it out, no-one could do you too much damage, and get away with it, on a crowded street after a Test match, if you walked quickly and made sure that no-one came near you. Sure, they could rob you, hurt you maybe, if they wanted to, but someone would be sure to see them, and from what I had heard of prisons in Guyana, no-one in their right mind would want to risk that.

It was very convincing in theory, except that I'd forgotten a couple of important points. The sun goes down like a red stone in Guyana, and apparently the baddies in Georgetown don't care who sees what's going on anyway. Witnesses are always too scared of repercussions to talk. (I hope the old lady who saved Alison and me in Jamaica is still OK.)

I asked a well-dressed young Negro if I was walking in the right direction to cross Main Street (where I would turn right to reach the Pegasus). He said I was. How long would it take, I asked. 'Too long,' he said.

After that, I was really hurrying, as you can imagine. There were lots of people on the walkway: youths kicking a soccer ball around, Rastafarians packing up their stalls, young and old people talking to themselves and staring into space, mothers nursing children, hearty old 'higgly' ladies (street sellers) selling the remnants of their baskets of fruit at give-away prices.

Whenever it looked as though some male, big or small, was approaching me, I'd stop and ask the way from a nursing mother, if I could find one, or hurry off as fast as I could without actually running. The couple of men who came close to me were probably beggars; they certainly weren't menacing, and I just waved my hands, palms upwards. 'I never carry paper money with me away from the hotel,' I'd lie, although I doubt anyone would have understood what I was saying. At the best of times, Guyanese and Australians have to speak slowly to make each other understand what they are saying. That's pretty true of all West Indians, I found. I have never been more conscious of the distinctive Australian accent.

Why did I carry money with me (a minimum of US$20) at all times? Because I can't handle the thought of being flat broke overseas. No matter the circumstances, while you have money, you still have some chance of getting back to your base, to your friends and travelling companions. If you have to, you can buy your way back with the promise of more of the same; at least that's the theory. Any way you look at it, $2500 Guyanese (less than US$20 in March 1991) is a lot of bargaining power in Georgetown. Also, of course, a powerful temptation.

That's why I think no-one, including his cricket team-mates, was surprised when Greg Matthews lost his gold chain in Main Street. He was walking bare-chested in an old-fashioned country where you don't see too many bare chests in the public thoroughfares, and he had at least $25 000

Guyanese worth of easily recyclable gold bouncing around on his chest. And he was near a run-down public housing estate in a country where the average labourer earns $45 Guyanese a day, if he can find a job!

To say the police were unimpressed by Greg doesn't do justice to their disgust at the robbery report. Lawrie Sawle and Bob Simpson did not seem to be too impressed either, although they were too diplomatic, and too conscious of team unity and morale, to say so. But back to the odyssey of my safe passage from the Bourda to the Pegasus.

In the dusk, a succession of open manholes worried me more than a group of chanting Rastas (how'd you fancy falling into a Georgetown sewer?), and when I passed St Agnes Parochial School and the Guyana Responsible Parenthood Centre, I knew I was home safe. Who in the neighbouring tenements would molest a grey-haired grandfather of nine?

I joined the rowdy crowd shouting good wishes to a Guyanese wedding party outside the downtown Watercriss Hotel, and found a sprinkling of holidaying Australian cricket supporters among the crowd. 'Any problems?' I asked Susie, a happy-faced nurse from Brisbane, taking time off from a job in London to follow Australia in the Windies. 'Only with the Aussies,' she replied with a grin, which helped me put my own survival problems in perspective.

I breezed past the Brain Child Photo Studio, the Ptolemy Reid Rehabilitation Centre and the Scottish Flower Masonic Lodge and turned into Main Street. How could anyone worry about anything while walking between the Forbes Burnham Chess Hall and the British High Commission, the Brahma Kumaris Spiritual University and the Commission for the support and re-election of President Hugh Desmond Hoyte, the venerable gentleman who had been our host at a government reception only a few nights previously?

Outside the Umana Yana (a huge thatched hut across the road from the Pegasus, used as a ceremonial meeting place), three pert, black teenage girls, neatly dressed in pink blouses and grey skirts, accosted me. 'Excuse me sir,' said one, apparently the leader. 'But could you give us a flash?'

'Oh, come on,' I said, embarrassed, and walked on quickly. It was only in the Pegasus minutes later that I realised the schoolgirls were talking of a photograph with the camera I had hanging from around my neck, a camera worth at least as much as Greg Matthews' gold chain.

So much for not putting temptation in the way of unfortunate people who, I am convinced now, 'choke and rob' much more from hunger than from greed. Forced into similar circumstances, I am confident many Australians would do the same. I certainly don't feel any superiority or resentment for Guyanese who lash out and try to take something they will never earn enough money to buy. They have been forced into a situation in which they have nothing to lose.

The Essequibo River trip was the turning point as far as my attitude to Guyana and the Guyanese were concerned. In some senses it was a nostalgic trip backwards in time, in others an educational step forward into a deprived, primitive world which could teach our modern, consumer society a thing or two about hope and perseverance.

We started soon after dawn and finished well after dusk, covering more than a thousand kilometres in all, first in a battered four wheel drive van to Parika, on the east bank of the Essequibo River, then in an equally battered power canoe down the Essequibo to Bartica, a nineteenth-century frontier town, at the junction of the gold- and diamond-rich Mazaruni River.

From Bartica, seemingly taken straight from historical pictures of the New South Wales and North Queensland goldfields, we power-canoed 50 kilometres up and down the Mazaruni, the site of underwater mining, sluicing and dredging supervised by lithe, goggled, wetsuited scuba divers who would have been quite at home in a James Bond movie.

We had a late lunch at Camp Rainbow, a camp below two waterfalls built and maintained by exuberant Negro teenagers, then power-canoed back to Bartica and Parika and, long after dark, to Georgetown. It may sound like something straight out of the tourist brochures, yet it was anything but that.

Aboard our canoe we had a pretty combative crew including Terry, a grey-haired, retired American chemical engineer, who coyly admitted to being oldest aboard (I am 63), but was goddamned if he wasn't going to do everything better than anyone else; Mike Coward, the former *Sydney Morning Herald* cricket writer; and Mike Raynor, the adventurous photographer, who was determined to go where Terry couldn't follow, even if it killed him.

Richard Ousman, a Muslim Indian, organised the trip and provided the lunch of curry and barbecued chicken, as well as the mixed bathing at the waterfall which brought Terry unstuck. Brothers Salim (Jim) and Joseph Kayum, also Muslim Indians, manned the canoe powered by an Evinrude motor maintained by their brother Bill, 30, in Parika, and financed by their sisters in Canada.

Before boarding the canoe, Rich showed us a '100 per cent haunted house' near Parika, an eerily imposing, two-storey shell of a place facing the road, with big empty windows that seemed to stare at you like eyes. No-one would live at the house, neither for love nor money, Rich said, with what seemed a genuine shiver. Evil spirits, ghosts, devils, 'the walking dead' inhabited the house.

'It's obeah, African witchcraft, an evil spell, which causes the furniture to fly about and strange lights to shine,' he said helpfully. 'It scares people to death just being there. They are trying to get a priest to cast the evil spirit out, but they can't, because it is not a Christian spirit. I think they will have to kill a chook and sprinkle blood on the floor.'

We inspected a 300-year-old Dutch fort and a barn-like Reform church on the western bank of the Essequibo and then visited an Amerindian village and school. The Amerindians, small, slim, olive-brown people, with very black hair and pointed chins, are as close as there are now to the original inhabitants of the Americas. They're treated like a threatened species (which I suppose they are) by governments in the area, and allowed to travel at will along the rivers and valleys of Guyana, Venezuela, Brazil, Surinam and other South American countries.

When we passed their canoes on the Essequibo, with the men and boys paddling and the women plaiting cane and reeds, the Amerindians hid their faces from Mike's camera, but on shore, outside the simple, homemade huts of their villages, they were friendly and outgoing, although I doubt they understood a word we said.

The women sang what I assumed were ancient tribal songs, but could have been local pop songs, as they stood knee-deep in the river, battering brightly coloured clothes between stones. It was like a diorama in a pre-history exhibition, but I couldn't help noticing that the women pegged out the clothes to dry with plastic pegs, and there were transistor radios playing in their huts.

While the two Mikes arranged some cricket photographs with the photogenic Amerindian children at the Saxacalli village, I spoke to Salim Kayum about his life on the river. He said he was 27, and lived in Parika with his Indian wife and small daughter. He was a happy man, he said. He had no enemies, and an interesting job. He had been working on the Essequibo for nine years and was learning more about it every day.

Salim said he did not know how much he earned a week because his parents, his brother Bill who looked after the engine, his 16-year-old brother Joe, who was the crewman, his sisters and himself all had a share in the profits. 'We make a living,' Salim said, for all the world like a struggling Jewish businessman in a Woody Allen skit. 'Fruit and vegetables are cheap on the banks of the river, and the fish in the river are free.'

Bartica has something of a split personality: a river-town with wharves, warehouses and boat-building yards near the meeting of Essequibo and Mazaruni, with the Old West of wide, dry, dusty streets between slab-front stores and rum-houses (one was 'Blondie's Pub') a few hundred metres inland. There were grey-clad convicts slashing the long grass in front of the police station with cutlasses when we there, and it wouldn't have surprised me to have seen Gary Cooper adjusting his six-guns as he stepped down into the street.

Interestingly, what obviously had been an elaborate war memorial at the cross-roads outside the Bartica cricket ground was now a squat block of white-washed stone. Printed on one side was the blunt message: 'Memorial dedicated to the heroes of what we were, what we are, and what we shall be'.

If I were nominating the current heroes of the region or, for that matter, the whole West Indies, I'd find a place for the frogmen of Guyana who dive alternate shifts, sluicing the mud from the banks of the Mazaruni River for gold and diamonds. They spend a fortnight at a time in the jungle and then hit 'Blondie's Pub' and others in Bartica to celebrate, or to forget.

Nobody told me, but I suspect the Negro teenagers, male and female, who staff the Rainbow tourist camp below the two small waterfalls we visited on the Mazaruni are members of an Evangelical Church group, or a Reform School task force.

Either way, they had that instantly recognisable, shiny-faced zeal common to both species. It was great, JUST GREAT, to know us, and if someone had started a robust hymn or Christian marching song on the way to the falls I would not have been surprised.

My particular escort (we each had an individual escort, at some stages two) was a tall, broad-shouldered, very black Negro named Andrew, who wore long pants, a grey guernsey and cloth cap, despite the heat and humidity.

Andrew spoke slowly, carefully, and seemed eager that I should not miss any of the very real beauty of our surroundings. He forced his way into the tangled undergrowth beside the path to retrieve orchids and pointed silently at lizards and birds. Once he halted, finger to lips, while we watched what seemed like a million butterflies covering the path in front of us. Then he clapped his hands and they all flapped away, like a 'flying carpet', he said. I was struck by the image, so much so that I had made a note of it, and wondered if he had heard it from some other visitor. I wasn't underrating his sensibilities, disbelieving his sincerity, putting him down, or anything like that. I simply felt there was something strange, off-key, about his reactions and conversation.

Finally, he turned, looked at me in the eyes, and asked, 'Tom, do you believe in God?' Surprised by the abruptness of the question, and the familiarity with which he asked it, I hesitated, then said I did. 'Are you sure?' he asked, as though both our lives depended on it. I said I was, adding that I couldn't see what it had to do with him.

'Good,' Andrew said with feeling, ignoring my objection. 'I am delighted we are both in the Brotherhood of Christ. It makes us real brothers; we will enjoy Paradise together. All humans make mistakes, but once we join the Brotherhood of Christ we are saved. No devil can stand against us.'

Remembering Collingwood's defeat of Essendon in last year's VFL grand final, I wasn't too sure about that but, on a steep and slippery path in the Guyanese outback, I wasn't about to try any smart remarks. I hadn't had much to do with devils, I said. What did he mean exactly?

Andrew's sincerity crushed my flippancy. 'We all have devils,' he said. 'Mine were drugs and my bad temper. I used to drink strong [cheap over-proof] rum and smoke ganja [marijuana]. I used to fight every chance I got, in the street and in the boxing ring. I nearly killed a man in the boxing ring at Bartica and everyone treated me as a hero. They wanted me to fight in Georgetown. [Andrew and practically every other Guyanese I spoke to called it 'G'town', but if I tried to record all the various Windies accents and dialects, I'd be lost. Often it is all I can do to understand them].

'I am still not a good man, but I am trying to be one. One day I hope to be a Pentecostal minister, or at least a full-time worker for the church, but I am afraid that will take a long time. I have no education, and I am still a fighting man. Often I am still an angry man.'

In fact, Andrew became angry when Rich initiated a swim in the pool in front of the first waterfall we visited. No-one had bathers, it seemed at first, so Rich and most of the others, including three girls from Camp Rainbow, swum in their underwear, the girls in bright bikini panties and brassieres. That's where Terry, the aged American, failed to match Mike, the brash Aussie photographer. Terry wore boxer shorts over his underpants.

Andrew, built like Muhammad Ali, a regular brick outhouse, to adapt an Australian expression, refused to strip. 'It is cheap,' he said, gesturing particularly at the girls who, quite innocently, were having a wonderful time in their undies. 'It takes a hundred generations for us to learn to wear proper, Christian clothes, and now we take them off in front of tourists.'

Which makes you wonder how Andrew, an extremely dignified and proper young man, would handle the beaches in Australia, if he visited them. It would be wonderful if we could find out one day, maybe when he is a Pentecostal minister. He has almost no chance, of course; virtually no chance in hell or Guyana, whichever you prefer. Andrew cannot read, and can barely sign his name.

I interviewed Roy Fredericks, sports adviser to the president of Guyana, in the secretary's office at the Georgetown Cricket Club on 25 March. Roy, a dashing left-handed opener, played 59 Tests for the West Indies between 1969 and 1976, including 15 against Australia. He scored eight Test centuries, including one against Australia: 169 in Perth in 1975-76, his highest Test score. In all, he scored 1069 runs against Australia, including five half-centuries, at the respectable average of 38.18. 'That was my best Test innings, the 169 in Perth,' Roy said.

Australia had the best speed attack in the world in those days, Dennis Lillee and Jeff Thomson; they'd never give up, they kept pegging away, Thomson straight at your throat, and they had such fine fieldsmen to back them up. Greg Chappell caught me off Lillee the first ball after tea. I edged a cover drive and Greg took a splendid left-hand catch, high at second slip. With an ordinary fieldsman it would have been a four.

The Australians have always been fine fieldsmen; it is still a big part of their game. It is what enables them to maintain the pressure and usually makes them tougher opponents than other teams. It is why Australia is so good at one-day cricket. If I have any criticism of recent West Indies teams it is that they have become less determined in the field.

Roy sighed. Obviously he would have preferred to discuss cricket more than anything else — indeed he had insisted we meet at the Bourda during the Test — but as an adviser to Prime Minister Hoyte and a former minister in his government (Sport 1981-86), he conceded he probably knew more about Guyana's problems than almost anyone else I would meet.

'Guyana's main problem is a lack of top-level administrators,' he said. 'Skilful people leave the country because they can get better pay elsewhere. Our government sends people overseas to learn things, but if they come back at all, it is only for a few years, then they're off again for good. The country gets very little return from the skills it paid them to learn.'

Had Roy been tempted to stay overseas, like (for instance) his West Indies captain and fellow Guyanese, Clive Lloyd? 'Of course, I was tempted,' he said.

I played county cricket with Glamorgan between 1971 and 1973 and I liked Wales. The Welsh are nice people. I like their dark, bitter beer. I made eight overseas tours with the West Indies, three to England, two to Australia, and one each to India, Pakistan and New Zealand, so you understand I saw a bit of the world, I had plenty of opportunities. But I always liked Guyana best.

Guyanese people are friendly and carefree, like no-one else. They don't bother with show. They like to enjoy themselves, like meeting people, foreigners especially. In some countries overseas, foreigners are unpopular, but not in Guyana. We make everyone welcome.

For their hard currency? If Roy was annoyed by my devil's advocate style of questioning, he was too polite to show it. 'Admittedly our currency is bad,' he said.

Everyone knows that; what hope do you have when your dollar is worth only about seven or eight cents American? A gallon of gas [petrol] costs $215 Guyanese and you have to import all key machinery and other manufactured products.

What can we do about it? Well, our government is doing what it has always done, placing the emphasis on youth and education. Education is totally free in Guyana — better than that, parents are subsidised to keep their children at school. That must make a difference eventually, particularly now that Guyana is on the way back as far as foreign investments are concerned. Foreign investments are not only increasing, they're becoming more diversified, the investments in mining and lumber looking particularly promising.

Roy is 49, slightly built, with grey, receding hair and a goatee beard, wearing tight brown trousers, white suit top and black moccasin shoes. He was a dapper and instantly recognisable figure to everyone in the Members' stand. A chain smoker, he seemed to light another cigarette every time he was greeted as 'comrade'.

'My main responsibility is cricket,' he said. 'I'm not really a politician. My main work is with the West Indies Board of Control. I've been in the job since 1987. I came back to Guyana in 1977 as national cricket coach. Cricket's my game, not politics.'

Maybe that was just as well, the way the wind was blowing in Guyana and in the world as a whole! Practically every day, in every hotel the Australians stayed at in the West Indies, there was a conference of earnest public servants. The newspapers, many of them government-owned, were full of important-sounding proposals and resolutions. The winds of change were obviously blowing up a storm.

It was fanciful but, for a long moment, talking to Roy in Georgetown, I was a world and a generation away, notebook in hand, hunched over Dennis Lillee in the Australian dressing room at the WACA ground in Perth. It was tea on 13 December 1976, the second day of the Second Test against the Windies. I was 'ghosting' Lillee's comments for Australian newspapers and, because of the time difference, needed an early comment. 'You always have a chance against Fredericks,' Dennis said, considering what was to prove Australia's losing position. 'He always has a go.' As it happened, Dennis took Roy's wicket with his very next ball.

In the Georgetown stand, Roy laughed and lit another cigarette. 'I am not really a socialist,' he said.

Certainly not a communist, like some people seem to think. Once things are perfect it doesn't matter whether a person is a capitalist or a socialist. Regardless of policy, the important thing is people; people are the only thing which counts. I don't think Guyana has ever been a

*socialist country; it was just working towards it, until everything seemd
to happen to stop us.*

*A lot of Caribbean countries, not just Guyana, are against right-wing
governments and people governed by right-wing governments, but it is
still the most friendly country in the Caribbean. Guyana is home to me
and I like it, not necessarily the way it is, but the way it can be, the way
it should be.*

Roy Fredericks, his wife Joyce and daughter Alicia, 14, live in
Georgetown. Daughter Denise, 17, is in New York, doing the first year of
a computer course.

I never thought I would feel nostalgic about Georgetown and Guyana, but
already I do. It is like the unpleasant towns, dangerous jobs, or bad
company you survived as a youth. You forget the bad times, and always
remember them as vastly more enjoyable, more fun, than they actually
were. Mind you, there was a big, incredibly colourful macaw which used
to perch on a tree near my bedroom window in Georgetown. How many
times in the rest of my life will I have a macaw perching beneath my
window?

Then there was the matter of the 'labba'. It is a Guyanese meat which
tastes like sweet beef in curry. I ate curried labba practically every meal
during my first week in Guyana. When you're on a good thing stick to it,
particularly as far as meat goes in the West Indies.

Then one night, dining in style with Johnny Woodcock of the London
Times at the best dining room in the Pegasus, I showed my local
knowledge, and moved one notch up the gastronomical scale, by ordering
roast labba. 'Good heavens,' said Johnny, normally the most unflappable
of men, when it finally arrived. 'That looks like the hindquarters of a
RAT!'

It did and, as it happens, to my horror it was. The labba, I discovered,
is a rodent with a white stripe down its back, slightly smaller than the
American skunk, slightly larger than an Australian rat, about four times
the size of an Australian mouse. The Amerindians hunt them in the jungle,
and regard them as a delicacy. From that moment on, I didn't eat much,
and lost quite a bit of weight during the rest of my stay in Guyana, but that
didn't do any harm, rather the reverse.

'Third World' nothing! I've been to G'town, mon; and who else do you
know who has been down the Essequibo River, to Bartica, and beyond?

THE SECOND TEST:
THE WINDIES FIGHT BACK

The West Indies rocked Australia with a crushing ten wicket victory in a complete form reversal after the one-day internationals, providing a superior display of batting, bowling and generally aggressive cricket. Richardson pulverised the attack for 182 majestic runs in one of the classic innings of Test cricket to set up the victory in whirlwind fashion. The Australians virtually lost all chance of even salvaging a draw in just one session on the second day when Richardson was at the height of his massacre. He totally negated the diligent batting performances of Marsh, Border and Mark Waugh, and a five wicket haul by Border was the

Seats with a view at the Bourda.

Australian highlight. Any Australian hopes of saving the game disappeared with the controversial run-out of Jones in the second innings, an incorrect decision by umpires Clyde Cumberbatch and Clyde Duncan which was compounded by a lack of sportsmanship from the West Indians and a lack of knowledge of the rules of the game by the Australian players. Jones was given out under a misapprehension that he had been dismissed, and was run out after heading towards the pavilion. The error cost the experienced Cumberbatch any further matches in the series, at the request of the West Indians, but that was little consolation for Jones or the Australians who trailed 1-0 in the series.

This was the first West Indian victory against Australia since 1965 when rival managers Simpson and Gibbs competed. Ironically, that Test began with a major umpiring controversy when one of the most experienced of the West Indies umpires, Kippin, withdrew on the eve of the match at the instance of the local Umpires' Association, which objected to the appointment of a Barbadian umpire, Jordan. The local association was angered that both umpires were not Guyanese and the match was threatened but saved by the appointment of former Test all-rounder Gerry Gomez, who held an umpiring certificate but had never umpired a first-class match! Wisden reported that 'the act of the local umpires ... served only to cost West Indian cricket in general a loss of prestige'.

The Australians, having won the one-dayers so handsomely 4-1, approached this Test with the opportunity to seize a distinct advantage. The West Indians were under mounting pressure to make changes to the team, particularly after young left-hander Brian Lara batted so productively and aggressively for 91 against the Australians at Pointe-à-Pierre in a one-day match for Trinidad and Tobago the previous week. The batsmen under pressure were Greenidge and Hooper. The lacklustre bowling of Marshall and Walsh in the one-dayers also caused the Trinidadians to lift their voices for the inclusion of young Tony Gray. The venue and history also seemed on Australia's side: the Guyanese populace contained many Indians who preferred any team to beat the West Indians, whom they considered arrogant — doubtless a reflection of the absence of an Indian in the line-up and a reprisal for comments by Richards the previous year that West Indian cricket strength owed almost everything to the Negro influence. The Australian team also benefited from the fact that the West Indians had a dismal record at the Bourda ground.

The only pre-match concerns for the Australians were a knee injury to Jones and the make-up of the attack. Jones had been playing with a right cruciate ligament complaint and it flared on the eve of the Test. 'I have just been hoping to get through this tour and I am sure I can. But as soon as I return home I will need an operation. It is deteriorating too quickly,' he conceded. The right knee had taken excessive pressure following the complete reconstruction of his left knee three years previously because he transferred all the pressure on it when turning while running between wickets, his trademark particularly in one-day internationals. The ailment was the latest in a succession of injuries since the knee reconstruction. He almost lost the sight of the right eye when hit during an early tour match in England in 1989, damaged his shoulder which restricted his throwing the next season, and then arrived on the 1991 tour with a hairline fracture of the right forearm, courtesy of a blow in the final Ashes Test at Perth.

The composition of the attack caused genuine confusion before the Australians named the same eleven which drew in Jamaica. The selectors were extremely tempted to play Reid despite his lack of work and confidence following the back ailment, mainly because of his potential as a match-winner. Whitney had done nothing wrong with his tireless efforts but he lacked penetration, having failed to capture a wicket off 38 overs in the opening clash. The other worry centred around Matthews, whose lack of wickets in six Tests since his comeback was increasingly frustrating for the enthusiastic and dedicated all-rounder as well as the selectors. Seven wickets in six Tests was hardly inspiring and the selectors considered using Border as the spinner and including Steve Waugh, who was batting brilliantly, on the basis that if he captured a wicket with his medium-pace it would be as effective as Matthews' average results for the summer. But conservatism prevailed — and failed.

The convincing Australian victories in the one-day series possibly worked against them for this Test. That may seem a strange assessment but their repeated and undisciplined losses steeled the West Indians for the Test. Manager Lance Gibbs ordered an unscheduled training session two days before the Test and the players discussed the need to bounce back in the Test series to silence the critics and to prove to the world that they were still champions. The West Indians travelled with scant frivolity or contact with anyone outside the unit in an obviously premeditated plan. The atmosphere was one of 'us against them'. And that meant the team against the Australian players, the rest of the cricket world, the unsupporting and critical crowds, the media and even the bus driver, who received an unholy dressing-down two days before the Test. He duly arrived on time but then departed when nobody was in sight. The players arrived half an hour late at the hotel foyer to go to training, and when informed the bus had gone, angrily hailed taxis. The bus driver took the brunt of the blame when he rolled up again as they were driving off and the incident merely added to the group opinion that everyone was anti the West Indian team. The motivation certainly worked.

Border perhaps sensed the awakening of the sleeping giant. On Test eve he suggested:

I think there is no question that they are shattered by the 4-1 loss in the one-dayers and that they will come out with all guns blazing in the Test. We don't expect any favours and we won't be giving any. We must respect the West Indies because they haven't lost a series for so long and they don't like losing.

Georgetown, the once majestic capital of Guyana where grand buildings of British reign now were derelict and a buoyant economy now reduced the people to a poverty-stricken existence, proved an ideal place to stick together. Wandering the streets alone or even in small groups was inviting trouble, as Matthews and Whitney discovered. Desperation, not greed, motivated daylight robberies and any tourist was fair game for the pitifully bereft. For the Australians, the golden rules for venturing out were to travel in large groups, take as little money and valuables as possible and stick to the main streets. Matthews ignored the advice and lost a gold chain and his wedding ring attached to it when he was robbed in a side-street while taking a stroll with Whitney. A 'dude', as Matthews described him, walked across the street and when within half an arm's length, grabbed the chain from around Matthews' neck and darted 20 metres along the street and down an alley. The Australian pair alerted police and patrolled the area in a divisional van without success. The episode ended happily however when locals tracked down the culprit and the goods and returned the valuables to an extremely relieved Matthews.

On a lighter note, team manager Lawrie Sawle took the advice of not carrying too much cash to the other extreme on the eve of the Test. The party organised the usual pre-Test team dinner at a superior Chinese restaurant, the Caribbean Rose, and the players enjoyed the best meal on offer in Guyana. At the end of the evening Sawle was surprised to receive a bill, normally paid by the West Indian Board in advance for official team dinners. He dutifully attempted to settle the bill, only to discover that he, with all the help from the players, didn't have enough cash! That was understandable in a way, because you needed a wheelbarrow to carry any substantial amount of Guyanese dollars, with an exchange rate of 120 to one US dollar. Not many people walk around with 60 000 Guyanese bills, and to Sawle's embarrassment he had left his chequebook and credit cards safely locked in the vault at the team hotel. The restaurateur, a cricket buff suddenly flush and famous and a couple of tickets to the cricket better off, obligingly took Sawle's word that he would return the following day with the necessary ... and a couple of autograph sheets. The players took the advice of locals and ate out only on a couple of occasions but at very enjoyable restaurants. Nobody wanted to be striken with any ailment lest he needed treatment from one of the official medical team, Dr Billy Fung-A-Fat!

DAY ONE

A typically hard-nosed manipulation of the over rate enabled the West Indies to take control of the Test on the opening day despite a resolutely patient 94 by Marsh. The Australians struggled to 6 for 249 at stumps on an excellent batting pitch against a relentless pace quartet led by veteran Marshall. But the primary concern was the over rate, which flew in the face of pre-series promises to attempt to bowl 90 overs within the scheduled hours of play. The West Indians bowled only 71 overs in ideal conditions in the regulation six hours, and even after an extra hour fell seven overs shy of the target when fading light halted play. The ploy, which is killing

Test cricket, proved as successful as it has done for 15 years and gained the desired result. The West Indians philosophise that the result justifies the means but the rest of the cricket world condemns the method and awaits positive action from the International Cricket Council to outlaw the practice. The exercise is nothing more than time cheating, a manipulation to keep the fast men fresh while frustrating the batsmen. The Australians scored at three runs an over but were never allowed to find rhythm. When a batsman looked like taking the initiative, the tempo slowed alarmingly with some of the go-slow tactics assuming farcical proportions. When a bowler was hit for four he often remained at the end of his delivery stride until the ball was returned to him, rather than making his way back to his bowling mark. Richards regularly pondered long and hard to set his field and occasionally, too often in fact, he jogged from slips to the bowler for a chat. Most captains do this, but as an exception, not the rule. And no effort was made to be ready when a new batsman entered the arena. This went to the extreme when Matthews arrived at the crease late in the day. He was at centre-pitch, having taken guard, before the West Indians broke from a huddle and he received his first delivery almost three minutes after the fall of the previous wicket.

The annoying aspect is that the West Indians can bowl at a recommended over rate when required, notably in the one-dayers. One of the suggestions before the ICC is to impose run penalties for failing to bowl the required overs within the scheduled hours of play. If, for instance, there was a penalty of four runs an over for every over remaining at the scheduled stumps time, the West Indians would have been looking at providing the Australians with another 64 runs because they were 16 overs shy of the target. Not even the West Indians would allow that to happen — the opposition total scooting from 6 for 249 to 6 for 313 — and that would force a drastic reassessment of tactics.

Marsh provided the backbone of the Australian innings with a display of his characteristic courage and powers of concentration and determination. He laboured for 325 minutes for his 94, his highest score in seven Tests against the West Indians, but faced only 201 deliveries in a period of 65 overs. The effort continued a purple patch and followed his previous innings in the one-day internationals of 81 off 107 balls in 173 minutes, 113 off 140 balls in 202 minutes and 106 not out off 158 deliveries in 216 minutes. But he was never allowed to increase the tempo or gain rhythm because the West Indians bowled only 24 overs in the opening session and only 22 in the second session. When stumps should have been drawn there were 16 overs remaining, and an hour later when darkness prevented any further play, seven overs of the scheduled 90 still remained. Marsh was somewhat embarrassed by his lengthy innings and equally frustrated by the incessant delays. 'It is pretty boring,' he said.

I don't know what the crowd makes of it: watching them bowl to me must be very hard to take hour after hour. But the fact is that there are no rules. We have to accept that and we have tried to adopt the attitude that we are going to have to put up with a very slow over rate. But as a batsman it makes it very hard work: you just spend so much time waiting between deliveries. I can't say it contributed to my dismissal but I was really mentally exhausted at the end.

Marsh's contribution became increasingly important as he withstood a ferocious early barrage when Mark Taylor (0) and Boon (7) were removed within only 13 overs with just 24 runs on the board. Taylor was out in the second over of the day when he played back to a delivery from Patterson which kept low and trapped him lbw. While Marsh was enjoying a productive period, Taylor was struggling, having played only three innings in 22 days since his innings in the opening Test at Jamaica. The lack of time in the centre obviously caused problems, particularly as his two most recent innings were in one-day internationals when he batted for a combined 36 deliveries for only eight runs.

Boon's dismissal caused considerable confusion when umpire Duncan, standing in his maiden Test, belatedly responded to simultaneous appeals for lbw and caught behind off Marshall. The schoolteacher reacted to the concerted appeal and a disgruntled and bemused Boon was on his way for only two, having been the stumbling block for the West Indians in the opening Test with his unbeaten century. But how was he out? Duncan apparently was the only man who was sure. He went to the official scorers at the luncheon break to inform them of his decision because one of them had Boon out lbw and the other caught by Dujon. Radio broadcasters were divided, while the television critics believed Boon probably was out lbw. But the television replay suggested that Duncan was the man who erred, not Boon. The ball was not in line with the stumps, clipped the top of Boon's pad and continued on the rise over the stumps to the wicketkeeper. That eliminated an lbw verdict. But Boon's bat and gloves were nowhere near the ball, equally eliminating a suggestion of a catch. The pugnacious right-hander was on his way nonetheless, a cruel blow to the Australians who slumped to 2 for 24 in the 13th over of the game.

Marsh and Border began the rebuilding program with a union of exactly 100 runs in 147 to steady the innings without ever taking the initiative for any length of time. Border began in aggressive fashion but he suddenly lost his timing and concentration. An excellent over of genuine pace from Patterson seemed to unsettle him and when Marshall returned to rekindle memories of his fiery best, Border was totally on the defensive. Marshall decided to attack the left-hander by bowling around the wicket and Border edged the first delivery to Dujon but was given the benefit of a slight doubt. Marshall was in no doubt as he ran the length of the pitch

Skipper Allan Border on the attack.

waving his finger to signal the dismissal; he was stunned to be denied. He then produced a gem of a delivery which cut back to skittle Border's stumps. This was the Marshall of yesteryear, charging in with express deliveries which skidded on to the batsmen with monotonous accuracy, and spicing the action with an occasional deadly accurate bouncer directed at the throat. The Australians went to tea at 3 for 133 but with only 46 of the day's quota of overs gone. Marsh and Jones lifted the score to 188 before Marsh edged a delivery from Patterson to Hooper in the gully to end a valiant defiance. His 94 included a dozen boundaries and he richly deserved a century, falling in the end as much to mental fatigue as the quality of delivery from the speedster.

Jones looked set for a big score as he batted confidently and with comparative ease against the pacemen, earning praise from Clive Lloyd who commented that he looked a class batsman capable of heady achievements in the Test arena to match his superior limited-over cricket achievements. Mark Waugh, who surprisingly didn't encounter many short-pitched deliveries during his settling in period, was likewise at home on the docile pitch, which suggested even before play that batsmen would dominate and confirm the bookmakers' odds of a draw. The second new ball became due as the scheduled stumps time ticked by. Marshall excelled again when he bowled Jones off an inside edge for 34 after the right-hander had batted cautiously for ten minutes less than three hours to gain his runs. Marshall boasted the wickets of the third, fourth and fifth batsmen in the line-up and finished the day with 3 for 52 off 17 overs in a complete reversal of form from the one-dayers.

The complexion of the game changed dramatically after Jones helped the score to 4 for 237 with a 64 run partnership with Marsh and a 49 run stand with Mark Waugh, giving hope that the Australians

Ian Healy, hit on the shoulder, grits it out, as he did in both innings.

would finish the day on top. But Jones departed and Matthews followed only one run later to plummet Australia to 6 for 238 with Mark Waugh and the tail-enders to contend with a new ball. Matthews, who enjoyed so much success at number seven against England, rashly attempted an off-drive to the fourth delivery he faced and presented Dujon with a regulation catch off the very impressive Ambrose. The angular paceman was a constant concern to the Australian batsmen, who seemingly pre-determined to defend against his awkward deliveries as they considered him the man most likely to destroy the line-up. Matthews fell victim and it was left to Mark Waugh, who batted stylishly and confidently, and Healy to seek the safety of a belated stumps as the shadows protruded across the pitch.

SECOND DAY

Richardson's second successive Test century, set at a tempo usually reserved for carefree limited-over exhibitions, turned the Test on its head during an extraordinary final session of brutal bombardment of the Australian attack. The West Indians finished the day at 1 for 226, only 122 runs in arrears after dismissing the Australians for 348.

The heir apparent to mentor and skipper Viv Richards clubbed his century off only 116 deliveries with 13 boundaries and two sixes; he gained solid support from Haynes, whose unbeaten 87 would have commanded headlines under normal circumstances. The pair was ruthlessly aggressive whereas the Australian batting had been conservative on the perfect batting pitch, although (to be fair) the West Indian bowling was overbearingly superior compared to the inept response. Only McDermott and Border looked capable of restricting the run flow, let alone capturing a wicket.

The contrast in the action was extreme with the Australians fighting grimly for two sessions only to see the West Indians pulverise the bowling in a cavalier manner to erase two-thirds of the total by stumps. Mark Waugh and Healy displayed considerable fortitude to establish a record seventh wicket partnership at this ground with a 101 run combined effort. They batted sensibly and methodically to frustrate the West Indian attack throughout the opening session while adding 79 runs off 25 overs, giving rise to Australian hopes of a score in excess of 400. Mark Waugh was particularly impressive, using crisply timed drives and cuts to reach his half-century in difficult times off 99 deliveries. He was in total control until he slashed at a delivery from Patterson to be caught at the wicket by Jeff Dujon for 71. The liaison with Healy was invaluable in the circumstances, surpassing the previous highest at this ground of 95 by Bob Simpson and Steve Rixon in 1978.

The loss of Waugh ended any hopes of an imposing total and the Australians lost their last four wickets for only nine runs in 4.3 overs, in much the same dramatic fashion as the opening Test in Jamaica when they lost 5 for 12. When Waugh departed, the whole platform of stability collapsed in an irrational way. Healy, who batted so well for 53 in almost three hours, ran himself out in suicidal fashion when he pushed a delivery to substitute fieldsman Roger Harper, who threw down the stumps from extra-cover. Perhaps Healy had forgotten Harper, who is regarded as the best fieldsman in the world! The departure was a waste after almost three hours of intelligent batting, particularly as it left the tail-enders totally exposed without an established player at the other end. McDermott's effort to play correctly wasn't productive when he was trapped lbw for only a single when his strong shoulders perhaps should have attempted to punish the bowling, and Hughes had no answer to a leg-cutter from Ambrose which uprooted his off stump for a duck. The Australian tally of 348 was disappointing because the batsmen who gained a start and a good sight of the ball — Marsh, Border, Jones, Waugh and Healy — didn't completely capitalise on the excellent pitch.

Patterson finished with 4 for 80 to add to his first Test figures of 5 for 83 and again he wrapped up the tail. The senior batsmen acknowledged him as the fastest of the bowlers without being overly concerned by his sheer pace, but he was dynamite against the tail-enders and included four top-order scalps in his nine wickets in two Test innings. Ambrose again was the best bowler, despite figures of 2 for 64, and the analysis was evidence that the Australians treated him with such respect they wouldn't take risks against him. Marshall excelled on a placid pitch while Walsh lacked penetration at this stage of the series and had only one wicket in two Test innings while conceding 154 runs.

The Australians realised they had to complete 56 overs for the day, paying the penalty for the earlier slow over rate by the West Indians, and tried determinedly to put the pressure on the batsmen to avoid the trap they fell into in the second innings at Jamaica when they squandered a 107 run lead within two hours. McDermott trapped Greenidge lbw for only two and after 13 overs of accurate bowling and exemplary fielding the West Indians went to tea at 1 for 28. But then the floodgates opened in a demoralising demolition.

Richardson and Haynes added 198 off only 41 overs after tea by pounding an assortment of deliveries — accurate or wayward, half-volleys, bouncers or full-pitched deliveries pitched on the stumps or on either side of the wicket — to plunder 26 boundaries and two sixes, reducing what appeared to be a defensible Australian total to a cakewalk.

Richardson, who boasts an extraordinary record against the Australians, clubbed seven boundaries and a six in a half-century off only

Richardson, well on his way to a 'big' century, just like the cricket ball.

60 deliveries. He added a further six boundaries and a six off another 56 deliveries to register his seventh century against Australia, elevating him to the top of the table, one ahead of Clive Lloyd and Larry Gomes. His blazing bat has ruined several Australian campaigns — he scored 528 at 58.66 in Australia two years earlier — and this century followed his 104 not out in the opening Test in Jamaica. He gave fair warning of his ability to wreck this attack by keeping in form with 90 off 94 balls in the third one-day international and 94 off only 88 balls in the fifth limited-over match a couple of days earlier at the Bourda ground. His driving was brutal, his timing and placement impeccable and his attitude ruthless. The 29-year-old made the Australians look like second-raters as he hit one after the other out of the attack.

Richardson's aggression rubbed off on Haynes, who was only 64 when his partner reached his century but went on to finish unbeaten on 87, adding 23 while Richardson added only 14 in the final seven overs. They dealt contemptuously with Whitney and Hughes immediately after the interval as they took 39 runs in six overs from each bowler in an explosive onslaught. Mark Waugh's two overs cost 18 runs. Matthews, who showed courage to return to action after badly dislocating a finger while fielding a thunderous drive in the outfield, bowled 15 overs for 64 runs.

The union, which reached 216 by stumps, easily eclipsed the highest for the second wicket in Australia-West Indies Tests of 167, set by this pair in Adelaide in 1989-90, and the highest in the Caribbean by the same pair at Bridgetown, Barbados, of 145 in 1983. Richardson scored 131 not out and Haynes 145 in 1983-4 and Richardson 106 and Haynes 83 in 1989-90 so the Australians were accustomed to the punishment.

There was more in store the following day.

THIRD DAY

Richardson played one of the great innings of Test cricket to mastermind a West Indian run feast which set up an historic Test victory at this ground. The batting blitz provided 306 runs in the day to lift the West Indian score to 9 for 532 and gave a lead of 184 with ample time to press for victory. Richardson's 182 was scintillating and suberbly supported by Haynes' 111 in a mammoth partnership of 297, the second highest for the second wicket in West Indian history. Local heroes Hooper, Richards and Logie chipped in with half-centuries to capitalise on this foundation and the only bonus for the Australians came from the unlikely spinning fingers of Border, whose belated five wicket haul included the rare feat of three wickets in four balls.

But the innings belonged to Richardson, who wrecked six weeks of methodically crafted advantage by the tourists. He took less than six hours to dismantle that advantage with an innings as brash and brutal as Sir Garfield Sobers' masterpiece against Dennis Lillee and Co. at the MCG in 1970-71 in what Sir Donald Bradman described as the greatest innings he had seen. Three harsh judges, who themselves have decimated Australian teams in the past, were at the Bourda ground to approve and acclaim Richardson's effort. Roy Fredericks was in the Members' Stand, Clive Lloyd in the commentary box and Richards on the players' balcony as Richardson pulverised the Australian attack with a style and power of which any of the trio would have been proud.

They cast admiring eyes over an innings which included 26 boundaries and two sixes as the lithe batsman penetrated the field with precision drives, powerful cuts and pulls and impeccable timing. The eagle eye, slashing blade and attitude of aggression is indigenous to the Caribbean cricket character and although he has played many fabulous innings, this was the moment Richardson stepped from the shadow of Richards to assume the title of Master Blaster.

Richardson was modestly aware that his time had come as Richards talked of pending retirement. He suggested that the sheer adrenalin of playing against the Australians was the incentive he needed to stir himself for action. 'I don't know what it is but I always have wanted to play against the Australians and emulate the feats of Viv Richards. I didn't know if I could ever do it, but I reckon now I am getting close,' he suggested, as if to play down his surge past his boyhood idol.

Lloyd described the innings as one of the best he had seen while Fredericks, who scored a century in the opening session of the Perth Test in 1975-76 against Dennis Lillee, Jeff Thomson and Max Walker, went further to suggest Richardson should be acknowledged as the best batsman in the world. And Richards smiled in recognition of an innings of

Richardson is mobbed by adoring Guyanese fans after he reaches his century in quick time.

which he would have been proud a decade ago and confided: 'The man sure can bat!'

Border, who saw the action from even closer quarters, also heaped praise on the batsman and the innings. 'That was one of the best innings I have seen,' the veteran said. 'He didn't let up from the moment he went to the wicket and his innings alone got the West Indies into the position they now find themselves. It was a classic.' The Australians will long remember this innings, as much as they will regret it in the context of this series. They bowled as poorly as a unit as at any time during the previous three years in a Test arena and had no answer to the genius of Richardson. Only McDermott, who before play went to hospital for blood tests which cleared him of major problems after complaining for several days of dizziness, and part-time spinner Border could be satisfied with their efforts.

The brillance of Richardson diminished the value and excellence of the 111 by Haynes, his fifth century against Australia and the 16th in his illustrious career. He carved 17 boundaries off 211 deliveries before becoming Border's first victim with a defensive edge to Mark Waugh at silly point. Haynes and Richardson added 297 for the second wicket, eclipsing the 287 by Greenidge and Larry Gomes at Lord's in 1984 and remaining second highest only to the massive 446 between Conrad Hunte and Sobers against Pakistan in 1957-58 at Kingston, Jamaica. The performance ranked as the tenth biggest second wicket partnership in Test history, which puts its magnitude into perspective.

Richardson finally fell lbw to McDermott, receiving a standing ovation from the small but appreciative crowd and a longing look of admiration from a tiny schoolgirl who toddled onto the ground to escort her hero to the shade of the dressing rooms after almost six hours in the heat of battle. The West Indians added 343 runs from the time he took block, only five runs shy of the entire Australian first innings total.

'My hero.' Richardson escorted off the Bourda by an admiring schoolgirl.

Hooper, of whom so much is expected by the West Indian

selectors, saved his best for his native Guyanese fans with a half-century off 77 deliveries with six boundaries, while Richards assassinated Matthews with three straight driven sixes and four boundaries in a whirlwind half-century off 59 deliveries. They added 90 runs for the fourth wicket before Hooper presented Mark Waugh with a bat-pad catch off Matthews for 62. That was Matthews' first wicket in 100.3 overs and 350 runs since he dismissed Graham Gooch at the SCG in the third Ashes Test on 28 January, and he had that to mull over as the West Indies went to tea at 4 for 443.

He struck again immediately after the break when he bowled Richards off the bottom of the bat for 50. Logie and Dujon were not about to miss out on the batting paradise, however, and added 85 runs for the sixth wicket before Border belatedly re-entered the attack. He trapped Dujon in front of the stumps for 29 with the final delivery of an over and then had Logie caught at the wicket by Healy with the first delivery of his next over for another deceptively swift innings of 54 off only 76 deliveries with eight boundaries. Ambrose prevented a hat trick but Border bowled him the following delivery to boast three wickets in four deliveries, joining Richie Benaud, Johnnie Martin and Graham McKenzie as the only Australians to perform the feat in Tests against the West Indians. If that wasn't enough, the left-armer bowled Walsh to reap 4 for 0 in nine deliveries! He finished the day with figures of 5 for 51 off 25 overs and was suitably embarrassed with his success and annoyed he didn't appear at the crease earlier.

This was his second best return in Test cricket and followed his career best match analysis of 11 for 96 against the Caribbean champions in Sydney in 1989. 'I am a bit of a bunny when it comes to bowling myself, but I do seem to do well against the West Indians,' Border explained.

I just felt that as a left-armer I could bowl into the bowlers' footmarks and cause them a few problems. I only wish I had got the wickets earlier. They made 9 for 532 and I got 5 for 51: it looks ridiculous. I probably should have more faith in myself but hindsight is a wonderful thing. I don't know what it is. I always think how much I would like to bat against myself! Maybe I have negative thoughts about my own bowling: when I play grade or Shield cricket I get pogoed everywhere. But I just seem to get wickets against the West Indians.

Border had little to laugh about on the rest day, aware that the only prospect was to bat for two days to save the Test. He put the challenge to the players and told them that they would discover if they were a truly good side during the following two days.

This is a position we haven't been in for quite some time so we need to show tremendous fight. For the past couple of years we have been the ones dictating the game with a positive approach rather than a negative thought process. So it will be an eye-opener to see how we handle the other side of the coin, an education if you like in coming back from a very difficult position and walking away knowing no matter how well the opposition played they couldn't beat us. If we can get out of this I think we will show all the signs of being a very good side. To bounce back after this brilliant effort by the West Indians would be something to be proud of and to prove to ourselves and everyone else that we are genuine fighters who won't surrender. If we lose, well, we will deserve to lose because we would have been outplayed.

The answer hit home with a thud the following day, but not until Jones and Hughes played a practical joke on the West Indians at the start of the Australian second innings. The Australians discovered a dead snake before play and, having posed with it for photographs with the locals, decided to show it to the West Indians in a most unexpected way. They placed the once poisonous reptile on the ground where wicketkeeper Jeff Dujon usually stood in an inconspicuous way between innings. Dujon duly discovered the snake but wasn't overly concerned as he realised it was dead. But Richards hadn't sprinted so fast for many a year when he saw the snake after joining the slips cordon! Dujon, ever ready to enjoy a laugh, didn't bother to tell his skipper it was a dead snake and didn't remove it from the field until Richards unwittingly stumbled on it.

FOURTH DAY

An inexplicable umpiring blunder which wrongly ended the innings of Dean Jones took the gloss off another magnificent bowling display by the West Indies to take them to within three wickets of victory. The run-out controversy hogged the headlines and will forever haunt umpire Cumberbatch — the outspoken members at the ground won't let him forget it — as it involved a key batsman at a vital period of play and paved an easier avenue towards victory for the home team. Whether the dismissal influenced the outcome of the Test remains conjecture: it had nothing to do with the demise of the other six batsmen on the day, all of whom were victims of another day of fast bowling frenzy from Marshall and Ambrose. The Test was as good as dead when the Australians limped to stumps at 7 for 178, still 43 runs shy of averting an innings defeat.

The Jones run-out was an international incident, if only because it highlighted the lack of knowledge of the laws of the game by the umpire concerned, most of the Australian players and most of the West Indians. One senior West Indian player confirmed that evening that he 'and at least one other player' was aware of the law but decided to leave the verdict up to the umpire rather than intervene. He privately apologised to Jones.

The main culprit however was Cumberbatch, whose decision cost Jones his wicket, regardless of any uncharitable silence from members of the opposition. Jones, who batted competently for almost three hours in the first innings, had scored three runs off six deliveries when he was bowled by a magnificent delivery from Walsh. Jones dejectedly flung his bat under his arm and began removing his batting gloves as he walked away from his crease towards the Georgetown Club pavilion, oblivious to a no-ball call and signal from umpire Duncan. He obviously didn't hear the call or see the signal because of his reactions. He was about ten paces from his crease when Border realised a no-ball had been called and he yelled to Jones to regain his ground. Fast-thinking substitute fieldsman Roger Harper was too slick and he pounced on the ball which had come to rest only a metre from the shattered stumps, grabbed a stump in his hand and ran out the bewildered Jones who was frantically attempting to regain his ground.

Umpire Cumberbatch at square leg ruled Jones out, despite exaggerated signals from umpire Duncan to alert him to the original no-ball decision,

Dean Jones heads to the pavilion in Georgetown after being bowled by a no-ball in Australia's second innings.

suggesting that the novice umpire was in fact aware of a miscarriage of justice. The decision to end Jones' innings contravened two laws of which an umpire, especially a senior umpire of 11 Tests' experience, should be aware.

The first law which should have ensured Jones was not out is Law 27(5) regarding appeals. It states: 'The umpires shall intervene if satisfied that a batsman, not having been given out, has left his wicket under a misapprehension that he has been dismissed.' That clearly was the case in this incident.

The second law, 38(2), is more specific: 'If a no-ball has been called, the striker shall not be given out unless attempting a run.' This also was patently the case here.

Border and Jones erred in not querying the decision while Jones remained on the field but the reason for that was that neither of them was aware of the laws, which was an indictment on both senior cricketers.

Richards had the opportunity to recall Jones but didn't. That should not be held against him because he didn't see the incident, having turned his back on the action to engage in a 'victory lap of honour' when the stumps were shattered. He didn't see the run-out and explained that later. He

A telling picture. Windies wicket-keeper Geoff Dujon does not appeal when Jones was 'run out'. Gloves down, while his team-mates celebrate, his puzzled expression says it all.

would have been under considerable pressure had one of his team-mates mentioned the dismissal was suspect under the laws of the game because he then would have had the opportunity at hand to withdraw the appeal, as covered under Law 27(7): 'In exceptional circumstances the captain of the fielding side may seek permission of the umpire to withdraw an appeal providing the outgoing batsman has not left the playing arena. If this is allowed the umpire shall cancel his decision.'

'I didn't see the incident because I was too busy celebrating with the crowd. When I turned around I thought it was a legitimate decision, but I must admit I didn't know the rule until tea when everyone was talking about it,' Richards explained.

Everyone certainly was talking about it, and the members' stand was abuzz with condemnation of the decision immediately umpire Cumberbatch raised his finger. Terry Brindle, Tom Prior and I stood in the members and were amazed at the immediate and volatile reaction of the fans who clearly understood the laws and who were angered with the decision. How could so many people instantly recognise a batsman had been given out under a misapprehension when a senior Test umpire didn't?

The management of Sawle and Simpson approached the umpires at tea and asked for an explanation, but came away with the news that they were 'embarrassed and upset', as indeed they should have been. Simpson was disappointed because 'it had a dramatic effect on the game and I would have thought it is the first time it has happened in Test cricket'.

The umpires, exposed to the members as they sat in the secretary's office behind glass partitions — with the treasurer counting the day's takings beside them in full view of the bar! — tried clumsily to explain the decision. They contradicted themselves, with Cumberbatch suggesting Jones was attempting a run and Duncan saying Jones was heading to the pavilion!

Cumberbatch said: 'It is really a matter of whether the batsman was trying to take a run. From my angle, the way he left the crease suggested to me he *was*.' Duncan said: 'I don't think the question of misapprehension comes into it. The fact is that he suddenly tried to get back into his crease ... if he was under a real misapprehension surely he would have continued *towards the pavilion*.' Not with his skipper shouting at him, he wouldn't! 'It is hard for anyone to hear what is going on out there: the crowd is very noisy and it may be that players have difficulty hearing a no-ball call. That is why we always give hand signals. From my end I was confident that the player had seen the signal and knew it was a no-ball,' Duncan said to complicate his own version.

Cumberbatch was left under no misapprehension about his future in the Test series. The West Indians were decidedly critical of the Trinidadian businessman and the players and management left little doubt that they were disgruntled with his handling of the game. The Australians refrained from making a protest but were made aware of the West Indian stance as a consolation for the injustice.

The public obviously concurred with the thumbs down signal. One senior official at the Georgetown Club suggested Cumberbatch spend the rest of the series reading the laws of cricket, and even the public was annoyed enough on the final day to mockingly hoist an effigy of a hanging umpire with a sign: 'Sorry Dean Jones. Better luck next time.'

The bottom line, regardless of the Jones run-out, was that the West Indians bowled superbly on this important day and the Australian batsmen were incapable, in this moment of truth at least, of rising to the occasion. The entire day was a disappointment. The last West Indian pair of Marshall and Patterson batted for 40 minutes to add 37 valuable runs and inflate the lead to 221, leaving the Australians the challenge of surviving for approximately 167 overs to draw the Test. But that proved beyond them because of some excellent fast bowling by the Caribbean champions. Mark Taylor began confidently but was trapped lbw by

The Guyanese public show what they think of the umpire after the Jones run-out decision.

Ambrose for 15 with only 32 runs on the board in 11 overs. This was the second occasion in the Test that he fell victim to a delivery which trapped him in front of the stumps and it exposed Boon to a memorable delivery from Marshall. Boon helplessly defended a ball which speared back at him, flicking the edge of his bat on the way to Dujon. Taylor and Boon, who managed only two runs, were vital dismissals as they are two batsmen capable of occupying the crease for long periods. But they were out of the ball game with only 43 runs on the board in 15 overs, leaving the onus again on the broad shoulders of team leaders Border and Marsh.

Marsh batted for two hours and five minutes and looked set for as long and productive a stay as his first innings, only to attempt to pull a Walsh delivery at 22, thus deflecting the ball on to his stumps. That was the end of the best chance of batting out time and scoring heavily at the same time, and when Jones was run out for three in controversial circumstances with the score on 73, the match seemed destined to finish in the day. Border, like Marsh, mustered total concentration and batted determinedly with

Veteran fast bowler Malcolm Marshall fists his glee, while Greg Matthews departs the Test arena and the Australian team.

support from Mark Waugh who fluently struck 31 with four boundaries in an hour and a half.

Then the wheels fell off the wobbly wagon. Waugh edged a delivery from Ambrose to Dujon, who missed the chance but whose deflection ballooned the ball to Richards at slip. That ended a partnership of 57, then 40 minutes later the departure of Border signalled the death knell. After fighting for 209 minutes for 34 runs, Border gloved an attempted hook off Marshall to Dujon and trudged from the ground, aware than only a flash flood could prevent defeat.

Matthews, whose career was on the line after disappointing bowling and now a slump in his batting, managed 16 runs before being caught at the wicket off Ambrose and Healy. McDermott, who was bowled off a Walsh no-ball before he opened his account, survived until fading light halted play.

Ambrose and Marshall were as responsible with the ball as Richardson and Haynes with the bat for the West Indian dominance and they were outstanding on this fourth day. Ambrose was explosive with 2 for 31 off 17 overs while the veteran Marshall again was the instigator with 3 for 38 off 13 overs to follow his first innings tally of 3 for 67. For a cricketer whom many believed was at the end of his career, Marshall showed all the bowlers in this Test how to operate successfully on an unresponsive pitch with subtle variations and an occasional blast of outright genius.

Australian supporters endured a restless night counting the raindrops on the windows as the clouds gathered ominously over Georgetown. The count in room 511 at the Pegasus was 39 definites, three possibles. And the sun rose to do justice to the efforts of the West Indians as the fans gathered early for a sight of an historic victory.

FINAL DAY

Viv Richards happily put another feather in his cap by playing in his first winning Test at Guyana while the Australians mulled over their second loss in 22 Tests since defeating the West Indies in Sydney in January 1989. The ten wicket thumping was emphatic in every department as the West Indians batted and bowled throughout with more adventure and confidence while the Australians stumbled from one mishap to another. Border acknowledged the West Indian superiority in this game and said the Australians 'didn't play well because we were not allowed to play well in this match. The boys are disappointed but we know we can bat better than we did here and we certainly can bowl a lot, lot better.'

Richards was cock-a-hoop with the victory:

That was the perfect way of answering the critics who reckon we are too old and that we are an ageing team. There has been a lot of pressure with people saying that guys should be axed, and that is particularly so when you are playing at home. But nobody can complain about this effort. We bowled really well on a flat pitch and we scored so many runs so quickly that we had two days to wrap up the game. I feel really pleased, as if we have discovered something new. Yes, there is a rev in this team.

The Australians showed some spirit on the final day with Healy and Hughes forcing the West Indians to wait until mid-afternoon before claiming victory. Healy added 47 to his first innings score of 53 but once again surrendered his wicket in a silly run-out, this time failing to beat the return from Greenidge at fine leg to Dujon. Hughes batted for almost two hours for 21 before being the last man out, pulling a delivery from Walsh to Patterson at mid-wicket. The Australian total of 248, with 61 coming from the last two wickets, left the West Indian openers only 28 runs for victory with 45 overs remaining. Haynes followed his first innings 111 with an unbeaten 23 while Greenidge struggled for five runs and twice was hit by McDermott.

Richards acclaimed man-of-the-match Richardson an outright champion and also paid a tribute to Marshall who returned match figures of 6 for 98 off 38 overs on a pitch which produced 1165 runs. Border was similarly impressed. 'It is disconcerting that their fast bowlers captured 20 wickets while our fast bowlers took only two and the spinners eight — and that I took five of them!' he muttered.

The players were only too pleased to depart Guyana, but not nearly as much as some of the former champions now engaged in media activities. They were still limping after a 'golden oldies' match on the rest day. Bob Simpson and Greg Chappell, two former skippers, joined Clive Lloyd, Lance Gibbs and Roy Fredericks in a less than frantic one-day match with mixed results. Simpson was out for only half-a-dozen, while Chappell would hardly have approved of the reverse sweep which dismissed him, although he held a spectacular outfield catch. Laughter was the order of the day because most of the players had no intention of extending themselves to relive past glories. Former champion paceman Michael Holding best predicted the nature of play when asked where he was going as he left the hotel. 'To pull a hamstring!'

CALM BEFORE THE STORM

No less than 22 members of the official Australian party took part in a scuba-diving trip to Baleine Falls at St Vincent.

It was very much the calm before the storm of the final three Tests, the Australians down one Test in two, and trying to relax under a great deal of pressure. All 16 team members as well as coach Bob Simpson, physio Errol Alcott and four journalists (including News Limited photographer Gregg Porteous) were there for the six hour trip on two Dive St Vincent boats.

Scuba instructress Jean, an expatriate Australian and long-time sports buff, gave her impressions of 'my most interesting day for a long time'.

'Allan Border, who was on my boat, was a real mother hen. He was keeping an eye on team-members all the time. The night before, at the Barclay Bank reception attended by all the bigwigs in St Vincent, he was quite relaxed, happy and enjoying everything. He chatted away and appeared to gladly let [manager] Lawrie Sawle carry the load, the responsibility.

'On board, you could almost see Border square his shoulders and say to himself, "OK, AB, the load's on you; now listen up everyone, watch your Ps and Qs, we're representing Australia again." We were in the first boat, carrying the nucleus of the Australian team, and although he had Errol Alcott to help him, Allan was aware of everything everyone else was doing. He didn't relax for a moment. It was a disappointment really, because the whole idea, as Lawrie Sawle had said the night before, was to give the whole team a chance to relax. Everyone else did, except probably the most important man of all.

'Border wore the mantle of captain. He was on duty. We'd go into a little bay, for instance, and I'd say, "that's the local brewery", and he'd say "oh good". The night before he'd have been loquacious. He'd have asked what brand of beer did they brew and how did it compare with Fourex! I was very much aware that he was looking after the group. From what I heard, Bob Simpson was doing the same thing in the other boat.

'It wasn't as though our boat was irresponsible; on board we had Geoff "Swampy" Marsh, Dean Jones, Terry Alderman, Craig McDermott, David Boon, Peter Taylor, Merv Hughes and Errol Alcott, Allan's very busy number two.

'I was sorry for poor Errol in a way; obviously he wanted to be "one of the boys", and would have given his soul to be a Test cricketer, but just as obviously he never could be. There's a very distinct line between players and non-players in Australian sports teams and no matter how important the role of the non-player, he doesn't really rate. It's not the same. Even Bobby Simpson, who's played more cricket than any of them, except maybe Border, must have been aware of it at times. He'd done it, they were still trying to do it. I had the feeling Bobby Simpson would change places with them any time.

"Swampy" Marsh was my favourite; he reminded me what West Australians [like her parents and grandparents] are all about. Swampy is very West Australian and couldn't come from anywhere except a place like Wandering in the WA wheatbelt. When I told him I'd played a bit of basketball, he said it was a "bloody disgrace" that two of the Perth Wildcats' three American players had become naturalised Australians. "It shouldn't be allowed," he said. "West Australians should be playing for the WA team."

'Was he being racist? I don't think so; xenophobic more likely; he was nearly as crooked on "Eastern Staters" as he was on Americans. I don't know how long you have to be in WA before you are accepted as a local, but Mike Veletta joined our boat for the return trip and it was like old home week; Mike and Swampy obviously are very good mates. They'd bring tears to your eyes talking about their youth, parents taking kids to picnics, watching WA win the Sheffield Shield and that sort of thing. I like them both a lot, as I said, but gee they think they're something special, that ALL West Australians are something special. Victorians and other "Eastern-Staters" are far, far, inferior.

'How do Dean Jones and Merv Hughes, the Victorians, cop that? Well, I must say I was prepared to dislike Dean Jones because he gives this impression of thinking he's a bit special, you know, "watch me, and I'll show you how it's done," but now I don't think he's that way at all. He's a perfectionist all right, and a bit showy about it, but that's simply the way he does things. I'm sure if he thought there was somebody did things better than he did, he'd study them and try to improve on their style if he could.

'Mind you, I don't know who he'd think was better than he is, Sir Donald Bradman maybe. "Deano" is very matter-of-fact about being a very good cricketer. He is determined to be a lot better, however. I asked him about the run-out in Guyana and he looked serious and said "I will never be run out in the West Indies again!" He said it so quietly, and so seriously, it was like a man taking a vow.

'Merv Hughes? Let's put it this way, I don't know anyone who dislikes Merv Hughes. He's very popular with his team-mates; they all like to stir him, and he plays up to them, gives them what they want. Swimming near the boat, he was snorting and blowing water out, putting on a very funny act. The others called him "the hairy-backed whale" and so, for five minutes, he was one, spouting water in the air. They'd shout "thar she blows" and Merv would, as long as they kept shouting. He enjoys himself and likes playing the fool. He keeps making these ridiculous bird calls, but behind it all, he's quite a reasonable bloke.

'I certainly didn't hear any bad language or coarse remarks from Merv, although that's what everyone seems to ask me. He was a perfect gentleman as far I and the rest of the crew were concerned, as were Dean Jones and Terry Alderman. I don't mean the others weren't, but it was noticeable that they asked me for anything they wanted rather than [senior diver] Cally Richards and the other Vincentian crew members.

'Dean and Terry didn't; they talked to Cally a lot and, as he's mad on sport, particularly cricket, that made his day. Terry even asked him if he was related to Viv Richards and, though he's not, Cally will be talking about it the rest of his life. Merv was good too. He horsed around with Cally and the others and they loved it.

'Everyone in the Australian team went snorkelling at Coral Castle [a spectacular and colourful coral formation about five metres down in crystal clear water] and most of them had a dive, or a jump, into the pool below the falls later. Allan Border and the Waugh twins, Steve and Mark, sat on the rocks and watched, but most of the others had a go, although it took Greg Matthews about twenty minutes to make sure everything was right.

'I was wearing a blue tee-shirt marked "Staff" over my shorts and bathers in the boat, so he kept calling me "Miss Staff". Later, when the people who had cameras were having difficulty carrying them back to the boats without getting them wet, I offered to swim with them, holding them above my head with one hand. It was my job after all, nothing special; I've done it dozens of times. I said "trust me"; Greg Matthews said he wouldn't dare not to.

'David Boon and Bruce Reid were very quiet, David Boon because I think he became bored fairly quickly, and Bruce Reid because he's just naturally quiet, so much so that I doubt he'd say "boo" if he won Tattslotto. I think he's shy.

Mark Taylor didn't have much to say, but it wasn't because he was shy, just that there was nothing he wanted to talk about at that stage. He was too busy swimming and snorkelling. Obviously he is popular with his team-mates, however, and that's always a good sign.

'The Waughs? I don't know. They don't look at you and they don't look at each other. They're there and they're not enthused about it; they don't take any notice, but you feel that they know absolutely everything, every

Greg Matthews goes feet first at the Baleine Falls, St Vincent.

single, blessed thing that's going on. They never give a sign though, just sit there, or stand there, looking past you. You feel that maybe they're tensing to spring and take another one of those marvellous catches. If they were on the other side in *The Gunfight in the OK Corral* in the movies, they'd be the ones you'd have to keep your eyes on.

'Peter Taylor, on the other hand, is very outgoing, interested in everything. He's wide awake and asks questions which keep you on your toes. For instance, he asked me how deep the water is around these islands, and how deep it is close to shore, how abruptly the beaches fall away? Most people don't think of things like that. They think the beaches are long shelves of sand like they have in England or America.

'Peter Taylor also was interested in the local lifestyle and when I said quite a few of the locals were interested in small farming, he twigged immediately that I was referring to them growing their own tobacco, you know, strong tobacco, they call it "ganja" here. Peter didn't approve or disapprove; he was simply interested, not judgmental. In that sense, I think the New South Wales players were more sophisticated than the West Australians.

'Mike Whitney must be good for the team, I think. He's enthusiastic about everything, eager to take part, to get moving, to contribute. In that sense, he's like Mike Veletta. Neither of them is among the team's topliners, and they know it, but you know, and I'm sure Bobby Simpson knows, that it isn't for the want of trying. Forget about either of them breaking an arm for a team, they'd break a neck.

'Ian Healy is very chirpy, an up-front type, not at all shy. I could imagine him being a good salesman. The first thing he said to me was "hey, that's a good suntan you have" which was a nice thing to say, particularly because it was true, and he knew I'd like hearing it. Later when I was talking to someone else, he said "this girl would have to have the best job in the world", and I didn't mind hearing that either, because he wasn't just spinning a line. He told me about his new baby daughter, his first child, and how he couldn't wait to get home to Queensland.

'He comes across as very sincere, Ian Healy. He said he would prefer to play tennis or golf rather than a team sport like cricket. In tennis and golf you only let yourself down, you don't let down "the guys". In team sports, you let down your team-mates. You can ruin all their good work.

'The way Ian sees it, if he drops a catch, he costs a bowler a wicket; if he goes out cheaply, he can cost the team a match, or at least a draw. I asked him if he was talking about any particular match, a Test match for instance, and he said he wasn't. He was just talking in principles, but I think he still might have been blaming himself for that first innings run-out in Guyana.

'I don't think Craig McDermott felt quite comfortable about coming along on the trip. His wife is expecting a baby any day and he felt he should be back in St Vincent writing a letter or something like that, not swimming around in the Caribbean. He is only a boy after all, still making his way in the team.'

(McDermott was to prove the most successful bowler in the series, and that takes some doing by a white fast bowler in the West Indies. And at 26, he is only six years younger than Jean herself.)

'He's still finding his way. He was in our boat and had a good time when he settled down and relaxed, but still found time to worry why he hadn't developed a suntan like the others. He talks about health and fitness all the time. He looks up to Terry Alderman and had his nose and lips covered with zinc cream like him.

'When we put in to Wallilabou for lunch, Craig was concerned about what he should wear in the beach restaurant. "Should I put on a shirt?" he asked me. "Or am I all right in my bathers and towel?" I said "wear what you like, what you feel comfortable in; it's that sort of place. If you feel comfortable without a shirt, don't wear one."

'Terry said, "Wear a shirt; Simmo wouldn't like it if you didn't," and that settled it. Everyone wore shirts. They were all very conscious of what Bob Simpson thought, how he thought they should represent Australia.

'Mind you, Bob Simpson worked as hard as anyone else about "doing the right thing". He noticed the "Welcome Australian Cricket Team" sign at Wallilabou and immediately asked me who would have been responsible for it. I said the manageress, but the staff would have helped too, and he made a point of thanking them all.

'As a matter of fact, that was one of the best things about the day, that you could feel so proud of the Australians. I had forgotten how old-fashioned and chivalrous they can be. I wasn't allowed to pull up an anchor chain all day, it was "hey Merv", or "hey Deano, what do you think we brought you along for?" American tourists, in particular, expect you to do it all for them, and why not? They're paying for it after all!

'Allan Border even offered me his seat while I was driving the boat! Cally couldn't get over that. The Brits wouldn't think of being so courteous to a crew member. Neither for that matter would a West Indian. They wouldn't even see the crew member!'

I bet they'd see Jean. She's my eldest daughter and a knockout, even if I say so myself. Jean and her husband, Paul Fogarty, who is from Ballarat, have been in St Vincent for two years and have another year to go, while Paul, a doctor, completes his second eighteen month term at Kingstown Hospital. Then everyone, Paul's family and ours, hope they will come home, though Jean says they have a trip to Venezuela planned, a trip down the Amazon in Chile, and so on. You never know with kids these days.

They're so mobile, too mobile sometimes!

Jean and Paul have a house literally on the beach in St Vincent, a diet which features fresh fish every day — and, so far, at least one pair of visitors a month from England or Australia. Alison was determined we would not miss out, and we didn't, although I had to watch a lot of cricket to do it. Tough that, having to watch Australia play cricket in 'Paradise'!

THE THIRD TEST:
THE WAUGHS MAKE HISTORY

This Test always will have a place in history as the first time twins played alongside each other in a Test. Mark and Steve Waugh enjoyed that honour but the unseasonal weather wrecked hopes of a happy ending for the Australians in a disappointing draw at Queens Park Oval in Trinidad. The rain once again deprived the Australians of a hard fought advantage, as it had in Jamaica in the opening match, and only 265.3 overs were bowled in the game. The Australians batted diligently for a first innings total of 294, with Mark Taylor returning to form with 61 and the Waugh twins batting together in a breezy 58 run partnership in 90 minutes, with Mark finishing with 64 and Steve with 26 in a memorable liaison. Hughes then dreamed the impossible dream to capture 3 for 2 in 15 deliveries as the

Ground staff with more water than they can handle in the rain-ruined Third Test at Queens Park, Trinidad.

West Indies crashed to 5 for 56 in pursuit of the meagre 94 to avoid the follow-on but belligerent innings by Dujon and Ambrose carried the home team to safety. The Australians, with a first innings lead of 67, batted out time to reach 3 for 123 at the close of a miserable Test deprived of a climax by torrential rain. But for the second time in three Tests, there was controversy about leaking covers and a ripple of anxiety within the West Indian team as the top order crumbled in the first innings after such a monumental success in Guyana.

The Australians wisely utilised their ample time during the outrageously long travelling day from Guyana to St Vincent after the second Test. The players endured 16 hours before reaching the Sunset Shores Villa at 11.00 pm, having gone through customs in three countries and being forced to wait seven hours in Trinidad for a connecting flight. All this for what was originally scheduled as a one hour flight to Trinidad, a three hour transfer and an 80 minute flight to St Vincent. But all was not wasted. The team spent an hour of self-analysis in Trinidad to thrash out several disconcerting aspects of their second Test defeat. The mood was intense and the talk forthright, so much so that Simpson declared it 'one of the best meetings I have known since I have become involved with the team'.

> *There was solid, tough discussion and the best aspect was that all the contributions were positive with no holds barred. The boys really got down to the nitty-gritty. The consensus was that we hadn't played well in Tests since England in 1989, that we didn't play as well as we know we can in Guyana, that the batsmen were not aggressive enough and that we weren't patient enough in our bowling. It was very frank and forthright and the players left the meeting with a new resolve. I am sure the West Indies team will still commit hari-kari if they are put under the right sort of relentless pressure, as they were in the one-dayers, but we just must return to that really tight bowling.*

So the Australian selectors had much to occupy their minds when the players reached the idyllic island of St Vincent for the four day match against the West Indian Under 23 XI. The match was a showdown for Reid because of the urgency to return him to action, and equally important was the task of sorting out the lack of rhythm and aggression in Hughes' bowling. The Australians arrived in the Caribbean with the hopes of winning this series with a pace attack of McDermott, Hughes and Reid, but they hadn't been together and simultaneously effective at any stage of the tour. McDermott took a deserved rest, while the writing was on the wall that Whitney would be considered for the third Test only as a necessary substitute if Reid failed his form and fitness test. Whitney's big heart simply hadn't been enough to lift him a notch at Test standard in the opening two Tests and his figures of 0 for 216 condemned him to the backblocks. The same went for all-rounder Matthews whose batting had slumped since his outstanding contributions in the Ashes series and whose off-spin, flighted too much against the free-striking West Indians on the small grounds, paled into insignificance against even the part-part-time bowling of Border. Matthews was overlooked for the St Vincent match with Test figures of 27 runs in three innings and only three wickets at a cost of 91. The opportunity was there for Peter Taylor and Steve Waugh, the former because he was a spinner and the latter because he was an all-rounder.

The drawn match — in which the tourists came within a wicket and a handful of runs of victory in a rain-affected contest — quickly provided one certain answer when Reid captured 4 for 76 off 29.1 overs in the first innings total of 307, including the top three batsmen in the line-up. He improved the longer he bowled and added another two wickets to his haul in the second innings to assure the selectors he was ready to return to the Test arena. He was a greatly relieved and optimistic man after the match.

That is the best I have bowled for ages. I guess it was a combination of the physical and mental problem with the back ailment and it has taken a while for things to come together. But this was just what I needed. There is no soreness and I have bowled plenty of overs. It is a great confidence boost, particularly as I prepared myself especially for this game knowing that it was a do-or-die effort. It was very important to me and to Australia, because you start to wonder that if you don't front up it is all over for the tour. I couldn't cop that because I wanted a whole season of good cricket, not just have a season in Australia.

Reid admitted he bottled up his fears early on the tour although he knew he was struggling.

But then Bob Simpson spoke with me in Trinidad, took videos of my action and generally gave me a lot of help. I realised that the administrators wanted me to play as much as I wanted to play, and that they were as dismayed as I was about my unavailability. They were keen for me to play in the second Test but eventually I was overlooked and I was very disappointed about that, not just for myself, but because we lost. Now I want to get in there and set things straight.

That sort of attitude shone through in St Vincent. Peter Taylor also promoted his cause with two excellent stints at the bowling crease, claiming 3 for 54 off 21 overs in the first innings and then 5 for 37 off 25 overs in the second innings of 9 for 162. He had a purple patch to capture 4 for 4 off 12 deliveries in the middle of the innings when the Under 23 team needed 144 to avoid an innings defeat, but failed to wrap up the vulnerable tail-end to detract from his efforts.

But if the Australians were to add backbone to the batting which failed twice at Guyana without weakening the bowling to a great degree, the performance which stood out was the brilliant batting of Steve Waugh. He stylishly compiled 85 off 122 deliveries with ten boundaries to add to his only other first class scores on tour of 96 not out and 15 against the President's XI in the opening match at St Kitts, and followed his 26 off 38 deliveries in the last one-day international a fortnight earlier. The right-hander was in such dazzling batting form, with the advantage of being a capable medium-pacer, that he shaped as the logical replacement for Matthews. The prospect of little assistance from the Queens' Park Oval pitch sealed the issue on the eve of the Test.

The bonuses for the Australians came with Mark Taylor's return to form with his second century of the tour: 122 in six hours of determined concentration after a barren period at international level. Jones also sparkled with 60 entertaining runs in an Australian total of 451 and the Australians headed to Trinidad with a rekindled enthusiasm and refreshed bodies and minds. A special spirit was back in the team and not since England in 1989 had the banter between players been so spontaneous. The team meeting, the opportunity to relax at such an idyllic island with swimming, snorkelling and sightseeing, and a totally uninhibited surrounding demanded a refreshed spirit. Young Island, a private paradise only 200 metres from St Vincent, was a favourite nightspot for the team, as was The French Restaurant on the 'mainland'. It lay beside the jetty from which a ferry (after gaining permission from Young Island to allow you to land) would transport visitors across the clear blue water. Mark Waugh thought Young Island was so impressive he slipped across there one day when he should have been elsewhere. A couple of players spotted him and the all-rounder paid the penalty of an eight kilometre run. He was so exhausted that he damaged his ankle and had to play in the third Test with that lingering handicap! St Vincent was also the scene of a fun night at the yacht club at Blue Lagoon where luxury yachts bob on the glistening water at sunset, one of the most memorable sights of the tour. Errol Alcott joined Terry Brindle, Gregg Porteous and myself for dinner one evening for an impromptu relaxation, the former having finally cleared himself of all obligations — it is amazing how health returned on this paradise island after weeks of ailments — and the News Ltd trio having finished work for the day. The inland is a mass of banana trees and if there was one local commodity which seemed assured it was bananas. Imagine the stunned silence, followed by uproarious laughter, when informed by a blushing waitress that 'yes, we have no bananas!' When the poor lass simply couldn't get her tongue around the word crêpe, all members of the party insisted on ordering it and it must have been a source of bewilderment for Simpson, dining privately at another table, when he looked up to see four of the Australian contingent, in a superb setting on a balmy night in paradise with no commitments for a change, with tears rolling down their collective cheeks! This was the funniest dinner of the tour and the communication problem between the waitress and the Aussies reminded Brindle and me of a similar problem we experienced in Barbados. After a brief walk around the bustling centre of Bridgetown we decided to quench our thirst at The Waterfront, a popular restaurant and bar overlooking the harbour with Nelson Square opposite. The Waterfront in Sydney doesn't need to worry about competition because that famous view of Sydney Harbour is infinitely more pleasant than that offered by its namesake in Barbados. 'Two beers thanks,' I requested as we sat under a cooling fan, mopping the torrents of perspiration from our brows. We waited patiently as the barmaid busied herself slicing bananas and concocting all sorts of fancy potions, which we assumed were for one of the many tourist groups at the packed bar. Some time later another waitress approached and asked if we were being served and we explained that we had given our order for two beers. 'I'll fix it,' she said and plucked two beers from the fridge, placing them in front of us at the same time as the other waitress put the finishing touches on two pina coladas. OUR pina coladas!

The Aussie accent can be guttural, but how she managed to decipher two pina coladas from two beers remains a mystery. She obligingly took back the exotic drinks and was relieved when new customers immediately ordered two pina coladas. Brindle and I were bewildered when she didn't give them two beers!

Merv Hughes is the key man in the team when it comes to jokes and frivolity and he also is the one who lifts flagging spirits or takes the wind out of the sails of anyone feeling smug with a performance. And so it was when Mark Taylor celebrated his century. Hughes reminded him that he still boasted a higher Test score against the West Indians, and had a better average! The comment begged a reaction and it came immediately: 'I now really have something to aim for in this series: to beat Merv's highest score of 72 not out against the West Indians in a Test. That really bugs me,' Taylor grumbled as Hughes and the other players incessantly ribbed the opener. Hughes had done his homework, knowing that Taylor's highest score was 58 in the opening Test of this series and that his average of 21.67 marginally headed Taylor's 20.00. The banter was significant, if only because it stirred Taylor to greater achievements. The release of tension was also important because there was a feeling that people were becoming too intense and too involved for the playful asides which linked the team so closely during the glory ride in England two years earlier. But the spirit was back, along with important centre wicket form.

One of the most significant developments at St Vincent was the rejuvenation of Hughes, who recaptured his self-confidence after a substandard performance in Guyana. He endured a severe case of self-doubt about his ability and place in the Australian team during that Test and again in the match against the Under 23 XI. But self-analysis, moral and technical support from Simpson and encouragement from his team-mates snapped him out of a dangerously deflated period.

The bristling fast bowler, who built his reputation on aggression and confidence, confessed the fear of losing his Test place had haunted him as he explained he never had suffered so many self-doubts about his ability. 'Negative attitudes breed negative results and for the first time in my international career I have wondered where my next wicket would come from and if I had lost everything I had which made me a Test bowler,' the giant pondered as he sought the solitude of his room at a very early hour.

I have done a lot more than just think about losing my place in the Test team: I have been worried sick. Everything was going well in the first innings of the first Test when I captured four wickets but since then everything has gone wrong. I bowled absolute shit in the second Test and the lack of confidence really kicked me in the guts. You know you can do it at this level but if your confidence is down you start to worry about all sorts of things. Steve Waugh came up to me in this match and said I was bowling well and that I would get a wicket any time. Then I looked at the scoreboard and saw I had none for 70 and all the self-doubts returned and I wondered where I would get the next wicket. But the more I bowled the more confident I became. The half-trackers became bouncers even on this pitch and I grabbed a couple of wickets, bowled economically and felt very pleased with myself at the end of the day. I have just been going through a rut. It doesn't matter whom you are playing against in these circumstances, it is just a matter of regaining confidence. I know I bowled badly in the Test but when I couldn't get a top-order wicket against the Under 23 team I was shattered. But I took stock of myself and thought about the ability I had. I had self-doubts but realised eventually that I could bowl better than I had been and then started to turn things around. I am confident now that I can be more aggressive and more value to the team. This is the first time I have doubted myself at international level. I don't like it, and I intend to do something about it to make sure it doesn't happen again.

Simpson took video of Hughes in action against the Under 23 team and, having sorted out the technical problem, explained his attributes and importance to the Australian cause to correct his attitude and confidence. 'Merv looked at the video and immediately recognised what he was doing wrong, without any suggestion from me,' Simpson said.

As soon as he saw the tape he shook his head and said he was bowling with his shoulder and arm and not with the weight of his body. He was basically bowling off the back foot. That was why he was not hitting the pitch as hard as he normally does and to his credit he went out and tried to put his whole body into his bowling action even though his run-up and delivery stride still didn't co-ordinate as well as he would have liked.

The improvement was swift. Simpson then privately and publicly boosted the paceman who boasted 107 victims in his 27 Test career.

For some reason he stopped being aggressive on this tour, probably having misinterpreted the idea of bowling line-and-length, and so he cut his pace in a bid to work to our plan of attack. We need him to bowl well. Not just line-and-length, but at genuine pace. Once he sorts out his run-up I am sure he will be back to the bowler who has done so very well against everyone in the past few years. We know he can do it, and I think he realises that too now.

The players were keyed up for the third Test and keen to make amends for Guyana. The Trinidad Hilton was a pleasant enough headquarters for the team, although Neville Oliver of the ABC had his doubts during the first two visits. Oliver initially arrived at the hotel on the hill for the second one-day international, booked in as the clock ticked towards midnight and carried his heavy suitcase to his alloted room alongside the rest of the press corp. Finding the room was difficult enough because the floors in the hotel are numbered upside down. You must press the down button on the elevator to reach the sixth floor and the up button to travel to reception on the ground floor because the rooms are built down the side of the hill which overlooks the vast Queen's Park Savannah (which is encompassed by the world's longest roundabout). Oliver's strangled scream alerted us that something was amiss but he saw the funny side of being given the most spacious room in the hotel — a room with only a telephone in the middle of an empty room!

He wasn't laughing the following week on our return visit, especially after a lengthy delay at reception because the press hadn't been booked in despite confirmation only four days earlier. That sorted out, Oliver lugged his suitcase and equipment along the corridor for 200 metres to a room at the maximum distance from the elevator. He wasn't amused to discover the front desk had given him the wrong key! Back down the corridor and up in the elevator to reception, his deep radio voice increasing in volume. Almost an hour later the crimsoned-faced Tasmanian collapsed at the Aviary Bar overlooking the dazzling night lights of Port of Spain in urgent need of refreshment. This was not his day. The players, who on $15 a day found this plush bar far too expensive, were just leaving for a trip to the popular pub at the bottom of the hill. The Pelican became the hideout for the players and the press but it had one drawback: the hill. Getting down the winding path was no big deal but returning past the guards and their vicious dogs up the steep ascent was torture for the fittest of players, let alone poor Neville who had just completed a routemarch to settle into his room. Neville couldn't understand the difficulty of getting into a room at the Hilton. He had more trouble there than he did getting into the Governor's residence in Georgetown, Guyana, a few weeks later. He arrived with his tape recorder in a briefcase and was suitably impressed when a security guard asked if he was carrying any weapons, explosive devices or other potentially dangerous equipment. 'No' was the simple reply. 'Oh, then that's okay — you can go straight in,' came the reply without any suggestion of looking in his suitcase!

FIRST DAY

The Waugh twins were the focus of attention before play as they prepared for an historic match as the first twins to play together in the same Test. They had played together regularly for New South Wales and earlier in the season shared a world record fifth wicket partnership in first class cricket of 464 and a record for any wicket by two Australians. Mark finished unbeaten with 229 and Steve unconquered on 216 against a West Australian attack in Perth of Reid and Alderman. The twins also have centuries to their credit on opposition teams: Steve scored a dazzling century off 101 deliveries for the Australians while Mark helped himself to a century for English county team Essex. They previously represented Australia together in one-day internationals but on 5 April at the Queens Park Oval they stood side by side in an Australian Test team. Only six sets of Australian brothers have played Test cricket together, and standing on the same centre wicket square as television commentators were the last pair to compete together, Ian and Greg Chappell. The air was pregnant with anticipation at the picturesque ground, the atmosphere made twice as heavy by the gathering clouds which were to devastate Australia's hopes.

The Australians, having been sent in to bat, battled diligently to 1 for 55 before the heavens opened a few minutes before lunch, sparking a bevy of groundsmen into action to deposit a mass of covers. But when the deluge abated and the ground staff crudely but effectively removed a sea of surface water from the covers, the Australians were left to bemoan a damaged pitch.

The covers had leaked, leaving five damp patches on the pitch, including one on a good length in line with the off stump at the outer end. The explanation was that the covers had been pierced by boot sprigs before play after being spread out on the cement cycling track which encompasses the oval. The bottom line was that once again a Test pitch was damaged because of leaking covers and an important event suffered an avoidable loss of activity. The damp spots guaranteed no further play was possible despite the clearing skies and warming sunshine, and the situation was a pitiful repeat of the opening Test at Jamaica when four sessions were lost (when the sun was shining) because the covers leaked. First class matches at St Kitts and St Vincent also were interrupted because of cover leakages; clearly the entire issue of wicket protection in the Caribbean required urgent and drastic action.

Border and the Australians were furious that such frequent mishaps continued to hinder their campaign and suggested it was an unacceptable occurrence in a country which boasted the dominant team in world cricket for the past 15 years. A similar event in Australia or England would incur international outrage, but here it happened twice within three Tests and was too readily accepted as an unfortunate mishap instead of a blight on the game, the authorities and the stature of West Indian cricket. 'It is ridiculous,' Border said as he surveyed the damaged zone. 'If the West Indies want to be fair dinkum about their cricket here they must address these problems. It is just not good enough.'

He was hardly impressed by a suggestion from former West Indian Test captain Clive Lloyd that the International Cricket Council set up 'a Third World cricket crisis fund' to ensure such basic matters are brought up to standard. Lloyd suggested the money be raised from a one-day international at the start of every series around the world and set aside each year to be channelled into areas which need upgrading. Border retorted:

> Where is the third world? There are no such problems in India or Pakistan and really not in Sri Lanka. The only place this sort of problem regularly occurs is in the West Indies, so who would get the benefit of such a fund? I think the simple answer is for the ICC to demand a certain standard and insist it be met.

Sawle made strong recommendations in his tour report about the lack of adequate covers and the ramifications for the touring team. Border refrained from an official complaint at the time but posed a valid question: 'How can the public be expected to pay to come to the cricket and despite the sun shining be told there will not be any cricket because of a damp spot on the pitch caused by inadequate covers? If you don't get the people, you don't get gate receipts and you automatically lose support for the game.' The sparse crowd on the opening day, despite the West Indian team's 1-0 lead in the series, was typical of attendances around the islands. And there was every chance that the decline would continue, especially if officials couldn't guarantee that wickets were protected and that play would resume once the sun emerged.

So the Australians left the Queens Park Oval under clearing skies after only 23 overs of action with Mark Taylor (28) and Boon (6) waiting to renew the battle. The Australians were progressing comfortably after losing Marsh for 10 when Ambrose caused a delivery to rear unexpectedly and divert from Marsh's defensive bat to Hooper at second slip. Boon batted for 56 minutes before his opening run and Taylor, who scored a patient century in the build-up game against the West Indian Under 23s, also struggled with the slowness and unevenness of the pitch as he attempted a dozen cuts without contact before finally hitting the target with 10 runs from a Marshall over. But the momentum stopped when the rain started and the Australians were left to lament the uncharitable weather in the Caribbean yet again.

SECOND DAY

April showers flooded the ground after only seven overs on the second day and the only ray of sunshine came with swift action by the West Indian Cricket Board, with support from both teams, to scrap the rest day, thus providing as much play as possible on the remaining three days. The Australians advanced to 1 for 75 with Taylor on 35 and Boon on 12 before the heavens opened the floodgates, but this time the mended covers were swiftly in place to protect the area while the outfield disappeared in a sea of water. The good news was that the damp spots from the day before had dried under the previous afternoon's sun and that at least that unhappy incident had no adverse effect on the Test after the opening day.

The unseasonal rains, which dumped twice the average monthly rain on the ground within two days, were unkind to the Australians: 30 overs in two days was a recipe for a draw at a time when the Australians needed a win to level the series. Border was realistic about the situation: 'It is hard to get enthusiastic about a result in this Test, although anything can happen. At least the West Indian officials have seen fit to get an extra day's play in and that can't be bad, even if we use it for batting practice and then have a bit of a bowling workout.'

Perhaps the dismal weather had demoralised the captain because it was difficult to understand his softening of attitude during these couple of days. The intensity and desperation for victory left him for a few days and he talked of escaping the tour with a Test win instead of with a series win to become the world champions.

I just want to win a Test. If we beat these guys at home it will be a good series given that we have won the one-dayers, beaten England in the Ashes and won the one-day series in Australia. It would be a good summer's work. I am not paranoid about this top dog tag. It is more important that we prove ourselves a good team and get Australia moving forward again.

A moment off guard was the only explanation for those remarks, because Border was quickly back on the front foot with the management when it was suggested they play a one-day international instead if the rain continued and prevented action during the next couple of days. 'No way!' he declared. 'This is a Test and we want all the work we can get in the Test arena.' Sawle quickly put paid to the idea:

As far as we are concerned this is an official Test and we want to use whatever time is available for our players to get Test match practice with two very important Tests to come. And I believe that once a Test has started it should be finished, not superseded by a one-day international for the sake of it.

The proposal gained momentum as the rains continued because local officials estimated that the two disrupted days at the most profitable Caribbean venue already had cost them $150 000. Only one tour in 20 years in the Caribbean — Pakistan in 1988-89 in a three Test series — earned a profit and this rain-ruined Test was a bitter blow to the finances of West Indian cricket. As executive secretary Steve Comache explained: 'Any other business would have filed for bankruptcy years ago ... cricket here is surviving on goodwill.' The gods finally smiled on the treasurer when the downpour ceased and gave way to sunshine to enable the Test to resume.

THIRD DAY

The Australians worked their way into a handy position at stumps but not without telling blows to two senior batsmen. Boon suffered a broken left index finger and Jones a suspected broken middle left toe as the Australians reached 6 for 279 and a position of complete safety. Boon was hurt when he was hit on the hand at the start of his innings on the opening day and if there was any doubt it was fractured, a delivery from Ambrose then crushed his hand on to the bat handle when he was 13 to confirm the break. Jones sustained his ailment when a yorker from Patterson hit him flush on the toe and, to add insult to injury, he was given out lbw!

The injuries were part of a tough day of competitive cricket as the West Indians strove to gain the ascendancy, aiming to catch the Australians in a listless mood after the rain. But the batsmen, acutely aware of the dangers of a slump with three days of Test cricket to play, knuckled down and played handsomely to take the honours on the day. Boon, who had trouble even gripping the bat, played on doggedly for almost three hours to contribute 27 in a 69 run partnership with Taylor. But he could do nothing but present Logie, fielding at bat/pad, with his 50th Test catch when defending a rearing delivery from Patterson.

Taylor recorded his highest Test score against the West Indians with 61 after four hours of gritty concentration and application, an obvious legacy of his time in the centre while compiling a century at St Vincent. He reached his second half-century of the series off 140 deliveries and was beginning to attack the bowling when he fell victim to a Marshall delivery which kept low. Taylor, having hit two boundaries off the previous six deliveries to take his tally to nine for the innings, mishit a pull shot because of the low bounce and presented Walsh with a regulation catch at mid-wicket. The Australians needed to consolidate at 3 for 116 before lunch and Border and Jones did the job with a 68 run stand in two hours. Jones, as he had in Guyana, looked composed and prepared to bide his time for his runs rather than play risky shots. The method succeeded until Patterson hit him on the toe with a yorker to end the innings at 21, another failure by his own high standards. He was finding the umpires unkind in this series, particularly as this dismissal followed his controversial run-out in the second innings in Guyana. 'The toe hurts nearly as much as being given out to that delivery,' Jones grumbled as he limped from the ground at stumps.

Border and Mark Waugh survived the second new ball and began increasing the tempo until Border's hard work came to a disappointing end when he was run out by a direct hit from Hooper from the covers. Border's 43 followed his previous Test scores of 31, 47 and 34 and while it was pleasing that he was establishing an innings it was increasingly discouraging that he wasn't capitalising on the starts. His exit did pave the way for 90 minutes of history when Steve Waugh joined twin Mark at the crease at 3.52 pm. They played stroke-for-stroke to skip past a half-century stand in only 72 minutes and looked set for a truly memorable union until Steve drove at a wide delivery from Walsh to present Dujon with a regulation catch. That ended a 58 run partnership and left Steve cursing himself. 'I am really dirty about getting out,' Steve said of his innings of 26 off only 54 deliveries. 'We have a sort of telepathy between us and we don't need to say much out in the centre. We just take runs, hit shots and get on with it. I was hitting the ball really well until I played a poor shot, and it was really disappointing because we could have set ourselves some sort of standard in our first Test together,' he said.

Mark Waugh continued his giant strides towards stardom with his fluent and effortless style and he reached his second half-century of the series in 156 minutes with the prospect of more runs the following day. Walsh carried the West Indian attack in an outstanding show of stamina and accuracy after Marshall bowled only four overs and left the field for an injection because of a stomach upset, and Ambrose needed tablets for a similar complaint. He bowled 30 overs and captured the wicket of Steve Waugh while conceding only 45 runs — an important form reversal for the laconic paceman.

FOURTH DAY

The Australians dreamed the impossible dream of dismissing the West Indians for fewer than 94 to enforce the follow-on and for 25 overs the West Indians were having nightmares. Hughes recaptured his best form in a remarkable about-turn from the second Test and he took 3 for 2 off 15 deliveries in an inspired spell to have the Caribbean champions tottering at 5 for 56. Hughes added Richardson to his haul before Dujon, Marshall and Ambrose ensured a draw with a spirited latter order fightback after averting the follow-on. The day was full of drama and a cascade of ten wickets tumbled for only 101 runs in the opening 150 minutes of action. The pressure certainly was on the West Indian camp and at one stage during the collapse a predominately Indian section in the members' pavilion baited agitated West Indian manager Lance Gibbs. The ill-feeling was directed at Richards, who was dismissed attempting a lusty hit off Hughes. 'The Master Blaster no more,' the crowd persistently shouted as Richards strutted from the field at the height of the collapse. Gibbs could take no more and a public verbal slanging match developed, such was the tension within the West Indian camp. Gibbs is a generally placid man and it was obviously upsetting that so many West Indians, even given the Indian descent, were openly anti the legendary batsman and the team. Cricket for the West Indians in the Caribbean has its tough side for the local players as well as the tourists.

The day dawned with no warning of the dramas to follow and drizzle prevented play for the opening hour. But when the game resumed the action came thick and fast. The Australians lost their last four wickets for only one run in nine deliveries in yet another tail-end collapse to be dismissed for 294. Mark Waugh fell lbw to an improved Marshall for 64 and McDermott's batting woes continued when he was caught at point for a single when uppishly driving Patterson. Hughes didn't trouble the scorers and Healy, having run out of partners after contributing nine in an hour, finally edged a lavish cut to Dujon off Marshall. Patterson yet again took the statistical honours with 4 for 50 by ripping through the tail but Ambrose (1 for 51 off 29 overs) and Walsh (1 for 45 off 30 overs) bowled just as well without similar rewards.

The West Indian reply began shakily without a hint of the mid-session collapse sparked by Hughes. McDermott rattled the stumps of Haynes for only one with 16 runs on the board; then Reid produced the sort of rearing delivery the team had been waiting for to have Greenidge caught at second slip by Mark Waugh off a defensive edge for 12. Richardson and Hooper negotiated the bowling to ease the score from 2 for 18 to 2 for 42 at lunch. With only 52 more runs required to avert the follow-on to virtually kill the contest, the intensity abated during the interval. But Hughes upset the tranquillity in the West Indian viewing area when he took the ball immediately after lunch. He began his fiery spell by trapping Hooper lbw for 12 and having Logie caught in second slip by Mark Waugh for only one.

The confrontation between Hughes and Richards was compulsive viewing: a raging fast bowler with a full head of steam against a champion batsman who seemingly had set himself to blast every delivery to the boundary or beyond. Hughes beat Richards a couple of times and prolonged eyeball-to-eyeball glares-and-dares intensified the showdown. Richards then opened his shoulders with a thumping drive which was stopped brilliantly by Steve Waugh and Hughes applauded the West Indian skipper for hitting a delivery in the middle of the bat. That was enough to encourage outright war, but on this occasion Hughes won handsomely with a slightly slower delivery which Richards hammered straight to Steve Waugh in the covers where the brilliant fieldsmen held the hot chance.

Richards swaggered from the field chewing gum in an exaggerated manner as a section of the members' chided him and another jeered and mocked him. The West Indian balcony now was deserted as batsmen scurried to pad up while those dismissed in the recent collapse gave assistance. Hughes had taken three vital wickets in 15 deliveries and in the midst of the collapse Richardson enjoyed an unlikely escape when Jones, one of the best fieldsmen in world cricket, dropped a simple chance at covers from the bowling of Reid. Richardson, only 16 at the time and with the score on 3 for 50, mishit a drive and guided the ball directly to Jones but the fieldsman didn't pick up the flight of the ball against the background of the concrete stand and grabbed at the ball at the last moment, only to drop it. The error was costly because the end of Richardson combined with Hughes' wickets would have plummeted the West Indies to 6 for 56. Richardson found Dujon a supportive partner and they carried the score to 86 before Hughes found the outside edge of Richardson's bat for Mark Taylor to hold a neat catch at first slip. Richardson's 30 in an hour and a half was invaluable in the context of the game.

The Australians claimed four wickets for 44 runs in 11 overs in 54 exhilarating minutes after lunch but Dujon and Marshall woke them from the impossible dream by skipping past the follow-on target. The impetus evaporated as Dujon settled in to guarantee the Australians didn't pursue the advantage to claim a sizeable first innings lead with an eye to a declaration on the final day to press for an unlikely victory. He lost Marshall for a dozen when a Border full toss sailed to McDermott at mid-on. The West Indians were still vulnerable at 7 for 110, a deficit of 184. But Dujon played faultlessly and discovered a willing if unfashionable partner in Ambrose. Dujon's correct technique and Ambrose's unorthodox but effective swipes frustrated the Australian bowlers, particularly McDermott who stood idly in the outfield for the entire final session as Reid, Hughes, Border, the Waugh twins and even Jones took turns at the bowling crease. Dujon reached his half-century off 100 deliveries and Ambrose recorded his highest Test score when he passed 44, the score he registered against Australia at the MCG in 1988-89. He was proving a major hurdle to the Australians following his 33 in similarly difficult circumstances in the opening Test at Jamaica, and he fully deserved his maiden Test half-century off only 78 deliveries with six boundaries. His effort came to an end three runs later when he guided a delivery from Mark Waugh to Border after sharing an 87 run partnership with Dujon in a tick more than two hours to bury Australia's faint hopes of stealing a win. The West Indians afforded a relieved grin as they boarded the bus that evening after an unexpectedly difficult day at the office.

FINAL DAY

Australia took scant solace from having the better of this Test which fizzled into a tame draw to leave the West Indians 1-0 up in the series with only two Tests remaining. They batted and bowled considerably better than their opponents but once again the weather ruined any chance of a result. The loss of five sessions cruelled their chances and the players were left to wonder what might have been without the hefty reduction. At the close they boasted a 200 run lead with seven wickets in hand on a pitch which was playing tricks.

The final day was a letdown in many respects. Dujon, who resumed on 70, failed to add to his score when a century would have been a fitting reward for his efforts. McDermott trapped him lbw and in a fine sporting display the pair exchanged friendly blows as they crossed in centre pitch. The memory lingers as the last overtly spontaneous gesture of sportsmanship in the series as the Barbados and Antigua Tests turned sour. McDermott added Patterson to his list to wrap up the innings for 227, providing the Australians with a lead of 67. But Hughes was the bowling hero, finishing with 4 for 48 off 17 overs in a welcome return to form.

The West Indians were out to squeeze a psychological advantage from a disappointing showing and quickly removed Mark Taylor for 2 when the left-hander again succumbed to the pull. This time he chopped a Patterson

Keith Arthurton hands his illegally wide bat to the umpire for measurement in the Board X1 match at Barbados.

delivery on to the stumps in the second over of the innings. Marsh contributed a dozen in 85 minutes before he was trapped lbw by Marshall, then Boon, battling with a broken finger for 97 minutes, lost his stumps to Walsh after scoring 29. The tourists went to lunch at 3 for 81 and Jones and Border batted out the remainder of the day to reach 3 for 123 before a premature declaration to enable an early end to play. Jones, batting at number four in a bid to spend as much time as possible in the centre to regain his confidence, batted for 145 minutes to remain unbeaten on 39 while Border continued his steady contributions with an unbeaten 27.

The Australians had not played to their full potential but the team effort gave rise to enthusiasm for the remainder of the series. The team headed to Barbados for a four day match against the West Indies Board XI at Kensington Oval, the famous venue of the fourth Test with Marsh at the helm in a match the Australians agreed should be played with as much dash and daring as possible. But the build-up was a major flop as the Australians came off second best with bat and ball in a demoralising display as the rains continued to follow the tourists from island to island.

The match involved further controversy when West Indian batsman Keith Arthurton used an illegal bat during the match and despite being alerted to it, the umpires took no action. The confrontation occurred in the second innings when Dean Jones queried the width of the bat. Novice umpires Steve Lewis and Dalton Holder approached reserve umpire Lloyd Barker, who was to umpire the Test, and he measured it and declared it a quarter of an inch above regulation size. Cricket bats must not exceed 12 cm in width. Nobody deserved credit for what followed. Arthurton should not have used the bat in the first place and the umpires should have insisted that he replace it with a legal piece of equipment. The Australians also were at fault, having initiated the complaint but refusing to follow it to a logical conclusion, instead preferring to let the matter drop. Marsh said he preferred the issue be settled off the field, although Jones didn't back off, saying he warned Athurton about the width of the bat in the first innings and said he would take action if he used it again. 'He did, and I did,' Jones said. 'It is against the laws and traditions of the game. Bowlers aren't allowed to scratch the ball to gain an unfair advantage and batsmen are not allowed to use oversized bats. It is time this sort of thing is exposed.'

Rival skipper Carlisle Best supported Jones' comments without suggesting that Arthurton was aware he was contravening the laws and spirit of the game. 'The important thing is that the issue has been brought out into the open without any harm being done. But manufacturers must take note and make sure the bats are without reproach.' Umpire Barker, who as reserve umpire was powerless in the situation, said he was pleased Marsh didn't upset the spirit of the game by causing a major incident on the field. 'We umpires will end up having to weigh the ball before every over and measure bats when players come on to the field if this sort of thing keeps up,' he said. 'I can't remember this happening before but it is very important that such matters are investigated.'

The incident was an unfortunate exposure for Arthurton, who ironically was caught behind in the first innings and trapped lbw in the second. It started a fortnight of accusation and counter-accusation of all sorts during the stay in Barbados.

But the Australians had much more to worry about than the width of Arthurton's bat after a dismal build-up to the Test. Phil Simmons and Clayton Lambert belted an opening stand of 125 on the opening day with Simmons going on to smash 22 boundaries in an innings of 122. The Australian attack lacked penetration and spice on the placid pitch; Steve Waugh took the first innings bowling honours with 3 for 76 off 21 overs.

Rain robbed the players of all but 35 minutes of play on the second day as the Kensington Oval became submerged within 20 minutes of a downpour, having absorbed 130 mm of rain in a week which saturated the outfield and over-extended the drainage system. The only joy in a poor Australian innings of 207 was an accomplished 92 by Mark Taylor, who batted for almost six hours in another long and productive stint at the crease. The uncertain footwork which betrayed him in the middle of this tour began to regain surety after consistent advice from Simpson and he looked the only player ready to face the West Indian attack in a Test within a few days.

Terry Alderman, the forgotten paceman on tour, finally ended his hibernation with a second innings analysis of 5 for 40 off 17 overs, dismissing the Board XI for 189 in the second innings to end the match. His wickets included two lbw verdicts, a return catch and a direct hit and his enthusiasm was admirable after a bitterly disappointing tour. Reid responded to the challenge too, capturing 3 for 27 off ten overs to guarantee himself another Test.

But the Australians, having done so well in Trinidad, naturally employed the same 11 players for the Barbados Test after considering the pitch, which promised little encouragement to a bowler of Alderman's declining pace.

Barbados is the mecca of West Indies cricket when it comes to meeting heroes of the past. This island of 430 kilometres has produced almost a third of the West Indies Test cricketers, headed by the famous three 'Ws' — Sir Frank Worrell, Everton Weekes and Clyde Walcott — and the legendary Sir Garfield Sobers. Greenidge, Haynes and Marshall were the current champion trio in the Test team.

One of the best known cricketers to emerge from this island was Wes Hall, the former express fast bowler who these days is the Minister for

Sport and Tourism. Hall has a wonderful way with words — well, he is a politician! — and he used them eloquently as the official speaker at the West Indian Board dinner, at a party he provided for all kind of Australian tourists to the island, and when explaining his plans for the benefit of cricket in Barbados and the West Indies. He has achieved a considerable amount for sport in Barbados, reducing the tax on sporting goods and being the figurative architect of new sporting complexes. His dream is to establish a cricket museum and a cricket academy, similar to those in Australia. He is particularly keen on a Hall of Fame (nothing to do with his name), similar to that at the Melbourne Cricket Ground.

It's said that you can go to Australia or England and look at museums and galleries which show the history of the game, yet in the West Indies we have nothing. The young lads today don't know the deeds of Weekes, Worrell and Walcott, Griffiths and Hall, Clive Lloyd or Viv Richards. All they know is what Richards is doing in the middle today, but nothing of his great contribution over the years. There's no history available in cricket in the West Indies and what I would like to do is establish a gallery where every youngster can look at the legends of the past and want to emulate their deeds, aspire to their greatness. As it is, the only thing going for West Indies is the kid in the street who wants to be a cricketer to replace the current man with no idea of what West Indian cricket has achieved nor of the men who have preceded them.

Hall emphasised that 'this game of cricket is about players, personalities and history' and he is determined that so much of the character of the Caribbean won't be lost to future generations. 'It costs money but I can only hope that the folklore of the game and the future of the game in this country can be developed within a few years ... if not, West Indies cricket will have no past, and a doubtful future.' Hall also planned a cricket academy, claiming that the major difference between the Australian Youth team and the West Indian youngsters they thrashed the previous year was the professional development in Australia and the uncultivated talent in the Caribbean.

He planned a trip to Australia in 1992 to look at the academy in Adelaide and provide himself with information and ideas for a similar set-up in Barbados.

We have many wonderful young cricketers in the West Indies but we don't have the sophistication of the Australians. I want to establish a similar set-up in Barbados but every nation in the Caribbean must be involved. Barbados will go it alone if necessary but the idea is for everyone to join forces to develop our youngsters throughout the islands. It makes me weep that a man like Rod Marsh can call on every great former player to teach young Australians every aspect of the game and

135

that we're still wandering around the islands hoping to find a player with talent and not being able to do anything about it.

Hall really enjoys meeting former team mates and opponents and he spent a considerable time with former champion all-rounder Alan Davidson, who led a tour party for the final two Tests, during the official West Indies Board dinner at the Hilton. The evening was a highlight of the tour, if only because of the table allocations. The teams were split up with a member of the Australian team and a member of the West Indies team delegated a table together, with the guests simply sitting where they chose. Giant Curtly Ambrose and stocky David Boon didn't have much to say to each other throughout the tour with the former rocketing missiles and the latter evading them most of the time. They had a great night at the same table without ever saying a word to each other. Desmond Haynes and Geoff Marsh was another matchmaking blunder, but given the events on the field in the fourth Test, it could have been worse had Ian Healy been at Haynes' table!

The chance to meet a lot of friends came, beginning on the opening day of the Australian match against the Board XI. No sooner had Terry Brindle and I deposited our briefcases than New South Wales chief executive Bob Radford and former West Indies opening batsman and former assistant manager to Australia, Cammy Smith, came calling. Cammy (one of the nicest men in world cricket), Radford and the press pair known as the 'terrible twins' headed to the members' bar to reminisce. Getting a drink was no problem because behind the bar was a familiar face: Test umpire David Archer, who owned the catering rights to the ground with a firm called the Ump's Inn. A few days later in the Barbados Cricket Association viewing room we caught up with Charlie Griffiths and Conrad Hunte, Walcott, Weekes, Comacho, Joey Carew, Seymour Nurse and Joel Garner, who was studying accountancy in England. When the Test began other legends roaming the members' included Sobers (who spends most of his time these days on the golf course), Hall, Lloyd, Holding and Gibbs. We even ran into David Murray, the former wicketkeeper who has turned his life around after a drug problem. Wayne Daniel was hard to miss; Gerry Alexander, Gerry Gomez, Denis Athinkson, Jackie Hendricks, Maurice Foster and David Holford also were there to add to the social atmosphere.

If that wasn't enough, John Snow hit town with a tour group and David 'Bluey' Bairstow was scouting for business in his new enterprise of making ties. Colin Cowdrey slipped in as part of his mission for the International Cricket Council, and Pakistan's Mudassar Nazar also was on tour for a benefit match.

And then there were the Aussies! Bob Cowper journeyed from Monaco with Melbourne Cricket Club secretary John Lill and wife Rosemary, and longtime mate John 'Junior' Curtin and wife Karen, who organised a wild

50th birthday beach party for 'Junior'. Australian Cricket Board media manager and domestic team manager Ian McDonald also arrived with a tour party of sixty-seven! The group included Geoff Marsh's father Ted, Test umpire Tony Crafter and ACB member from New South Wales, Alan Crompton, as well as an assortment of supporters from all over Australia. They were keen, you had to admit, because they watched the Australians train before the Test and then sat in the three 'Ws' stand waiting for the West Indians to practise.

The functions came thick and fast in Barbados, but none was more pleasant than the party at the beach house of West Indies media doyen Tony Cozier. It seemed all those mentioned above were there along with many more, including famous English writer Ian Wooldridge and veteran cricket correspondent John Woodcock. Australia's famous crew of Richie Benaud, Ian and Greg Chappell and their wives also were there to enjoy the ample food and inexhaustable alcohol supply, the calypso music, good company and delightful views of clean ocean waters crashing against the rocky cliffs on the almost deserted side of the island of Barbados at St John. The Board dinner that evening ended a hectic day, for those who made it! ACB chairman Col Egar and Victorian representative Jack Edwards and wife Angela arrived the following day to add to the Aussie flavour at the end of the tour, while Mark Taylor's parents arrived in Antigua just in time to watch the opener score his man-of-the-match century.

Barbados provided welcome outlets for everyone and The Ship Inn became the team's favourite restaurant and watering hole. Their English style steak and kidney, potato, and chicken and mushroom pies and the outstanding carvery guaranteed repeated custom. The friendly staff was taken aback only once. That was the evening McDonald's touring party arrived in Barbados and, informed of the nearby Ship Inn, descended for dinner. The original plan of a table for six developed into a table for forty-eight! The food at Iles de France was exceptional while a beer at the Dockyards with the crystal clear water almost lapping on to the bar was most relaxing. The younger members of the group — and that was almost everyone else — also ventured to a few nightspots which stayed open to accommodate the extensive tourist market, while Bert's Bar was a favourite at the time of the Foreman world title fight and Ian Woosnam's US golf title because of the direct telecast via satellite on big screens.

The Rockley Resort where the team stayed during the Barbados games comprised clusters of condominiums scattered around an 18 hole golf course. The self-contained suites were pleasant enough but offered no view of water, a prerequisite for such an island resort. The players eventually referred to their rooms as cells because of the tiny windows which allowed only a narrow view from the dining area. But they were comfortable enough for Comacho, Lloyd, Rudi Webster and Haynes to own one each. Haynes was regularly sighted within the resort as he drove to and from his condominium in his luxury new car. He retained a sense of humour until the incidents in the fourth Test, at one stage catching Terry Brindle by surprise. Brindle was waiting outside reception and looking wistfully upon the golf course when a car pulled up and the driver jumped out. 'Taxi sir?' he asked as he woke Brindle from his dream. 'No thanks, mate, I was just ...' Brindle began before realising the car was a bit flash for a taxi and that the sparkling teeth of the driver opening the boot belonged to Haynes.

The golf course did prove a bonus for Merv Hughes, who gleefully handed over his title as 'the worst male golfer in the world', an unflattering crown bestowed by Allan Border. Hughes defeated Mike Veletta in a series of rounds to relinquish the title, publicising the fact with a relentless news release to every member of the touring party. But cricket, not golf, was the game at hand.

COLOUR, CRICKET AND CALYPSO

Dr Robert Lee is a fifth generation Chinese-Trinidadian, single, in his mid-thirties and widely travelled. For two years, he has been his government's AIDS Counsellor in Port of Spain, and a delegate to the region's necessarily frequent AIDS conferences. Ferociously protective of his individual patients' privacy, he thinks the time is long overdue for a few home truths about sex in Trinidad and Tobago, more particularly about unsafe sex in T and T and the West Indies as a whole.

For instance, Trinidad has about 700 current AIDS cases in a population of just over a million, compared with Norway's less than 200 in a population more than four times Trinidad's. 'What are we supposed to deduce from the figures?' Dr Lee asks with a snort.

That Trinidadians are more than 14 times as sexually active, more than 14 times as promiscuous, as Norwegians, or that they are 14 times as careless and uncaring? I don't think there can be any doubt, particularly when venereal disease figures are collated with the AIDS figures, as they should be. VD, classed as 'passive' in Norway and in Scandinavia as a whole, is raging in Trinidad, and in the Caribbean generally. Syphilis, gonorrhea, herpes, genital ulcers and warts: you name it, we have it in epidemic proportions.

Dr Lee says that, as far as he can tell, 'safe sex' is still a foreign concept to the majority of both sexes, of both Indian and African ancestry in T and T. 'It is a "macho" world here,' he says.

Negroes, African males, will not take the time to use condoms because they think it reflects adversely on their virility. Similarly the 'boys' night out' concept, a bout of sexual promiscuity with 'easy' girls, or prostitutes, is an African tradition.

It reflects badly on a man, even a man in a stable relationship, if he doesn't indulge in an orgy at least occasionally. This greatly increases the incidence of sexually transmitted diseases. Men, not one or two but dozens, have told me, I believe truthfully, that they were infected in such situations. They then go home and infect their wives, or steady girlfriends, who infect the children they are carrying, and so the whole sorry cycle continues, and increases. 'Multiple sex partners': in just three words that is the root cause of the African STD [sexually transmitted diseases] epidemic.

The situation with the Indian majority in Trinidad is that it is considered insulting to a male for a female to ask him to use a condom. It reflects badly upon his respectability and sense of responsibility, both extremely precious to Indian males. This not only increases the birthrate, it increases the spread of AIDS in families, involving the wives and children of bisexual men.

It is a waste of time telling West Indians, whatever their origins, not to have sex, extremely difficult to persuade them to use condoms. The women will agree in the clinic, all right, but once they're home it is a different matter altogether. Many of our patients, of all races, are Fundamentalist Christians, and they usually won't use condoms. Neither will practising Catholics, and Indians say they will but they don't. The African girls may intend to, but they forget. You wouldn't believe some of the excuses we hear!

Dr Lee, who has a wry sense of humour, is in great demand as a lecturer.

He says he disagrees with the figures which say Trinidad and Tobago is 42 per cent African, 38 per cent Indian and 10 per cent other races, including British, Europeans, Americans and, way down at the bottom of the list, 5000 Chinese. 'My estimate is that the true figures are Indians 42 per cent and Africans 38 per cent, with the others about the same,' he says. 'The Indian birthrate is outstripping the African by as much as eight to one in some areas. This is offset to some extent however, by increased Indian migration to America and Canada.'

There was a continuing, and embarrassing, scandal in Port of Spain early in 1991, while the Australian cricketers were there, about Indian T and T citizens trying to enter Canada claiming 'refugee' status. A Canadian MP, with a large number of Indians in his constituency, who visited Port of Spain was criticised as an 'opportunist' and 'publicity seeker' when he announced he would investigate allegations of 'victimisation' and prejudice against Indians in Trinidad and Tobago.

The MP should have visited Trinidad's Queens Park Oval, one of the West Indies' most famous cricket grounds. There, in the one-day internationals, the predominantly Indian crowd booed Viv Richards when he led the all-Negro Windies team on-field against the Australians.

The Indians barracked strongly for the Australians during the matches, the second of which gave the Windies their solitary win of the one-day series, and later during the Third Test, which was spoiled by rain. The Queens Park crowd's disloyalty was bitterly resented and widely criticised in the press by loyal West Indians, particularly by West Indian Negroes.

In not one taxi to the oval, invariably driven by an Indian-Trinidadian owner, was I not wished 'Good luck, Aussie. I hope you win.' Pressed, the driver would usually add: 'These Negroes, they are very athletic; they can play cricket, but they are bad sports. They are prejudiced.'

One of my souvenirs of Trinidad is an anonymous message returned with my laundry: 'Good luck Australian team. You will win Mr Pior.' I wonder what sort of mail Allan Boder and Geoff Mash were getting.

What did Dr Lee think of the practically infinite varieties of his Trinidadian countrymen? Did he have any advice on multiculturalism for an Australian, by comparison a beginner at the game?

Dr Lee was tempted, I could tell, but finally he dead-batted my leading question. He'd give me any medical advice I asked, he said with a sly grin, but considering his specialty, hoped that I didn't need any. As far as individual races and origins went, he probably felt more comfortable with Chinese than others ('I'm related to so many of them,' he joked, and indeed, he introduced me to half a dozen). Generally speaking, he said, he considered himself a Trinidadian first, and a Chinese second.

He tried to judge Negroes and Indians, and Australians for that matter, strictly as he found them; there were good and bad everywhere. It was ignorance and prejudice of any kind, racial, religious, social or sexual, he was against and tolerance and acceptance that he was for.

'When a girl eats sand or faeces because she has been told it will end a pregnancy, or make her sterile, you don't worry what caste or tribe she is,' he said. 'When a child is abandoned at a hospital because its mother thinks there is something wrong with it, and she caused it, and she doesn't know exactly who was its father, well, you don't particularly notice what colour it is.'

But you know. 'I suppose you do,' Dr Lee conceded.

But it doesn't influence you, or it shouldn't. I think it is fair to say there are points for and against any group. The Africans, the Negroes, are more easy-going than the Indians, easier to get along with, and generally speaking more popular. As against that, in most cases, they're not as ambitious, and don't work as consistently as the Indians. I won't say the Negroes are not as bright as the Indians, that would cause an uproar I don't need, and I'm not sure it's true, but they certainly don't get the results the Indians do. And they're nowhere near as smart with money. Money doesn't seem to stick to African fingers like it does to Indian ones.

How about the Chinese? I must admit I'd been feeling kindly to them since a Chinese-Guyanese member complained loudly in the Georgetown Cricket Club when Dean Jones was so shamefully given out in the second innings, run out after being dismissed by a no-ball.

'We Chinese survive, even in Guyana,' Dr Robert Lee said, and indeed they do.

The Indians, however, were the ones who were out to get Viv Richards in particular, and with him any member of the all-Negro West Indies team who showed the slightest sign of faltering. Opener Gordon Greenidge, wicketkeeper Jeff Dujon and fast bowler Malcolm Marshall all had their Indian critics and, in Georgetown, scene of their crucial Second Test win, there were bottles thrown at Courtney Walsh and other Windies players who ventured near the fence, and an umpire was hanged in effigy in front of a largely Indian crowd.

The sports editor of the *Guyana Chronicle*, the semi-official voice of the (overwhelmingly pro-Negro) government, warned: 'We do not dispute the right of the individual to support whatever side he wants, but that support should not degenerate in boos and jeers ... and even more repulsive was the senseless throwing of bottles at our own West Indian players.' It would be too much to say the Australians were the meat in the 1991 Negro-Indian sandwich, but undoubtedly there was no way they were not involved in a racial, intra-West Indies argument.

In the 9 February 1990 issue of the *Outlet* newspaper released in his home island of Antigua, Richards was quoted as saying: '[the West Indies cricket team] is the only sporting team of African descent that has been able to win repeatedly against all international opposition, bringing joy and recognition to our people.'

His statement didn't bring any joy whatsoever to his fellow West Indies citizens of Indian descent, particularly those living in Trinidad and Tobago. Basdeo Panday, leader of the United National Congress (UNC) opposition party in T and T, said Richards should be made to apologise for his insult to the great Indian cricketers of the past before again being allowed into the country.

'If the government claims it is against racism, then it must be against racism anywhere and everywhere that this evil shows its head,' Panday said. 'I would like to clarify the situation, emphasising the significant contribution that people of all races have made to the development and present stature of West Indies cricket.' Under pressure from the WIBC, Richards replied: 'I am sorry if I have offended any group of people.'

As it happened, he didn't play in the Trinidad Test against England anyway, due to trouble with haemorrhoids, and it was left to stand-in Windies captain Desmond Haynes to keep the racial pot bubbling with alleged 'sledging' of England's slow-coach batsman Alec Stewart. The English cricket press, never slow to respond to a challenge, criticised the Windies' excessively slow over rate, when it was apparent they could not win. London's *Daily Mirror* went so far as to headline the accusation 'CHEATS'.

I can imagine the West Indies reaction to that effort. When the

Australians were batting particularly well in their first innings in the First Test at Kingston, the Windies over rate slowed until it was practically motionless.

Frankly, I think the West Indies over rate is a disgrace and, to use an old Australian expression, Ned Kelly was a gentleman compared with some of the Windies umpires. We were much more sinned against than sinning this time around.

Just for starters, how about the caught behind decision against Greg Matthews in the First Test, the Dean Jones run-out in the Second Test, the Dean Jones and Geoff Marsh lbw decisions in Barbados, not to mention Gordon Greenidge being not out lbw when he was 42 in the same, deciding Test. As Jack Dyer would say, in Australian football, if you don't mind, umpire!

But, thankfully, it is Rod Nicholson's job to give the expert opinions; I was simply there for the 'colour', and the colour I like least is the colour of blood, particularly my own. We wuz robbed plenty of times in the Windies, but it is up to Nicko to give you the technical details, not me. I'll simply wax indignant and say instant TV replays have ended forever the cosy cricket custom of saying it's 'not cricket' to criticise the umpire and accuse your opponents of bad sportsmanship, racism and/or murder.

I've been a calypso fan since the early (second world) war years when I heard 78 rpm records of the Andrews Sisters singing 'Rum and

Steve Waugh hits out.

143

Coca Cola', but it wasn't until this year I heard some of the original verses:

> *There are some aristos in port of Port of Spain,*
> *I know a lot but I wouldn't call names,*
> *In the day they wouldn't give you a right,*
> *But you can see them with the Yankees late at nights.*

and again,

> *A couple got married one afternoon,*
> *And was to go Mayaro on their honeymoon,*
> *The very night the wife went with the Yankee lad*
> *And the stupid husband went staring mad.*
> *To buy, rum and coca cola,*
> *And go down Point Cumana,*
> *Both mother and daughter,*
> *Working for the Yankee dollars.*

It was interesting in Trinidad to learn of the amalgamation of kaiso, which came from African villages, and picong, developed in medieval France by strolling minstrels. Kaiso is the repetitive, narrative newscast, developed before its singers could read or write, and picong the sly, witty mix of gossip and insulting innuendo and repartee appreciated by the French, peasant and aristocrats alike.

West Indians of all races and racial mixes, learning a new language and boastful of their learning, loved to pile word upon word in an attempt to verbally smother opponents. 'Attila the Hun'(Raymond Quevedo), who later became a deputy mayor of Port of Spain, taunted an opponent:

> *I admire your ambition, you'd like to sing,*
> *But you'll never be a Kaiso King.*
> *To reach such a height without blemish or sport*
> *You must study Shakespeare, Byron, Milton and Scott.*
> *But I'm afraid I'm casting pearls before the swine,*
> *For you'll never inculcate such thoughts divine*
> *You really got a good intention, but poor education ...*
> *sans humanité.*

Every ground we went to, from Warner Park in St Kitts to the Recreation Reserve in Antigua, was bouncing to the beat of 'I Love Cricket' and it was rare to see West Indians without either earphones or a transistor growing out of their ears. Only part of the time were they listening to the play.

I doubt you could ever go past Trinidad and calypso for the voice of the Windies. I wouldn't try. In a nightclub, a dancehall, a bar or a tent, it is entertainment and history rolled into one.

In 'Four Cents a Day', written 40 years ago, Attila the Hun gave one of the reasons so many West Indians fought so hard for independence.

An Englishman came here recently
And started to grumble about his salary,
Two hundred dollars a month he told them flat,
With the cost of living he couldn't exist on that.
He resigned with regret,
Now his salary don't forget
Is more than what twenty workers get
And still they want them to be happy and gay
On that princely rise of four cents a day.

Visit the slums all over Trinidad,
The situation is repulsively sad and bad,
To see little children about the place,
With starvation imprinted on each face,
They ain't got any strength to shout
On their spindly legs they run about,
Hookworm got their bellies pushing out,
With all this suffering and misery
You call yourself a Christian community.

After Gordon Greenidge's double century in Barbados a cry from the West Indies people was heard. This muted paean appeared in *The Advocate* in Bridgetown on 23 April, titled simply 'Ode to Gordon'.

Pardon, Gordon,
Oh, pardon
All those who doubted your place.
Now they can see intact,
the grace,
the pace,
In the unhurried haste to 209!

How can a 'walking stick'
flick
so elegantly?
Or drive so smoothly,
Penetratingly,
Hook so disdainfully,
So gracefully
So mercilessly,
For four
upon four?

Greenidge pulls another boundary on his way to 226.

You with Richie,
closed the door
From an Aussie fightback;
It was 'Attack!' 'Attack!'
The Aussies just snarled,
Not even fighting back,
That bat, Gordon,
Engrave it in gold
For cricket lovers everywhere to behold!

Statistics will never tell
How often,
How accurately,
Its blade fell, and fell
As you sliced the air,
And scorched the turf.
Poor old Merv!

Soon forty? So what?
Ask Bruce Reid or McDermott
How it feels
To be on the opposite side of
A 40-year-old attack-bat.
Bat on, Gordon!

Randolph Chase, the author of the Ode, said in an accompanying note that he was 'aesthetically touched' by Greenidge's innings. Thank heavens he wasn't excited by it!

THE FOURTH TEST: ALL-OUT WARFARE

The West Indies won an eventful match by an imposing 343 runs to retain the Sir Frank Worrell Trophy and the title of undisputed world champion Test cricket team. But the on-field animosity and behaviour which marred the Test flew directly in the face of the spirit of contests between the two countries which prompted the Australian Cricket Board to instigate a trophy following the memorable series in 1960-61. The trophy wasn't on hand at the close, having been lost two years before, much to the embarrassment of West Indies officials. Lost with it seemingly was its significance as a tribute to competitive and sporting combat in a mutually respectful and good-spirited nature.

Great men of cricket watched forlornly as often conduct overshadowed some excellent play, tarnished by several controversial umpiring decisions. A Test which should have been remembered for an historic double-century finale at Barbados by Greenidge, two extraordinary first innings collapses, explosive fast bowling and a final day Australian wipe-out, instead left deep scars between the teams.

Sir Garfield Sobers, Clyde Walcott, Wes Hall, Richie Benaud and Alan Davidson, all honourable members of that famous 1960-61 band which inspired the Sir Frank Worrell Trophy and disillusioned spectators at this Test, recognised the end of an era. Tradition counted for little it appeared in the new era of modern cricket dominated by a a demand for success and the ensuing monetary rewards. The emotive and ugly actions and unnecessary verbal outbursts on the field mocked the spirit of Worrell at a time when the respective cricket leaders of the two countries, Walcott and Col Egar, laid a wreath on Worrell's grave on the 25th anniversary of the instigation of the trophy.

The conduct of vice-captain Desmond Haynes in removing his batting helmet, pointing his bat and abusing wicketkeeper Ian Healy after an appeal for a catch at the wicket seemed unnecessary, as Hall informed him in sombre tones. Challenges among players to settle differences behind the pavilion after play, incessant chants of 'coward' or 'cheat', and provocative appealing and umpire intimidation have no place on a cricket field.

The Australians were not blameless, lowering their standards by reciprocating in the verbal battles and eventually giving as good as they got as frustration with the manipulation of over rates and leaking covers gave way to angry reaction to constant taunts, unfavourable umpiring decisions and intimidatory jibes from the opposition.

But the breaking point of relationships came in an unsolicited outburst from Richards in the post-match press conference when he diverted from team and personal glory to attack Australian coach Bob Simpson. That ill-timed and unprovoked character assault sorely strained relationships on an official level, severed any lingering links between the teams and set the scene for even more unsavoury conduct in the final Test. But much more on that later.

The West Indians won the series, but at the high price of tarnishing their reputation as sportsmen. The response to a genuine challenge to their supremacy was a superb victory by ten wickets in Guyana. Despite the controversial run-out of Jones in the second innings, this was the result of playing superior cricket as batsmen and bowlers, for which the players received deserved and genuine congratulations. But this Test victory, equally impressive as it was by 343 runs, came at the expense of acceptable behaviour. The culprits one day may regret their actions when considering the ramifications. If the International Cricket Council needed any ammunition to provide referees with the power to suspend cricketers for on-field misconduct it can point the finger at this Test as the catalyst for such a dramatic innovation. ICC president Colin Cowdrey witnessed the Test and must have wondered at the deteriorating standards in the game, while Australian and West Indian administrators made it clear that the trend must be stopped to preserve the ethics of the game.

Control of player behaviour is the responsibility of the captain but in this Test, and the one to follow in Antigua, Richards appeared to condone the aggressive attitude of his players and then inflamed the situation with his criticism of Simpson. He abrogated his duties as captain in both regards but escaped without punishment from the West Indian officials. They remained impotent if saddened observers which only supported the case for an independent referee.

DAY ONE

Australia took all the honours in a remarkable opening day by dismissing the West Indians for a meagre 149 before reaching 2 for 56 at stumps. The heroes were McDermott and Hughes with four wickets apiece. Reid gave

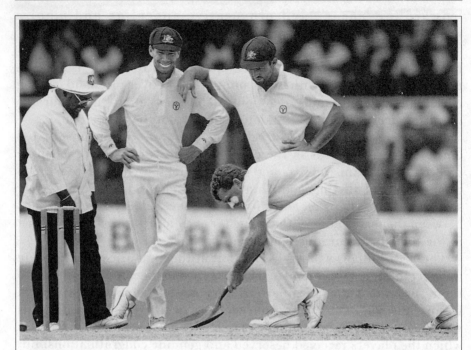

McDermott digs out the bowling crease before digging out the Windies batsmen in the first innings at Kensington Oval, Barbados.

fine support with two wickets after Border won the toss and inserted the opposition, the tenth consecutive time the captain has done so in Tests at Kensington Oval. The West Indian total was its lowest in 20 years at Bridgetown and only 40 higher than the lowest tally in a Test against Australia in the Caribbean of 109 in Guyana in 1972-73. But amid the clatter of wickets was the first and most disturbing outburst of on-field disharmony and misconduct when Haynes clashed with Healy.

The drama began when Greenidge hooked a McDermott delivery to Reid at fine leg to depart for 10 after 42 minutes of routine activity. Richardson, unusually nervous as he scratched around the crease and fiddled with equipment, didn't have a chance to settle in before he tentatively struck a McDermott delivery to Boon at mid-on where the stocky fieldsman jumped for a valuable catch. Hughes completed an imposing opening hour to plummet the West Indians to 3 for 22 when Hooper departed for a duck as a half-hearted drive speared to Jones at point.

The Haynes incident erupted soon after the drinks interval when McDermott beat the right-hander with a delivery which cut back sharply and forced wicketkeeper Healy to take the ball down the leg side. The Australians were convinced that Haynes was out for 10 with the score on 28 in only the 15th over of the day, claiming the ball deflected from the

The war of words begins between Windies vice-captain Desmond Haynes and Australian wicketkeeper Ian Healy.

inside edge via Haynes' thigh on the way to Healy. Haynes immediately indicated to umpire David Archer that the ball had clipped his thigh, while Healy suggested that the batsman allow the umpire to make his own decision. Archer rejected the appeal and Haynes then removed his helmet and approached Healy behind the stumps with his bat pointed at him as he vigorously mounted a verbal attack. Healy responded in kind to the tirade before resuming his position, McDermott already being back at his bowling mark and all other fieldsmen ready for the next delivery. Richards then walked from the non-striker's end to speak with Haynes in mid-pitch and they punched gloves in a distinctly West Indian-style show of triumph.

The tension mounted when Haynes delayed play a couple of deliveries later, eventually removing his helmet complaining of a foreign body in his eye. He approached Boon at square leg but received no sympathy before asking Richards to inspect the eye. He returned to the fray and survived until lunch when he sought out Healy for further debate as the players left the ground.

Healy refused to comment on the incident, believing 'what happens on the field stays on the field', but Simpson defended the wicketkeeper's involvement in the ruckus.

It's rather unusual to see a batsman come to a wicketkeeper in a situation like that and continue the onslaught as he left the field. From what I understand, nothing was said on the field to warrant that sort of reaction. It was one-on-one and all Desmond Haynes was told to do was to let the umpire do the umpiring. I am happy with Healy's behaviour on the cricket field and cannot understand the reason for Haynes' over-reaction.

The tension between the Australians had been mounting through the series and the players were unhappy with what they regarded as Haynes' dictatorial attitude and what they claimed was his belief that he could 'stir' whenever he pleased but that anybody who objected to him deserved a tongue-lashing. Haynes claimed that Healy had sworn at him when he had said there should not have been an appeal. 'Healy swore at me because I indicated the ball had hit my pad. He swore at me for no reason.' He also accused the Australians of bad language and said he was upset by constant ribbing, a suggestion the Australians repudiated. Richards backed his vice-captain: 'When you are speaking with big people, you have to be careful if you are only a little "pop".'

The obvious reaction was for the teams to support their own but that hardly excused the incident, regardless of who sparked it. Haynes' reaction was unnecessary and almost theatrical, alerting everyone to the scene. For most of his career Haynes has commanded admiration and respect for his demeanour and smiling attitude but several recent incidents have tarnished that image. In the series against England the previous season he was censured during the third Test in Trinidad for abusing Englishman Alec Stewart as he was leaving the field at the end of play. Such incidents moved former champion paceman Wes Hall, an admirer of Haynes and an important Barbadian figure as the Minister for Sport and Tourism, to seek out the local idol after the Healy incident.

Hall, who implored world administrators to enforce stricter codes of behaviour and for Test players to accept greater responsibility for their on-field actions, was appalled by the flare-up. He told Haynes his behaviour was totally unacceptable.

I told him that as vice-captain he was setting a bad example. I told him what I thought because he is a good fellow and he wouldn't like something like this to tarnish his name. I think I got the message through to him. He must look at himself and realise that a lot of people are watching him, especially with the television audience, and that he is setting a bad example for youngsters and giving himself a bad name. I accept that he was upset and the incident may have looked worse than it was, but when you go around lifting your bat and taking off your helmet and shouting at people you do tend to get noticed! What annoys me is that I've played cricket all around the world and I inadvertently probably have busted more heads and hands than any fast bowler. But I've never met anyone who played against me 30 years ago who is not my friend. I wouldn't like to think that Desmond or other West Indian players will spoil their chances of enjoying their retirement with similar friendships because of a few silly incidents at this stage of their careers.

Clive Lloyd echoed similar sentiments during the following Test at Antigua when the sniping and antagonism continued between players on both teams, suggesting the modern players were risking invaluable friendships with petty squabbling.

I played it as tough as anyone against blokes like Dennis Lillee and Jeff Thomson and the Chappells and Rod Marsh. But after the game we had a beer and to this day we still visit each other whenever we can and talk and laugh about the good old days. That is the best part of the game of cricket: the friends you make and the time after retirement to enjoy the memories with your pals. I fear the modern players will miss all that if the sort of behaviour and sniping continues as it is. I would have got out of the game a lot earlier if all it meant was making money and winning and fighting with the opposition. What enjoyment is there in that? Whom do you finally keep as your friends? If they don't like the game or the people who are playing it I think they would be better to come on this side of the fence and have a beer and let people who really do want to enjoy the game have a go. The end to this series is a bitter disappointment to me because of the on-field animosity, but I wonder if it will not be a bigger disappointment to a lot of the blokes out there when they retire and start to wonder who their old friends are?

But back to the match at hand. Haynes and Richards, who was increasingly aggressive with drives and pulls, eased the pressure with a 50 partnership in 90 minutes as Richards celebrated another milestone. When he reached 10 he overtook Geoff Boycott's mark of 8114 to become the third highest Test run-scorer behind India's Sunil Gavaskar and Border. But he lost concentration and hooked a McDermott bouncer from outside the off stump; the ball sailed to fine leg where Hughes judged a fine catch. The wicket was a vital breakthrough as Richards looked in fine touch during his 32 off 64 deliveries despite the precarious position. McDermott should have added Logie to his haul after the wristy right-hander edged a cut through the outstretched hands of Border at third slip after scoring only eight. But the miss cost only three runs when Reid reared a delivery off a good length to deflect the ball off Logie's glove and bat handle to Mark Taylor at first slip. The Australians claimed the fifth wicket with only 89 runs on the board, the third time in four first innings of the series the pacemen had skittled the top order. The other occasions were 5 for 75 at Jamaica and 5 for 56 at Trinidad when weather and belligerent lower order batting denied a victory thrust.

Hughes ended Haynes' diligent 212 minute vigil for only 28 runs with a delivery which took the edge of a back foot drive to sail to Mark Waugh at second slip. He added Dujon to his victims when the wicketkeeper presented his counterpart with a regulation catch after scoring 10. The West Indians went to tea at 7 for 109, having lost 4 for 51 in another eventful session.

The West Indian tail-enders added 46 runs for the last three wickets with Marshall (17), Ambrose (19 not out) and Walsh (10) making batting look far more comfortable than earlier in the day. McDermott finished with 4 for 49 off 22 overs and Hughes 4 for 44 off 16.1 overs to take the bowling honours, while Reid toiled hard for 2 for 50 off 21 overs to complete the success of the trio.

The West Indians needed a swift retort to regain valuable lost ground or face the prospect of a sizeable first innings deficit. Marsh and Taylor defied them for 55 minutes to compile 24 runs through evasive defence, managing an occasional crisply struck boundary. But Ambrose and Marshall struck within three runs to stagger the innings, the former dismissing Marsh for 12 with a rearing delivery when the opener fended to Logie at short leg, and the latter removing Boon for a second ball duck from a defensive edge which speared to Hooper at first slip. Taylor and Border survived to take Australia to 2 for 56 at stumps, a deficit of only 93 at the end of a productive day's work.

DAY TWO

Nobody would have guessed that by stumps on the second day the West Indians would be cruising in control of this Test with a 153 run advantage with nine wickets in hand. The somersault in fortunes was a combination of excellent West Indian bowling, disappointing Australian batting and a controversial lbw decision against Jones which turned the Australian innings on its head. The Australians were bundled out for a miserable 134, reviving bitter memories for Border who was a member of the 1983-84 Australian team which registered the lowest total by any team at this ground of 97. They lost 8 for 79 in 30.1 overs, including a staggering 7 for 39 in 14.2 overs to leave the West Indians with an unlikely lead of 15 runs. Greenidge and Haynes capitalised on that with a 129 run opening union before the tally reached 1 for 138 at stumps. Border suffered a broken heart and a broken thumb during the day as the Test, the series and the dream of being world champions crumbled around him.

Ambrose took only two deliveries to begin Australia's day of woe when a rearing delivery cracked Border's left thumb knuckle. From that moment he was severely restricted and in considerable pain as he grimaced with every impact of ball on bat. Ambrose generated express speed and disconcerting lift from the pitch off a good length and that made it exceptionally difficult for the batsmen to determine whether to play forward or back. Taylor chose incorrectly and was trapped lbw for 26 with only three runs added to the overnight score. Jones quickly discovered the difficulty of facing Ambrose when he, like Border before him, received a blow to the right index finger which prevented him from straightening it for the rest of the day.

The pair added 36 with intelligent and gritty batting as Jones took up the challenge with three sparkling boundaries to rapidly reduce the deficit while Border patiently lent support. Marshall, who had the better of Border throughout the series, then produced a delivery which scuppered the batsman as the ball scooted through ankle height to tilt the off stump. Border departed for 29 to be the highest contributor in the innings after two hours of toil, just at a time when Richards was fiddling with his attacking field placings.

The crucial blow came in Marshall's following over. Jones padded up to a seemingly harmless delivery outside the off stump, his foot a long way down the pitch and outside the line of the stumps. The shout from Marshall to the chorus of fieldsmen and fans was not nearly as deafening as the roar of approval when umpire Barker gave the signal for lbw. Jones was dumbfounded as he retained his pose and looked for the stumps behind him. He immediately sought a television replay which confirmed in his mind that the delivery could not have hit the stumps, the general

A tough call: Jones was given out lbw to Marshall after not offering a shot.

consensus of critics watching from behind the arm. To shoulder arms is always a gamble and Jones lost out to a very tough call from Barker. The dismissal broke the back of the Australian order as well as their spirit while sending the West Indian bowlers into a frenzy.

The last seven wickets fell for 39 runs in 14.2 overs from the time Marshall bowled Border with a shooter, with Jones and Steve Waugh (2) leaving the score at a miserable 6 for 100. The Australians lost Taylor, Border, Jones and Steve Waugh as top-order batsmen in the space of 11 runs in seven dramatic overs and there was no escape from that collapse. Steve Waugh fell to a defensive edge to Dujon off Patterson and then Walsh stepped in to mop up the tail with a stint of 4 for 9 off 4.1 overs. Walsh had Healy caught at the wicket for two and Hughes caught by Logie at short leg for three before yorking McDermott (2) and Reid (0) to end the massacre. Mark Waugh was stranded on 20, despite a bid to boost the total with three boundaries off only 33 deliveries. The entire innings lasted only 266 minutes and the Australian bowlers hardly had time to unstrap their ankle tapes before they were back in action and on the receiving end of some hard blows from Greenidge and Haynes.

Border was bitterly disappointed with the batsmen for letting down the bowlers and supported the decision to choose only three pacemen. 'Three fast bowlers knocked the opposition over for 149 and we had seven batsmen to capitalise on that. The batsmen didn't do the job and that put a lot of pressure on the bowlers who were back in action without any real time to rest for another attack.'

The bowlers were indeed a weary bunch by stumps, particularly without Border to assist with spin; he was at the hospital having his damaged knuckle X-rayed. Greenidge and Haynes adopted a positive attitude, in much the same way as for the opening Test when

Team leaders Allan Border and Geoff Marsh wondering what to do to halt the Greenidge assault.

they careered to a 118 opening stand to erase Australia's advantage. The 50 partnership skipped by in only 71 minutes and the only moment of concern came when Greenidge was 42 with the total on 72. Hughes penetrated the opener's defence to hit the right-hander on the pads as he played from the crease. Umpire Barker declined an estatic appeal from the Australians and Hughes, shuffling a victory leap down the pitch, stopped in his tracks in disbelief. If there was a moment on this day when the Australians felt betrayed by inconsistent umpiring this was it. How Jones could be out and Greenidge not out in the eyes of the same umpire totally confounded the players.

Greenidge and Haynes entered their 16th Test century opening partnership into the record books in 141 minutes as the Waugh twins entered the attack to quell the run rate with steady medium-pace bowling. Steve bowled 13 overs for only 21 runs in the session while Mark broke the union with the wicket of Haynes in five overs which cost only 10 runs. Haynes was 40 after 201 minutes with stumps approaching when he attempted to pull a short delivery from Mark Waugh only to glove a catch to Healy. Marshall entered the fray as a nightwatchman and by stumps the lead was 153 with a masterpiece on the menu the next day.

Border and the disillusioned players spent a quiet evening mulling over the lost opportunity. As Border put it:

After the first day you wouldn't have believed we'd be in this sort of situation. Obviously it's disappointing and we were a tad unlucky. Dean Jones received a shocking decision: David Boon copped a delivery which really kicked, Mark Taylor was out to a ball which kept low and I was dismissed by an absolute shooter which on that wicket was unbelievable given that you can break a thumb one ball and be bowled along the ground with another. Jones' was a vital decision. We could have come out of that first innings in a much better position with just a bit more luck, especially seeing Mark Waugh was there until the end and Deano was batting so well. But our batting was not disgraceful: the West Indians were just ruthless again in their attack.

The veteran skipper was matter of fact about the umpiring decisions which proved so costly. 'My philosophy is that you don't expect everything to go your way when you travel. The umpires are trying to do a good job but they are under pressure over here. You just have to accept this is going to happen and simply play better than the opposition and so far we haven't.'

DAY THREE

Gordon Greenidge made this day his own with an historic double century in his final appearance at his native Kensington Oval. The man known as 'GG' to his team-mates galloped into the history books as the West Indies took a stranglehold on the Test in a day which produced 269 despite the loss of only two wickets. The Caribbean champions were more intent on establishing an unassailable position. This Chinese water torture bore enviable results as the lead mounted to 422. The Australians toiled without fortune or favour, dropping Richie Richardson twice and having another concerted lbw appeal against Greenidge at 95 off Hughes rejected. But they had no answer to a 199 run third wicket union between Greenidge and Richardson, who missed his third century of the series by a miserable one run.

The innings by Greenidge should be covered in full, although he batted for an hour on the fourth day to finally lbw tumble to an exhausted but ever so relieved Hughes for 226. The bare statistics are as cold as Greenidge's stare: 677 minutes, 480 deliveries and 32 boundaries in the highest innings by a West Indian against Australia in Test cricket. He eclipsed the standards of Seymour Nurse (201 in 1964-65) and then Denis Atkinson (219 in 1954) in a methodical pursuit of immortality; both men were at Kensington Oval, the venue of their own triumphs, to witness the achievement. Greenidge also became the third oldest batsman in the history of the game to register a double century at this level: nine days shy of his 40th birthday he followed in the footsteps of Jack Hobbs (211 against South Africa at 41 years and 170 days) and Patsy Hendren (205 not out against the West Indies at 41). His 19th Test century and fourth against Australia came in 295 minutes off 214 deliveries and his 200 in 562 minutes off 395 deliveries.

But the bare statistics recount nothing of the magnitude of the effort, its importance to the outcome of the Test, or the significance to the man himself. The champion opening batsman, the best in the world for more than a decade, found himself the prime target of public dissatisfaction at the start of the series. The mumbles turned to open criticism when he managed only 58 runs at 9.66 in three Tests in Pakistan. A few failures at the start of the season converted the criticism to condemnation of his age at a time when youngsters were clamouring for inclusion in the Test team. The people who stood to applaud him only the previous season when, with his keen sense of timing, he celebrated his 100th Test with 149 at Antigua (joining Pakistan's Javed Miandad as the only batsmen to score a century in both their first and 100th Tests), now ridiculed him as an exhausted warhorse. That same sense of timing, and an irrepressible desire to silence his critics, drove him to the great heights in this innings.

Greenidge is a complex character. He gives the impression that he feels genuinely at home only when in the centre of a cricket pitch where he can command admiration with his wholesome array of shots. That may be a throwback to his early days when as a 12 year old he migrated to England, learning his cricket with Hampshire on the county circuit. He had a unique blending of the technically correct schooling of the English and naturally adventurous and aggressive skills of his Caribbean background. He grew up with the mind of an Englishman and the instincts of a West Indian and somehow he didn't quite fit into either society with ease. The English considered him a West Indian while his native countrymen thought of him as too articulate, too conservative, too proper in many ways, to be a genuine West Indian. Just where was his home when he wasn't fully accepted in either his native or his adopted land? He made it centre wicket in many ways, using his cricketing abilities to force acceptance and eventual admiration no matter where he played. But there always seemed a void. Clive Lloyd and then Viv Richards stole the limelight regardless of his exceptional feats for the West Indies and Desmond Haynes was the accepted King of Barbados even as Greenidge's junior partner. His wide smile and outgoing personality, and his lifetime in the area, guaranteed him of that. Greenidge, on the other hand, was seen as a professional cricketer who rarely smiled and played for Barbados only when necessary. He was the drifter. But he loved Barbados and sweated on Tests at Kensington Oval to show his skills. He was bitterly disappointed when the second Test against England at Guyana was cancelled in 1990, moving his 100th Test to Antigua and ruining scheduled celebrations of the event at

Greenidge, finding the strength of his youth, nearly broke the fence with this drive.

his home ground. Only once had he scored a century at Kensington Oval and he had to wait until 1989, 15 years after his Test debut, to score 117 against India and achieve that honour.

Against that background of criticism, combined with a genuine hurt and a sense of betrayal from the West Indian public, he steeled himself for one grand finale in front of his home crowd, aware that he wouldn't again walk from the pavilion to centre wicket in a Test for the West Indies. He was going to England for his farewell series but for all the folks at home, this was it. A century spiced with brutal drives, crunching cuts and powerful pulls combined with an impeccable technique would have been enough for most men to satisfy the public demand for overdue runs. This was, after all, only the second time in 24 Test innings that he had passed 50. But Greenidge had something really special in mind and he wanted to give the Bajans and the West Indians in general a reminder of his greatness. He ploughed on to his fourth double-century and onwards past every standard previously set against Australia at Test level.

And as he walked from the crease for the last time to a standing ovation, he lifted his bat in acknowledgement to the members and then turned deliberately to salute every section of the ground in a gesture of thanks and appreciation. Those fortunate enough to witness the innings will cherish it as a reminder of one of the greats of the game, a veteran reliving the best

Greenidge was mobbed by local fans in his triumphant farewell to his home island, Barbados.

of his career in one final curtain call. And for the next couple of days the fans, catering staff and officials wore badges proclaiming: 'I Love Gordon'. It was preferable to think he finally had touched their hearts and was not merely a by-product of swift marketing.

Greenidge naturally was exhausted as he sat in the dressing rooms clutching an icepack on a wonky knee and another on a massively bruised thigh. He wasn't talking. At the end of the match he sat in the same corner slowly packing his coffin for the trip to Antigua and his last Test on West Indian soil. He was circumspect as he explained his silence after a crowning glory the previous day.

> I feel too much anger, too much pain after all that has been said about me this year. Nobody wanted to know me before this innings and now those in the media who have called for my head suddenly need me. I didn't do this for them. I did it for the West Indies team, for the fans, for myself and my family and my friends who have believed in me. I am now satisfied.

And with a shake of the hand and a smile, Gordon Greenidge walked out of Kensington Oval to hear fans cheering his name as the hometown hero. That satisfied him even more.

The third day of action belonged to Greenidge but Richardson also grabbed his share of the limelight after Marshall's job ended at 15 with the score on 153. Richardson began playing shots from the outset without a hint of the nervousness which engulfed him in the first innings. But he virtually began walking towards the pavilion when he hooked a McDermott delivery to Hughes at fine leg when he was 15. Hughes dived forward to grab the ball and held it for a considerable period as he fell to earth, only for the ball to squeeze from his grip. The fine effort deserved better but Richardson survived and skipped to his half-century off only 69 deliveries with seven boundaries. The 50 partnership ticked by in 71 minutes and the 100 stand in only 113 minutes, as Greenidge methodically accumulated runs while Richardson wrenched the game from Australia's grasp. Not even the prospect of his third century of the series and a record seventh against Australia could temper Richardson's flare and he ignored the warning when McDermott again was luckless when Mark Waugh couldn't cling to a chance at first slip. Richardson was 97 at the time and he paid the penalty for his impetuosity two runs later when he played across a delivery from Mark Waugh to fall lbw for 99. The runs flowed from only 156 deliveries with 15 boundaries during a 199 run liaison with Greenidge for the fourth wicket. A dejected Richardson left the field but afforded a smile as he looked at the imposing score of 3 for 352. Hooper capitalised on the comfortable position to collect 25 runs before stumps and the West Indians gave the Australians much to contemplate on the rest day with a total of 3 for 407 and an advantage of 422 runs.

The Australians enjoyed a magnificent evening on a cruise on the Bajan Queen as guests of the Barbados Cricket Association, an official engagement which proved a spectacular way to forget the traumas of the day's battering. The party hastily gathered at Deep Water Harbour as arranged after play despite a long and frustrating day in the field, only for the voyage to be delayed as anxious officials waited for the West Indian players. Embarrassed and annoyed officials eventually conceded that only a couple of players, Haynes and Logie, bothered to turn up. Members of the West Indian and Australian Cricket Boards, dignitaries from other countries and other islands and the Australians and guests couldn't help but notice the absence of the majority of the West Indian players although few were surprised, such was their lack of social contact throughout the tour.

Border called on his players' personal pride as his ammunition to salvage a draw from the Test, and he used Greenidge as the classic example of what the Australian batsmen needed to aspire to do.

This now is an individual thing, not a matter of saying as a team 'We're going to get stuck in for Australia'. The individual must say 'I am not going to get out'. You have to say 'Gee, I'm as good. I'm going to bat for five sessions to save this game and I'm going to get a Test century' — that's the only attitude to have and I would be very disappointed if all the guys didn't think they could bat for five sessions to save the game.

Richards on the other hand considered his bowlers didn't need any more than five sessions to win and he made it clear he would make the weary Australians field for yet another session before beginning the really difficult task of survival.

DAY FOUR

The controversial first ball dismissal of Geoff Marsh and Border's fifth duck in 206 Test innings crippled Australia's hopes of survival in another fascinating day of action. Greenidge wrote himself into the history books and enjoyed a share in his third century partnership of the innings as the West Indians amassed 9 for 536 before declaring to give themselves 153 overs to clinch victory. Australia's 552 run victory target was irrelevant. The lbw decision from umpire Barker, sending Marsh on his way from the first delivery of the resistance, was a cruel blow which Sir Garfield Sobers and Clive Lloyd, as prominent West Indies figures, described as one of the worst they had seen from a delivery which they suggested wouldn't have hit another set of stumps.

The West Indians added 129 runs off 30.3 overs before the declaration as the batsmen enjoyed a carefree run spree. Greenidge fell to Hughes after his marathon innings, with a partnership of exactly 100 with Hooper to add to the 129 with Haynes and 199 with Richardon. The home team added 452 runs while he was at the crease and only another 82 after his exit. Hooper reached his half-century with five boundaries and a six but fell to Mark Waugh for 57. The increasingly effective all-rounder added Richards to his haul for 25 off only 21 deliveries. Logie chimed in with an unbeaten 33 off 50 deliveries with five boundaries while McDermott and Reid cheaply accounted for the tail. Mark Waugh took the bowling honours with 4 for 80 off 28 economical overs in the circumstances but McDermott was easily the best bowler and deserving of far better figures than 2 for 130 off 37.3 overs.

The Australian innings could not have started in more controversial or devastating circumstances. Marsh, a gritty batsman with immense powers of concentration and capable of protracted innings, took block for the opening delivery from Ambrose. The ball hit the seam and jagged a remarkable distance to almost cut the batsman in two as it thudded into his pads. Umpire Barker considered it out lbw, totally confounding observers and confusing anyone attempting to draw a line of consistency in his lbw decisions. Marsh couldn't believe it as he stood with his feet still rooted to the turf on or about leg stump, his butt protruding in the position he finished in when the ball hit his pads. The movement off the seam was so dramatic that it was impossible to entertain the thought that the ball would have hit the stumps. The only avenue from the trajectory was a path well wide of the leg stump. Television replays confirmed what seemed obvious to the naked eye — that this was a very poor decision, a vital decision. Former West Indian players were embarrassed and apologetic about the verdict which diminished the face value of the superior West Indian performance. Barker's judgement at crucial times in Australia's two innings — Jones in the first and Marsh in the second — certainly was open to question. That was of little consolation to Marsh who was demoralised by the dismissal and as frustrated as his father Ted who sat with shocked Australian supporters in the Worrell, Weekes and Walcott Stand.

Taylor and Boon doubled their mental drive to bat for three hours and a century partnership which promised a glimmer of hope. Boon enjoyed two escapes on his way to a half-century off 130 deliveries. He was bowled by a Marshall no-ball without offering a shot and at 40 he was dropped at second slip by Hooper off Patterson. His innings ended when an inside edge deflected on to the stumps at 57 from another express delivery from Ambrose. Border rejected the idea of a nightwatchman and instead took up his normal batting position at number four in a bid to adopt a positive approach despite a cracked thumb. The move backfired when Ambrose excelled with a kicking delivery which the left-hander fended to Dujon after only five deliveries. The veteran's dreams of saving the Test ended with only his fifth duck in 206 Test innings. Hughes then took over as nightwatchman and at stumps the Australians were 3 for 122, having lost the wickets of Boon and Border for 11 runs in the final hour of play.

FINAL DAY

The emphatic victory by 343 runs came with a burst within 12 overs after lunch when Australia lost 6 for 18 in a 51 minute capitulation after a bold showing in the opening session by Taylor and Jones. The entire team, with the help of 26 extras, managed only 208 runs or 18 runs fewer than Greenidge's solo performance and only three batsmen — Taylor, Boon and Jones — managed more than an hour at the crease against the unerring West Indian attack.

Marshall began the celebrations when he claimed his 350th Test victim in his illustrious career by removing Hughes from a gloved pull to Dujon for three. The pocket dynamo (by fast bowling physique standards) was a decisive force in the series after suffering the same baiting as Greenidge as a man nearing the end of his career after the one-day internationals. He finished the series with more wickets than his team-mates and his haul of 21 at 20.81 was a tribute to the veteran who celebrated his 33rd birthday on the eve of this Test.

Taylor and Jones joined forces after the early exit of Hughes and batted defensively as only 16 runs went on the board in the opening hour, with Taylor reaching his half-century off 151 deliveries. The pair then batted sensibly to take advantage of any loose deliveries and frustrated the West Indians by remaining together until lunch in a 68 run partnership.

The clatter of wickets after the interval began with another unusual dismissal of Jones — the luckless batsman seemingly found new or unusual ways of being dismissed in every Test — when he was bowled by a delivery from spinner Hooper. Jones played a classic forward defensive block to the delivery, only for the ball to hit the turf, curl around his bat and roll into the stumps to dislodge the off bail! Once again he managed a solid start and batted for a long period for 37 runs in 104 minutes but once again he failed to build on the foundation with a huge score. This was his fifth score above 20 but he remained without a half-century to his credit. Hooper struck another vital blow half an hour later when Mark Waugh spoiled his outstanding series by missing a faster delivery to be bowled for only three to spark a loss of three wickets in five balls without a run being added to the score. Marshall trapped Taylor leg before wicket

The end. Richards stands in triumph as Bruce Reid's wicket, Australia's last, falls.

in the following over and repeated the mode of dismissal before Healy had scored. The Australians had slumped from 4 for 190 to 8 for 200 in the space of 40 minutes after lunch.

Taylor's innings was unhappily wasted in the context of the outcome of the game but his 76 in more than six hours of stubborn batting was a tribute to his powers of concentration, improved technique and spirit. Walsh ensured early West Indian celebrations by removing McDermott and Reid to leave Steve Waugh stranded on four after 21 minutes of frustrated on-looking. Ambrose once again was the main destroyer with 3 for 36 off 19 overs which knocked over the top-order, while Marshall was magnificent with 3 for 35 off 17 overs. Walsh and Hooper chipped in with two wickets apiece to add support and Patterson's sheer speed kept the batsmen on their toes in an excellent team effort.

Border accepted the defeat on the chin and acknowledged the West Indians as the undisputed champions of the Test arena.

They proved again that they are the top side. I must take my hat off to them. I thought we had a big chance but they have blitzed us. We came here as challengers and have been beaten comprehensively. Nobody ever questioned that the West Indians were the top side but, as it has turned out, they have proved that in style. Their bowlers have been absolutely ruthless, relentless as well as being as good, in terms of applying pressure with line and length, as any West Indian attack I have faced. And, although the batting has been vulnerable at times, they have belted us in the two matches which have counted and nobody can argue with wins by 10 wickets and 343 runs. Sure, things haven't gone right for us. We were confident after the one-dayers but have been unsettled by rain, lack of form and an inability to press home whatever

How sweet it is. Veterans Malcolm Marshall and Viv Richards give each other the Shazam salute to hail impending victory in Barbados.

advantage we had to just win a Test. I said at the start of this series that we needed to play to the peak of our form but we simply haven't been able to do that — we have never had all the batsmen firing or all the bowlers fit and firing. I am not totally distraught because I knew what we were up against. I'm just sorry we didn't put up a better show.

Richards was elated with the win and the series result, particularly as the 'oldies' proved such a major factor. 'Our ticker was what got us through, especially the old tickers. We became stouter after people criticised us and we came good. That's what champions do. I think the Australians are a great cricket side and we had to work hard for this series win — they were very unlucky they caught us in such a rampant mood.'

Simpson congratulated the West Indians and commented: 'The West Indians just seemed to be able to get back into the game no matter what we did because they are a champion team and nobody can deny that. The results prove it.' After congratulating the West Indians in the dressing rooms he boarded the bus with the rest of the players and returned to the Rockley Resort to pack for the move to Antigua the following day, totally oblivious as he walked out of the ground to the scathing attack from Richards which was to sour the end of the tour.

DRIVING DOWN
VIV RICHARDS STREET

Driving into St Johns after our arrival at Antigua's impressive international airport, all the talk amongst the Australian press was of the bad feeling in Barbados and the unexpected outburst by Viv Richards at the end of the Fourth Test. Would there be repercussions, would the Fifth Test on beloved Vivi's homeground be a battle, bitterly contested to the final ball, or a fizzer?

I don't know whether it was accidental, or a silent protest at the course of our conversation, but the Antiguan driver took a slight detour down Viv Richards Street (one street past Andy Roberts Street) to pause outside a humble, green-painted cottage with windows and a religious message painted over the barred front door.

The driver told us the house was where Viv Richards grew up, and where his parents still lived. The message read: 'Yes! God is Good in Earth and Sky.'

Later, I went back to Viv Richards Street and tried to buy a tee-shirt showing a bearded, imperious looking Viv, wearing a red fez, Rastafarian colours and the title 'The World's Greatest Batsman', at a small sandwich shop near the Richards' house. The shop was busy, but not chatty and friendly, as I had become used to after leaving Jamaica, and the people behind the counter never quite got around to selling me the tee-shirt. To prove to myself that there were no hard feelings, I bought one later behind the public grandstand, near the Calypso Bar actually, during the Test.

There were hard feelings, however, and as Rod has said elsewhere, it would be idle to ignore it. To play fair, and to get both sides of the story, I decided to interview Dennis 'Slugger' Waight, the rugged, outspoken Australian from Curl Curl, New South Wales, who has been the Windies physiotherapist for 14 years, having been appointed to the job in World Series days.

Slugger is a rugged character who likes a drink and a yarn about boxing ('Muhammad Ali IS the greatest!') and football, and we have always got along pretty well together. But for once, Slugger didn't feel like talking. 'No, Tommy,' he said. 'Let's leave it a while. I have a sore tooth.' He did have too; he had it taken out, but eventually agreed to an interview. Even over a couple of six-packs of Red Stripe, it was like drawing teeth at first, but Slugger eventually said his piece.

'There's no "typical" West Indian cricketer,' he began.

They're not stereotypes like American basketballers, for God's sake. They're individuals, personalities; they change from day to day. Generally they're pretty good-tempered, you know, jovial, but most of them are serious about their cricket; it is worth too much to them to fool around and they can be very intense during a match. There is no horseplay then. They play hard and don't take any mercy.

Tony Greig started all that rubbish about them cracking under pressure in 1976 [at Adelaide Oval with Rod Nicholson 'ghosting' his newspaper column] when he said England would make them 'grovel' when they played them. Well, we all know what happened to England: the Windies gave them a terrible hiding.

Every side cracks under pressure occasionally; I think Australia did in its first innings in Barbados this time around, but as far as I am concerned, the Windies have been remarkably consistent. They've stood up all right, better than any other team in my time. When there's been a chance of a win, seven out of ten times the Windies have grabbed it. The Windies go in hard all the time, both batting and bowling. They take wickets so quickly, when they get a run on, that an innings is never safe, not even when you have 300 on the board, as Australia did in Guyana. It's the same thing with the batting; no-one among modern batsmen can score runs as quickly as Richie Richardson. Sure, he takes chances, and if you're lucky you can get him cheaply. But if you don't, there's a big 100 on the board and you're battling.

Viv used to be like that, and that's probably what's bothering him now; he doesn't set the place on fire like he used to. Mind you, he's still a great batsman, and there's no way you'll get me to say otherwise.

As a captain? Well, who do we compare him with, Clive Lloyd? Clive was a very good batsman and fieldsman who seemed to become more consistent as he grew older. He'd hold up under pressure, all right. You'd lose count of the number of times he saved the Windies when they looked to be in trouble. Larry Gomes could always be depended upon to shuffle around with Clive for a partnership of 70 or 80 or more.

Clive was more laid back than the average West Indian, more relaxed, the original 'Mr Cool'. He was a diplomat, a very smooth captain, who never seemed to let anything worry him too much, although of course sometimes it did.

Viv is completely different. He has his own ideas and is likely to express them no matter what. Viv is more intense, more excitable, and shows emotion much more readily than Clive ever did. Viv will lose his temper and go on a rampage, but then he cools down and everything is sweet again. He doesn't hold grudges, but Viv DEMANDS respect, Clive just expected it. He had more time to get his act together; he grew up in the job as captain of what became the greatest cricket team in the world. If ever there was a hard act to follow, he was it.

Just the same, Viv reinvigorated the side when he took over from Clive, the same way he did in this Test Series. There was a real danger of the West Indies going into a slump after Australia won the one-dayers 4-1. We got a real hiding, and everyone knew it. One more weak performance, and we'd have had to make changes, and morale would have suffered. But the win in Guyana took care of that.

With more than a little help from the umpires?

'There's always someone blaming the umpires,' Slugger said, with a shrug.

Just so long as it isn't us. When it is the other side complaining I know we're doing OK. If I was to discuss the umpiring, and I'm not going to, I'd say it was about time that some of the Australians woke up to the fact that the umpires hear what is going on out there, not just the opposing players. If you're sledging a batsman in his own country you have to be very careful how you do it. If you say the wrong thing, it could affect the umpire's attitude.

Our blokes don't mind fierce competition, in fact they thrive on it; but they say you can sledge without using foul language. As it is, the Windies get along better with England than they do with Australia; they say the Poms don't curse or swear at them half as much as the Australians do. That may sound funny, complaining about swearing and bad language — don't forget, I'm an Australian too — but the West Indians don't use much foul language.

They're wild men in a lot of ways, and you know what I mean; I'm not going to say any more, but they're pretty prim in some ways. They do rather than say; they don't use many four-letter words for instance.

And racism? They never use 'white' as a derogatory adjective? They don't refuse to mix with Australian players? How about Desmond Haynes and his threats to Ian Healy and other Australians?

It's hard to work out; he used to be a very easy-going guy, very easy to get along with, but he's a hard man on the field now. Maybe the Aussies have got to him. I know they've been having a go at him and, let's face it, cricket is very intense now, particularly with the 'World Championship' build-up, the crowds becoming involved and that sort of thing. The Windies have been copping a bit from the Indians too, you know.

The players don't like Desi pointing his bat at Healy and making threats, but they don't like the things Healy and other Australians close to the bat are saying either. The West Indians say the Australians say terrible things on the field, and it can't all be imagination. They can't all be lying. As a matter of fact, I don't think any of them are.'

He was taking sides then, against his own countrymen?

'You're wasting your time, Tommy, trying to "stir",' Slugger said.

All I'll say is that I am tired of being asked 'why are your countrymen so nasty?' West Indians operate on a much lower key. Aussies are louder and more aggressive. They're loud and boisterous, and Aussie spectators are even more so. West Indian spectators drink all day and don't get boisterous; the Aussies? Well, it was an Australian spectator who went and called the police to control Australian spectators at the Test yesterday [27 April]. It was an Australian who said the Australians were looking for trouble!

West Indians may be noisier in the stands than Australians, but they're more fun. You never see an Australian spectator in fancy dress, climbing up a pole for the amusement of the crowd [like the famous 'Gravy' did at the Recreation Ground in Antigua]. The Australians look for fights.

It sounded as though Slugger Waight, 45, ex-CBC, a rugby man from way back, had finally changed sides.

'Don't ever say that, not even joking, or stirring,' Slugger said.

I'm not changing sides, just describing things the way they are — and I'll tell you this now, people in the West Indies don't like the things which are being written about them, particularly the things written by English cricket writers, and white writers in general.

They say stories are phrased to make them look silly, to make them seem savages. That you're very patronising. Viv [Richards] has his own strong opinions and doesn't mind expressing them, and look at all the trouble that has caused. He and Bob Simpson don't see eye to eye at the moment, but that is one of those things which will be fixed. Both of them believe in discipline, and that is what the game needs now.

What Viv misses, and what all the Windies players miss, is the days when it was absolute WAR against the Australians on the field, but Thommo [Jeff Thomson] and Marshie [Rod Marsh] would always be first into the Windies' dressing-room for a drink after the game. Those were the days when Test cricket was fun.

Those too were the sentiments of Clive Lloyd when we said goodbye, see you later, in the Viv Richards stand, on the final day of the Fifth Test.

'I wouldn't want to play Test cricket now,' Lloyd said, seriously, deliberately, choosing every word carefully and knowing it would be quoted.

> *There's too much aggro, too much bad feeling. I'm not blaming anyone, not taking sides, I just don't think it's a game any more, it's not what we used to call cricket. Life's too short for all that sort of nonsense.*
>
> *Who'd want to spend the best 20 years of their life scowling at people, snarling and arguing? Life's too short for that.*
>
> *God, I hope they do something soon. It will be the end of cricket as we knew it, otherwise.*

Walking down to the beach near our hotel the next morning, for my last swim in the West Indies, I found myself next to Ian Chappell, obviously doing the same.

'A good win,' I said of the Fifth Test. 'What a shame it didn't happen earlier, and it could have!'

Chappell was unconvinced. 'Faint heart never won fair lady,' he said, and we went our different ways.

THE FIFTH TEST: RICHARDS RULES, SIMPSON SUFFERS

Viv Richards' tirade against Bob Simpson may have brought the game, West Indies cricket and Richards' status as captain into disrepute. The unprovoked character assault on a respected official from the touring team demanded disciplinary action from officials and a retraction and an apology from Richards. Yet the influence of the legendary batsman and his importance and high profile at the end of a successful series enabled him to turn his back on protocol, his country's administrators, the victim of his extraordinary accusations and a concerted Australian objection.

The episode exposed the West Indies Cricket Board of Control as a toothless tiger, seemingly prepared only to scratch at the surface but not prepared to bite at the heart of the matter. The officials dithered and Richards called their bluff by ignoring requests, not demands, to attend meetings and to diplomatically resolve the international incident which greatly embarrassed West Indies cricket. The Australians engaged in ten days of official endeavours to gain a satisfactory response from their counterparts and the West Indies captain, but eventually left the Caribbean without a semblance of a genuine apology. Richards also departed to lead the team in a series in England while West Indian officials prepared for a Board meeting at the beginning of June.

The Richards controversy doubtless was on the agenda, in much the same way as a similarly unacceptable incident was at the May meeting in 1990. An extract from that meeting is noteworthy.

The Board considered a matter involving the captain, Vivian Richards, which arose during the final Test in Antigua. It also considered a written apology by Mr Richards. The Board is of the opinion that, despite provocation, there could be no mitigating circumstances to justify the unprecedented step taken by the captain of the West Indies cricket team who, instead of leading his team on to the field on the second morning, was engaged in confrontation with a member of the English press. Mr Richards has been made aware of the Board's grave displeasure at his action and of the certain consequences of any future misconduct on his part. The Board also expresses its concern at the general deterioration of the conduct of some of the West Indies players and wishes to remind all players that strong disciplinary action will be taken against anyone found guilty of misconduct.

All of which counted for nothing. Richards seemingly abused his position as captain of the West Indies at a post-Test press conference, which, instead of being a platform to proclaim the virtues of a marvellous series win to retain the Sir Frank Worrell Trophy, became the vehicle of a private tirade against one of the most respected members of a guest team in his country. The unsolicited outburst against Simpson included:

He is a moaner and a bad loser. It is not a matter of what has happened on this tour or over the years. He is just a very sour sort of loser and I hope he changes. He has been shouting off his mouth. I have never shouted off my mouth. I dismiss anything that Simpson says. I'm not a guy who listens too much to Bob Simpson because we don't think we have a great respect for Bob Simpson. I have seen him over the years and seen the way he operates and I am saying that I am not a great lover or admirer of Bob Simpson. Every now and again he will say 'well played' or 'congratulations'. But you treat people as you are treated and I am going to tell you that Bob Simpson is not our cup of tea. You don't know what's in the man's heart.

Strong sentiments indeed. If he firmly believed this of Simpson he should have told him to his face, certainly in private, and not taken advantage of a press conference to publicly and internationally insult the opposition coach. He said there was nothing specific on this tour which aroused ill-feelings about Simpson but he reflected on an incident in 1978 when Simpson was Australian captain in the Caribbean during the World Series Cricket split. 'We got criticised in Australia when he said that Clive Lloyd told his guys to bully the umpires. But I saw him in action. He almost had his hand, his finger, up the nose of umpire Ralph Gosein. He can't deny it because I have the picture to prove it,' he said, claiming the incident was in Trinidad.

Simpson, who (having congratulated the West Indians on the Test and series win) was back in the team hotel when informed of the comments, was upset and bewildered by the outburst, and bemused by the reference to the incident in 1978. 'That picture was taken during a one-day match in Antigua when there was a dispute about a rule and I took a rule book out to show the umpire. We have laughed about that plenty of times including on this tour when we have met on our two visits to Trinidad,' Simpson explained. 'I am amazed, disappointed and shocked by this extraordinary outburst. As far as I'm concerned my only contacts with Viv

Richards have been pleasant ones: there has never been a cross word between us. It just saddens me to see Viv Richards make such an emotional outburst. I don't know what he is referring to,' Simpson said.

The official Australian response was prompt and pointed; it challenged the West Indies to back their plea for an end to unsavoury incidents in international cricket. 'The West Indies have made a great noise about the need of a code of behaviour: we want to know if they have the guts to take the lead and do something about their own captain,' manager Sawle said after receiving full backing from the Australian Cricket Board.

If Allan Border, who is a champion of Australia, said the same sort of thing about an opposition official there would be a call for his head as captain. Yet nobody here seems interested in taking Richards to task and that is bitterly disappointing as an administrator of the game in whatever country you may represent. We are appalled by the comments of Viv Richards about Bob Simpson and we expect the officials here to do something about it, and in a fast and very severe mannner.

The West Indies officials were too busy choosing the touring team to England the following day to hear an official complaint from ACB chairman Col Egar in Barbados, and announced only that Richards would captain the team to England. Sawle faxed the WICBC requesting an urgent meeting when the officials flew into Antigua the following day. He sat in the foyer of the Royal Antiguan Hotel, where the Australian and West Indian players were staying, for two hours before discovering that the West Indian hierarchy was staying at another hotel at the other end of the island. Chairman Clyde Walcott, executive secretary Steve Comacho and Board members were waiting there to interview Richards before contacting the Australian contingent of Sawle, Egar, Jack Edwards and Alan Crompton, who represented the ACB. Richards passed on his regret that he didn't have the time to attend the West Indian meeting and would be busy at training that afternoon. So the West Indian officials obligingly waited lest they upset the man.

The West Indies responded 36 hours after Richards' comments with this statement: 'Vivian Richards regrets any embarrassment which may have been caused to the Australian cricket team and to the Australian Cricket Board. The West Indian team hopes this incident does not affect relationships between the two teams for the fifth and final match.' The statement was unsigned and obviously not written by Richards, who wanted nothing to do with the issue.

The press release was totally unacceptable and Sawle insisted the response was completely unsatisfactory to the Australian cricket team.

I believe that nothing short of the West Indies Cricket Board disassociating itself from the remarks of the captain will be satisfactory to us. From Allan Border down through the team there is a feeling of outrage at this unnecessary and vicious attack on the Australian coach. I want to ensure the Australian public that the Australian team is 100 per cent behind Bob Simpson. If the purpose was to undermine the Australian team then it has been an abject failure. They are very disappointed that the West Indian captain took the privilege and licence of a post-Test match press conference to utter a tirade of derogatory remarks about the opposition coach. We doubt that winning a series has given any captain the right to abuse the code of ethics which the West Indian captain has done. The West Indies Cricket Board is in an enviable situation. At International Cricket Council level they approve and strongly support the concept of an international code of conduct with an international referee to adjudicate and impose penalties where deemed necessary. It appears at the moment they have the opportunity to implement the concept but won't. Bob Simpson, a great player of the past, a former Australian captain, has made a great contribution to world and Australian cricket. Because of that he is very well respected throughout the cricket circles of the world. He has been done a great injustice. It is up to the West Indian captain and the West Indian Cricket Board to correct it. The response received is a long, long way short of any correction or disassociation from the remarks and that is why we consider it totally unacceptable.

The members of the two Boards met for further discussions and Richards later issued this signed statement, issued as a press release on official West Indies Cricket Board letterhead, before any Australian official was notified of its contents:

I considered that the statements regarding Bob Simpson which I made during a press conference at the conclusion of the fourth Test reflected my personal views. Upon consideration however these statements were made in my capacity as captain of the West Indies. As my latter capacity takes precedence I hereby withdraw the statements which I publicly made in this regard.

The Australians were frustrated by the latest statement and made their feelings known to the West Indian officials once more, leaving the matter with them as they left the Caribbean. The Australians pursued the issue so vigorously and relentlessly on a matter of principle. The West Indian officials, privately angered by the Richards comments which put them under extreme pressure on an international basis, didn't stand up to be counted when confronted with the issue. They seemingly wanted the easy way out, allowing Richards to finish his career lest they upset him before cracking down on misconduct. The feeling within the Australian camp was that the West Indian desire for the introduction of an international referee and code of behaviour was simply a desire for somebody else to do their dirty work for them.

But what prompted the original outburst? There wasn't any obvious discord between the pair at any stage of the series leading up to the criticism. They always exchanged polite and seemingly friendly greetings at airports, functions, training sessions and matches. Perhaps Richards interpreted Simpson's comments on important cricket issues as criticism of aspects of West Indian cricket. Simpson, for instance, suggested that the West Indian trait of manipulating over rates to suit their own purposes was detrimental to the game; he suggested that the International Cricket Council instigate uniform rules for limited-over matches during the one-day international series and he spoke out about the inferiority of covers in the Caribbean. Those issues are important and, as coach of the Australian team, he has an obligation to support anything which would better the game, especially if Australia gained as well. If that is being a moaner, Simpson is guilty. Guilty of being a shrewd devotee with an eye to correcting anomalies in the game.

At no stage did Simpson make official objections about any issue. But he spoke privately to officials around the islands about many problems in cricket, and maybe Richards misread that as Simpson attempting to manipulate the game his way. Simpson also was outspoken about the manner in which cricket should be played, pressing for players to compete vigorously but always upholding the traditions of the gentleman's game. He always has done that, setting standards of attire, discipline and behaviour for the Australians which other countries have emulated. He also promoted Australia as often as he could, mainly for the benefit of the media, suggesting that the visitors had a good chance to defeat the West Indians in the series and that the West Indians were vulnerable. That may have been misinterpreted as 'shouting his mouth off' but it was part of Simpson's job to encourage and promote his players. Simpson has earned his stripes as a cricketer, a coach and a leader in the development and advancement of the game. He deserved better from Richards, and the West Indian Cricket Board for that matter.

We may never know the reason for Richards' comments at such an inappropriate and unsolicited time. But it was interesting to note that the only specific reference to an incident involving Simpson related to a match in 1978 when Simpson was captain of the Australian team at the height of the split with World Series Cricket. Could it be that after all these years the sores still fester between those who joined Kerry Packer's television brigade and those who stood by the establishment?

And if so, why at this particular time would a criticism be levelled at Simpson? Maybe it was a rare opportunity in recent years to seize on an Australian failure after so much success under his guidance. Others took that same opportunity as columnists in Australia, although to be fair criticism of Simpson has been incessant from some (former WSC) quarters. One could only wonder ...

What was encouraging was that the Australian Cricket Board fully supported Simpson, as did the players. They were furious with the criticism from Richards and Border didn't speak up only in deference to the ACB officials who wanted to direct their complaints through official channels. The incident bonded the team closer than ever and the future of Simpson remained far more secure with Australia than that of Richards in the scheme of West Indian cricket in the future.

The aggression overflowed in a nasty Test to conclude the series as the Australians retaliated in devastating fashion to defeat the West Indians by 157 runs with more than a day to spare. Umpires Lloyd Barker and Steve Bucknor eventually reported both teams for abusive language and repeated heated clashes on the field, while petty-minded and officious local administrators stirred trouble off it. The Test was a triumph for Mark Waugh and Mark Taylor who scored centuries and for McDermott and Hughes who bowled magnificently, but a sorry end for Richards in his final Test in the Caribbean. He was out for a duck and two in his farewell appearance at his native Antigua after officially opening a stand in his honour. The Australians dictated play throughout and asked the West Indians to create history by scoring 455 to win, a task beyond even this champion combination. And at the end of it all, after all the animosity and on-field ruckus, the tour ended with a call from both camps to end the bad blood and return cricket to being a gentleman's sport!

Antigua is a beautiful island with scenic coves and inviting beaches, excellent restaurants and a hunger for the tourist dollar. Transactions are in US dollars and traders require calculators to convert prices to their local Eastern Caribbean currency! The Royal Antiguan Hotel was a spacious domain for the team for this final match and offered 24-hour service, although it often took longer. But around the island there was ample to make the tourist drool: the natural harbour known as Nelson's Dockyard which is one of the wonders of the Caribbean, the dense hinterland, thriving shopping centres, wonderful restaurants, including Jaws, a seafood haven atop a mountain overlooking a superb bay, and five casinos.

But Australia's persistent demands for a retraction from Richards didn't go down well with Antiguan officials in the land of their idol and it came as little surprise that counter accusations flew at every opportunity. The first came from Pedro Corbin, an executive member of the Antigua Cricket Association. He complained that some of the Australians had upset the catering staff by putting their fingers in food to taste it. He added that a word to the Australians solved everything immediately, although he couldn't wait to inform the horde of English cricket writers, who had

Richards musters dignity as he leaves the field after his first innings duck.

arrived for the last two Tests, of the resurgence of 'the ugly Aussies'. The next complaint came on the morning of the third day's play when the Australians burst through the door leading to the dressing rooms, breaking the lock. The players arrived at the ground for warm-ups only to discover that the key given to them by local officials didn't fit the lock. After waiting for some time, Hughes and Alderman gave the door a nudge with their shoulders and broke in. 'We are only too willing to pay for a new lock for what already was a damaged door. We are bitterly disappointed that in the middle of a Test a visiting team could be locked out, having been given a wrong key, and with no officials around to help them get in,' Sawle said.

The English press seized the opportunity to unleash three years of frustration on the Australians: they were ugly Aussies again, committing acts of vandalism, upsetting kitchen hands with bad manners and the West Indian players with racist remarks and also making fools of themselves with a pitiful attempt to gain an apology from Richards. One would have thought the West Indians were on the way to England, such was the anti-Aussie and pro-West Indian account of it all.

The off-field hassles were not restricted to the players and officials. The press also had to contend with some distasteful episodes, notably at the end of the game. One official who seemed to have a finger in a lot of pies at the ground obstructed members of the press from reaching the post-match press conference as all pretense of hospitality and politeness disappeared with the final delivery. 'You are a white cockroach' the official indelicately hinted to an Australian member of the press corp. And this from a man allegedly dedicated to eliminating racial discrimination from the game and from the corridors of power in Antigua!

The build-up to the Test was odd. On one hand there was a letdown knowing that the series had been lost and with plenty of Australian supporters around on this pretty island and a day off after arriving on Anzac Day, the atmosphere was relaxed and enjoyable. But equally there was an underlying intensity to do well and to balance a few ledgers. Simpson explained the players' feelings. 'They are very unhappy about a lot of things, including things concerning myself, and I know that is going to add a bit of steel. They are too dirty on themselves to pack it in now. They want to show the West Indian public they are a far better side than they have looked in this Test series.'

The selectors made two changes to the line-up, bringing Alderman into the team to replace Reid, and spinner Peter Taylor for his first Test of the series at the expense of Steve Waugh. Alderman at no stage was suited to any of the pitches in the Caribbean and it was to prove the same here in his only major match on tour. Taylor was given the nod ahead of Matthews, and was needed because Border couldn't bowl due to his fractured thumb.

DAY ONE

Mark Waugh confirmed his status as Australia's newest batting dynamo with a remarkable century in a day of brash stroke-play by the Australians, who finished at 5 for 355 in their most adventurous and successful day of batting in the series. Waugh and Jones, who took the initiative with a sparkling 81, shared a 186 run fifth wicket partnership to take all the bowlers to task on a magnificent batting strip prepared by former West Indies champion paceman Andy Roberts.

Waugh, who suffered two nasty blows to the hand, combined classic shots with brutal hitting to reach his century off only 113 deliveries with nine boundaries and three sixes, the second 50 coming off a mere 39 deliveries with six boundaries and two sixes. He took his cue from Jones whose 50 came off only 58 deliveries with five boundaries and a six before his innings ended at 81.

Waugh's unbeaten 116, which included 109 in the protracted final session, rivalled his Test debut 138 against England in Adelaide in late January when he played a flawless innings to herald the arrival of a world-class batsman. 'I must rate it extremely high because obviously the West Indies have a better attack than England. With four fast bowlers it was going to be hard work but we had made a conscious decision to play shots and take it up to the bowlers and it worked for me,' he explained.

The reception for his century was memorable with the locals dancing wildly to loud music in appreciation of an exceptional effort. Mark Waugh suffered a nasty blow to the left index finger when in the 20s and another on the same spot soon after. But he forgot about the pain as he clouted the bowling to all parts of the field. Waugh, who has a habit of drawing a 'stick man' on his thigh pad to remind him of his centuries, had special delight notching this milestone. In many ways it completed his education. He was vulnerable to short-pitched bowling at the start of the series but proved in this innings that he was mastering that aspect of his game.

He developed as a pivotal player in the batting line-up and enhanced his reputation as a superior cricketer with the bat and in the field with the added bonus of being a useful medium-pacer. His assault on the West Indian bowlers included several shots usually restricted to one-day cricket, but as Waugh explained, the pitch was so even with the ball coming on to the bat, that the best results came from playing aggressively. A couple of examples of his aggressive attitude are worth noting. When he decided to step back to cut short-pitched deliveries he was called a coward. He did exactly the same next ball and smashed another boundary. Jones, batting at the other end, asked Waugh if he knew what he was doing. 'No, but they don't either and it is working so let's not tell them!' Later, as he neared his century, Waugh declared he would get his century by taking on Richards'

Mark Waugh acknowledges cheers for his century.

bowling, despite two men being on the boundary for the straight hit. Jones suggested he collect the runs in singles, but Waugh would have none of it and clouted the next ball over the mid-off fieldsman's head for six!

He was particularly ruthless on Richards, who conceded 46 runs off only seven overs during the rampage by Waugh and Jones. Waugh twice defied the fieldsman at long-on to cannon the ball over the boundary. Richards also suffered physically when Waugh belted a drive to him on 97. Technically the shot was a chance, but Richards did well to protect himself as he was knocked off balance and suffered a severely bruised hand.

The batting tempo increased after a disappointing start when Geoff Marsh (6) and David Boon (0) were back in the pavilion with only 13 runs on the board. Both were out attempting to put into practice the pre-match plan of attacking the bowling. Marsh was cutting when he edged the first of five catches of the innings to Dujon off Patterson and Boon's attempted hook ballooned to Greenidge in the gully off Ambrose.

Only 58 runs came in the opening session and 117 in the next, but the final session provided 180 runs with Waugh and Jones in full flight. The batting of Mark Taylor and Border, both of whom scored 59, was authoritative and impressive to pave the way for the two more flamboyant stroke-makers. Taylor's fourth half-century of the series was full of composure and class and he was unlucky to be caught down the leg side when sweeping a delivery from Hooper. Border, despite a crack on the left thumb knuckle, led from the front when he immediately began to pull and cut short deliveries from the pacemen. His 59 took only 112 deliveries and he and Taylor shared a 112 run partnership for the third wicket. They departed to the spin of Carl Hooper within 27 runs of each other and at 4 for 156 Mark Waugh entered the action at a delicate stage of the game.

Jones was the batsman to release the pressure valve. He blasted a half-century off only 58 deliveries in a display of brutal batting which included a six over the sightscreen and out of the ground to dent Hooper's confidence. He suffered a painful blow to the tip of the right index finger, in exactly the same spot that he was hurt in the previous Test in Barbados, and while he was restricted Waugh took up the assault. The century partnership swept past in only 78 minutes and only the second new ball ended the union. Jones, who received a cut between the shoulder blades when the ball cannoned into him as he took evasive action, looked set for a century when he greeted Patterson with a thunderbolt straight drive back over the speedster's head. But Marshall trapped him lbw to end a display of striking for which Jones and the Australians had been waiting all series.

DAY TWO

The nastiness emerged in an explosive day of intense cricket which provided Australia with a first innings lead of 189. The West Indians fought back gallantly in the opening session to capture 5 for 48 in 21 overs to dismiss Australia for 403 but McDermott and Hughes bombarded the batsmen in return to dismiss the champions for 214. Desmond Haynes was the only West Indian to pass 50, a bitter disappointment for the local fans who came to watch Richards in his final Test. McDermott destroyed their hopes and Richards' dreams of ending his illustrious career in the Caribbean on the high note when he trapped him lbw for a duck.

The pitch, which offered up 355 runs for only five wickets on the opening day, didn't have any bearing on the amazing tally of 16 wickets for 268 on the second day. That came about because of excellent bowling and many aggressive but risky shots and an occasional dazzling catch.

Mark Waugh remained unbeaten in the Australian innings on 139 but he found little support. Healy was caught by Dujon when hooking at a Marshall delivery at 12 and Ambrose and Walsh captured two wickets apiece to wrap up the tail in another miserable contribution by the last four batsmen. Dujon, an outstanding player for the West Indies during the past dozen years, celebrated his 250th Test victim when he caught Peter Taylor.

The on-field aggression began in earnest when McDermott went to the crease at the fall of the eighth wicket. He received his normal quota of short-pitched deliveries, including one which smashed into his left elbow and required treatment. The West Indians had made McDermott a target throughout the series and put him under extreme pressure whenever he took block. On this occasion they employed a fieldsman in front of each side of the wicket in close catching positions to unsettle him. The verbal exchanges were blatantly obvious and exaggerated and forewarned of a menacing reply.

Only one over before lunch, the keg exploded. McDermott bowled at blistering speed to rap Greenidge on the pads. Heated words were exchanged between the batsman and the bowler when the confident appeal was rejected. The pair continued their debate as they walked from the field at the end of the only over before lunch and the scene was set for an afternoon of fireworks. Nobody had to wait long for a resumption of hostilities. In McDermott's opening over after the interval he rapped Greenidge on the pads again and this time umpire Bucknor agreed with the lbw appeal. Greenidge and McDermott exchanged another barrage while Haynes and Healy entertained themselves with another conversation at the other end of the pitch.

McDermott then captured the vital wicket of man-of-the-series Richardson with a delivery which found the inside edge of a lavish drive to cannon into the stumps. At 2 for 22 the West Indians were on the back foot and when Hughes trapped Hooper lbw for only two to make the score 3 for 35, much depended on Richards to rescue his team. The man who made a century in the first Test played at St John's wanted to leave in a blaze of glory but he was in trouble throughout his brief stay as he played and missed and was hit on the pads in an extremely nervous and unconvincing display. He lasted only seven deliveries before a full-pitched McDermott delivery trapped him lbw for a duck. The stunned silence following the verdict of umpire Bucknor was broken only by the cheering of the Australian fans and then the humming of acceptance from those who watched the replay. Richards walked from the arena glumly but with a touch of class, aware that his team would need a huge effort to recover, once again, from an early collapse of 4 for 46.

The Australians suddenly found Haynes was in a belligerent mood. He survived an appeal for a catch by Healy off McDermott at 24, indicating the ball came off his shoulder when attempting a hook, and then engaged in a one-on-one tussle with Hughes. The two glared at each other for several seconds when an lbw decision was rejected before Hughes blew Haynes a mocking kiss and the batsman reciprocated. These two extremely competitive cricketers let off steam in a tense moment of play which finished humorously. Haynes wasn't to be unsettled and he belted a half-century off only 75 deliveries with eight boundaries, which, in the context of the crisis, was a blistering pace. He was ruthless on Alderman, who(having lost a yard of pace on this placid pitch and with no swing to aid him) was little more than cannon fodder. His seven overs cost 42 runs and Haynes and Logie hammered his deliveries to all parts of the field. Logie, who was hit on the helmet by a McDermott delivery, stayed with Haynes to contribute 24 runs in a partnership of 68 before he attempted to clip a delivery from spinner Peter Taylor and succeeded only in driving a catch to Jones at mid-wicket.

Dujon, so often the saviour with the bat in this series, then settled in while Haynes continued his assault. But when Haynes fell lbw to McDermott to end a spectacular innings which included 15 boundaries, Dujon went on the attack with 90 runs still required to avert the follow-on. He hooked sixes off consecutive overs from Hughes to race to 33 but the lion-hearted paceman had the satisfaction of capturing his scalp. The batsman belted a cover-drive off Hughes only to look in disbelief when Jones dived full-length and held a spectacular catch. Dujon still couldn't believe it that night. 'I don't count that as being out. Nobody is entitled to take that sort of catch from a drive which was four runs off the bat!' he said in admiration of the freakish catch which Jones held full stretch to his left and horizontal to the ground.

Marshall contributed 28 entertaining runs before falling to Mark Waugh and it was left to Ambrose and Walsh with a ninth wicket union of 11 runs to avoid the follow-on, which, Border explained later, he had no intention of enforcing because the bowlers were weary and because he wanted to bat the West Indians out of the match before having a shot of victory. Hughes dismissed Ambrose for eight the delivery after the follow-on was saved and then bowled Patterson for two to wrap up the innings.

The effort by McDermott and Hughes was tremendous, particularly as both were struggling with ankle complaints after landing awkwardly at the bowling crease during their explosive spells. McDermott set up the advantage with the wickets of Greenidge (6), Richardson (3) and Richards to have 3 for 14 off his opening seven overs. Hughes bowled magnificently after tea with ten relentless overs yielding 3 for 30 and he walked the length of the field to shake hands with McDermott as all the Australian fieldsmen gathered to show their appreciation of two outstanding efforts on a magnificent batting strip. McDermott finished with 4 for 42 off 15 overs while Hughes was tireless with 4 for 65 off 17 overs. Australia lost opener Marsh in the second innings for only a single, caught by Dujon off Ambrose, but ended the second day with a lead of 195.

DAY THREE

Mark Taylor dominated the West Indian attack in a return to the form of England, 1989, to ensure Australia set the West Indies a mammoth victory target. Taylor's 144, his first century against the West Indians, accounted for more than half the Australian second innings total of 265 as only three batsmen managed double figures! The West Indian attack, led by Walsh in a marathon display of controlled accuracy and aggression with support from Ambrose, fought inspiringly with Patterson and Marshall out of action for most of the day. But Taylor's century in front of his parents was all that Australia needed to leave themselves two days to clinch victory.

The Australians wanted to score rapidly to put the game out of reach of the West Indians as convincingly and swiftly as possible and nightwatchman Healy set about the task in cavalier fashion. He scampered to 32 off only 43 deliveries before falling to Patterson with the total on 49. The giant paceman grabbed his hamstring immediately after capturing the wicket and didn't return after his only over.

Taylor, whose footwork and concentration improved at Test level the longer the series progressed, reached his half-century with an array of drives and cuts off 139 deliveries in three hours. Boon, who had struggled since the opening Test, looked confident and composed in a 93 run partnership in two and a quarter hours but he became the first victim in a magical spell by Walsh after scoring 35. Walsh deceived the right-hander to bowl him in his tenth over and he repeated the mode of dismissal to

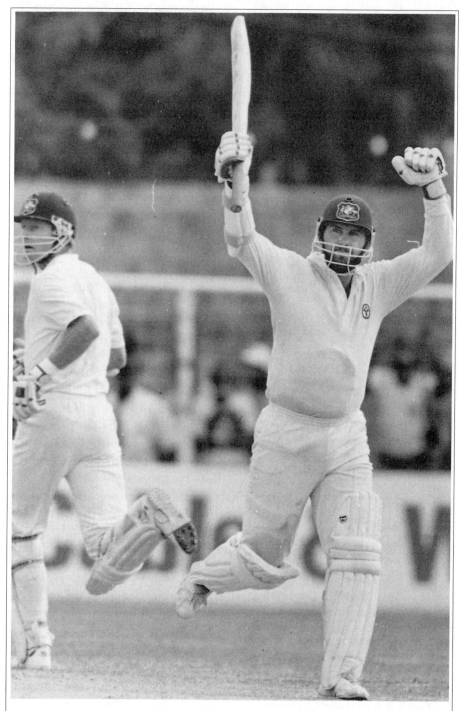

Mark Taylor punches the air in triumph after overdue century in the Final Test.

Bearded 'lady' Gravy entertains Antiguan supporters in one of his outrageous costumes.

remove Border for five in his 15th over and Jones for eight in his 18th over. The crowd rose to give Mark Waugh a hero's welcome and local identity Gravy escorted the batsman onto the field. Gravy is a celebrity in Antigua, an entertainer of exceptional skill who masquerades as all types of characters from Father Christmas to Mae West to provide entertainment at the ground. But his intrusion onto the playing arena during the game should not be condoned. He obviously upset Waugh, but not as much as the first ball lbw decision to give Walsh the outstanding figures of 4 for 22 off nine overs in an unbroken 18 over spell.

Taylor, who watched Border, Jones and Waugh depart while he moved from 81 to 89, decided to press on while he still had partners. He moved to his century in five hours with eight boundaries, recording his seventh Test century. After six hundreds in his first 14 Tests he had waited another 11 for his next. The stocky left-hander thrashed the bowling after his milestone to add another 44 off 50 deliveries before being the eighth man out for 144 from a snappy return catch by Ambrose. Despite a slump in the early part of the series when he was playing little cricket to work his way into form, Taylor finished the campaign with 441 runs at an average of 49, which, against this attack in a losing side, was a commendable performance.

Marshall passed Dennis Lillee's mark of 355 wickets when

Mark Waugh can't believe he's out lbw first ball in the second innings, but Courtney Walsh has no doubt.

McDermott gloved a bouncer to provide Dujon with his seventh dismissal of the match, giving the wicketkeeper 23 dismissals for the series to take his tally in 23 Tests against Australia to 67, the most by a wicketkeeper in Australia-West Indies history and two more than Rod Marsh.

But the bowling honours went to Walsh, who performed manfully in the absence of Patterson and with Marshall off the field until after tea. He captured 4 for 56 off 27 overs, including 21 consecutive overs in which period he captured 4 for 45. Ambrose ended a marvellous series with 3 for 64 but at no stage gathered the number of wickets in proportion to the amount of concern he caused, while Marshall's late two wickets gave him the greatest number of wickets for the West Indian pacemen (21) at the best average (20.81).

Border made no bones about the prospects as the players enjoyed a rest day. 'If we bowl well we will win it and if we don't the West Indians will create history — I can't possibly see a draw. I am not counting my chickens because I have seen the way these blokes attack in the second innings and if they get on top they would have an outside chance of winning. There is plenty of time remaining and the pitch is still playing well,' he said as the West Indians took up the challenge of scoring more runs in the fourth innings to win a Test than any team in history. The only occasions when a team had scored more than 400 to win involved India's 406 against the West Indies at Trinidad in 1975-76 and Australia's 404 against England at Headingley in 1948. The West Indies' 536 in the second innings of the previous Test doubtless made Border nervous.

DAY FOUR

Border, who equalled Sunil Gavaskar's record 125 Tests in this match, celebrated the end of a long series by leading Australia to a 157 run victory on the fourth day to reduce the series loss margin to 2-1. All the Australian bowlers chimed in with a wicket in a team performance while the West Indian batsmen tumbled as they went for the victory target with unrelenting aggression.

Greenidge and Haynes began in a whirlwind run-a-minute partnership of 76 which threatened to enable the West Indies to rewrite the record books. They hit hard and often on the super pitch and the Australians rarely beat the bat, further deflating their enthusiasm. But luck smiled on the Australians and frowned on Haynes when the opener was dismissed in a most unfortunate way. Greenidge thumped a straight drive off Hughes, only for the bowler to deflect the ball into the stumps. Haynes was backing up too far and was run out for 33, much to the relief and delight of the Australians. But another unnecessary incident occurred when Haynes and McDermott insisted on having a parting exchange when nothing needed to be said following such a clear-cut run-out.

Desmond Haynes is unluckily run out from the hand of Merv Hughes to give Australia a needed break in the Windies' second innings.

Greenidge also was the victim of a run-out, this time by almost the length of the pitch. He was in control with 43 off 73 deliveries with six boundaries and a six when he clipped a delivery to Boon at square leg and set off for a single. Richardson wasn't interested as he watched Boon stop and then gather the ball but obviously Greenidge didn't hear his negative response. The veteran opener didn't even attempt to beat Boon's return to Healy but he emulated Haynes with a farewell chat with a couple of the fieldsmen before leaving the ground. The Australians had both openers back in the pavilion by virtue of run-outs with only 92 runs on the board; even so Richardson and Hooper carried on with the aggressive approach. Richardson, who had shown throughout the series that he was capable of turning a match on its head with breathtakingly swift scoring, helped himself to five boundaries and a six to rattle to 41 off 70 deliveries, forcing Border to reassess the situation. He introduced Mark Waugh, the man with an uncanny knack of breaking a partnership, and the medium-pacer struck in his first over when Richardson lofted a cover drive to covers where Jones held another brilliant catch.

The situation was ripe for Richards to provide a fairytale end to his Test career in Antigua and the West Indies when he strode to the crease at 3 for 142, but Border was destined for the honours on this occasion. Richards attempted to loft an on-drive from Border's floated delivery and directed the ball straight to Alderman before mustering a sense of dignity to walk from his beloved ground. The sparse crowd gave him a fitting ovation for his contribution to cricket for his country, and a special thanks from Antigua, the tiny island Richards put on the map of world cricket.

After 35 runs in a mixture of careful defence and outgoing blows, Hooper fell to spinner Peter Taylor and McDermott trapped Dujon lbw for only four to send the West Indian hopes plummeting at 6 for 193. Logie and Marshall weren't in the mood to surrender and they took the long handle to the attack, particularly Border and Alderman, to boost the total to 271 by drinks in the final session. Marshall showed all the batting skills which made him one of the world's best all-rounders of the past decade and he reached his half-century off only 63 deliveries with five boundaries and two sixes. The milestone demanded another performance from Gravy, who once again was allowed onto the playing arena by unthinking staff. Gravy strutted around Marshall for a considerable period, despite the obvious annoyance of the batsman, before holding up play sufficiently to incur the displeasure of all the players. His intrusion broke Marshall's concentration and he was out next ball when Hughes trapped him leg before wicket. That sparked a sudden death end to the innings, the Test and the series. Ambrose ran himself out by heading for a single and then having no chance of beating a smart return from Jones at backward point to Healy. He departed for a duck and two deliveries later so did Walsh,

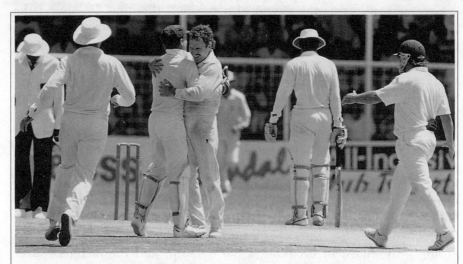

Wicketkeeper Ian Healy embraces Border after the important break.

caught by the wicketkeeper off the tireless Hughes. The West Indies lost 3-0 in an over and Alderman wrapped up the innings when he trapped Logie lbw for a valiant 61 in almost three hours. That was Alderman's only wicket of a personally disappointing Test tour and he suggested the following day that he would seriously consider retirement. The swing and seam bowler, so much the hero in two historic Ashes campaigns and the only bowler to boast two hauls of more than 40 wickets in Ashes series, endured a difficult tour. He was ill early on and despite fitness work he didn't recapture the zip of earlier years. He was a yard slower than a season ago and found no joy in the conditions in the West Indies where the wickets didn't suit and the ball didn't swing. He put up with many jokes about his trip, including the nickname 'Terry the tourist', but behind the smiling exterior he was bitterly disappointed he hadn't shown the West Indian public what a fine bowler he was. In two tours to the Caribbean he finished with only four Tests, five wickets and an average of 94.20.

Clyde Walcott, the chairman of the West Indies Cricket Board of Control, took the opportunity at the post-Test presentations to call for a return of greater sportsmanship and spirit in the game while Border and Richards also called an end to the 'bad blood' in the Test arena. 'I would sincerely hope that the cricketers and administrators could bring the game back to what it was in terms of on-field behaviour and spirit,' Walcott said. The plea from one of the famous three 'W's' of the 1950s was genuine if ironic given, as the country's leading administrator, he had the power in his own hands to do something about it but sidestepped that very week in the Richards upheaval. Walcott, 65, scored an historic 827 runs at 82.70 in Australia's first tour of the Caribbean, including 126 and 110 at Port of

Spain followed by 155 and 110 at Kingston. He was part of the calypso cricket era when fun was essential, but he became an integral part of the transformation of the chumps-to-champs era in the 1970s. He suggested on several occasions during the tour that he fervently wished that teams would play to win while enjoying the game as much as he did those many years ago and his final, public message gave hope of a direct input into ensuring it.

Richards acknowledged the unnecessary venom in the series but remained in many respects unrepentant. 'It seems to be not just what happened in this series,' Richards said.

It seems to be bad blood in cricket everywhere today. We must regain the respect for the game and realise that no individual is bigger than this game of cricket. The sooner something is done the better, because I find that certain people get away with things and others don't. I am not going to make this a colour or race thing, but I do say that some people get more flak than others and that the whole thing must be brushed up before too long to make this wonderful game we respect and love so much better.

Border was matter-of-fact about the behaviour in the series but ensured the West Indies took as much responsibility as the Australians for the on-field misconduct.

West Indies pace attack (left to right) Courtney Walsh, Patrick Patterson, Curtly Ambrose and Malcolm Marshall celebrate the series win.

I am not saying it is healthy or essential, but it is the way the game is played these days. It is not a waltz in the park any more. We are not the only ones who do it but we are more up-front in our attitude. I read about the Ugly Aussies but we are not Robinson Crusoe, the only man on the island. The problem is the way some people are playing the game. I play it hard and I don't go in for personal abuse. But I know that a couple of our players have had personality clashes with the West Indians. We were determined not to back down. The West Indians are an arrogant and aggressive team and they have every right to be. So we had two aggressive sides playing against each other and you must expect a few skirmishes. When those things happen I feel it is the ultimate respect because if one side is beating the hell out of the other there are few dramas. But if you are sticking them as much as they are sticking you, that's when it becomes aggressive.

The Australian skipper was disappointed with suggestions that the team had reverted to the Ugly Aussie image.

The teams didn't get on very well but the West Indians were not choir boys. Some teams mistake our aggression for something else, especially these guys. We recognise that they are the number one side and we are the challengers but if you take a backward step they will run all over you. We stood our ground and fought fire with fire and if they didn't like that it is their problem. We are not that fussed. They don't make any particular effort to get to know our players or to get on, so that's it.

The final word perhaps should be left to Rudi Webster, popularly known as the 'witch doctor from the Windies' in cricket and football circles in Australia. Earlier in the series he predicted an evil spirit would descend on world cricket when Australia returns to the top. The mental motivator, manager of the West Indies team in the World Series days in the late 1970s and then team psychologist until two years ago, believes Australia will dominate the game this decade. 'I don't see anyone coming near to them for a very long time,' he said as he canvassed the rise of the Australians and the inevitable decline of the West Indians. 'Once the Australians get back on top, and with the motivation and reserves they have which will drift through the Sheffield Shield and grade teams, they will be just as dominant as the West Indians have been for the past 15 years.'

Webster, who knows the Australian character extremely well after 17 years in Melbourne and experience with champion Australian Rules clubs Hawthorn, Essendon, Carlton, Richmond and Melbourne as well as his cricket commitments, sensed that the Australians are ready to regain the psychological superiority which totally demoralised every opponent for much of the history of the game.

Australians are very tough people and they don't like losing. Now they have started to win again, after so many dramas with World Series Cricket, the retirement of senior players and divisions with South Africa, I know it is only a matter of time before the qualities of the Australians will come through and make everybody pay dearly. Australia now is something about where the West Indians were a decade ago. They are excelling at things while the West Indians are falling away.

Webster, currently a consultant and adviser to the Barbadian Prime Minister, considered the nature of the Australian character would be a difficult obstacle for other teams during the 1990s.

I know the Australians don't like to lose and to become world champions is the strongest possible motivation, and once achieved, the title won't be lost without a great fight. The Australians have excelled in the three areas which were the strength of the West Indians — discipline, the ability to cope with pressure and a team spirit and will to win which will not be easily suppressed.

He dreaded the day when Australia regained its aggressive and irrepressible dominance. And the time was coming fast, he suggested. The Aussie toughness he came to appreciate so well is easily recognisable to his trained eye. And he doesn't like what he sees in this current Australian team which has many players capable of establishing a decade of dominance.

The best way to confirm Webster's fears is to look at the efforts of the Australians in this series, with an eye to the future.

Mark Taylor and twins Mark and Steve Waugh are three batsmen with a long time left at Test level; Dean Jones and David Boon now are veterans with considerable time remaining and Geoff Marsh and Allan Border have a few years left in them if they desire. And at home there is a host of young batting talent crying out for a chance.

Craig McDermott is the fast bowler of the future while Merv Hughes continues to give gallant support. The return of Bruce Reid would be a bonus while again there are many youngsters waiting for an

Craig McDermott attempting to windsurf in the Windies.

195

Test celebrations at last, with champagne and Red Stripe.

opportunity. Wicketkeeper Ian Healy is a really tough character, in many ways in the mould of Rod Marsh, and he is accepted by his peers as one of the big improvers in the Test arena in the past couple of years.

The youngsters, with so much desire to make it in the big time, surely will have opportunities to take the places of several of the tourists. The international days of pacemen Terry Alderman and Mike Whitney are numbered, while Mike Veletta's post as the permanent stand-by is up for grabs. The Australians also require a spinner of quality to put the icing on the cake, and the leg-spin of Adrian Tucker and Peter McIntyre must be encouraged.

'When I see all the young players scoring runs and taking wickets in Australia and realise they couldn't even make this touring team, I am even more convinced that Australia will be the dominant force in cricket for a long, long time,' Webster said.

And that was it. The teams went their separate ways almost immediately after the game. The West Indians booked out of the hotel early next day to prepare for the tour of England. The Australians whooped it up at a spectacular beach party organised by Ian McDonald and his tour group before they left the following day for beautiful Bermuda. Within a couple of days the West Indies seemed little more than a dream-cum-nightmare in very weary minds.

STATISTICS

ONE-DAY INTERNATIONALS

First Match
26 February, Sabina Park, Kingston, Jamaica. Australia won toss and batted. 12th man: M. Taylor (A) and P. Simmons (WI). Umpires D. Archer and S. Bucknor.

AUSTRALIA

	Runs	Mins	4s/6s	Balls
D. Boon b Walsh	34	81	2	70
G. Marsh run out (Hooper)	26	101	3	64
D. Jones not out	88	129	6	98
A. Border b Hooper	8	20	1	10
M. Waugh b Ambrose	67	78	7	61
S. Waugh not out	6	10	-	8
Extras (7 lb, 3 w, 5 nb)	15			
Four wickets for	244			

Fall: 59, 73, 98, 234.
Bowling: Ambrose 9-1-46-1; Gray 10-0-53-0; Marshall 6-0-27-0; Walsh 7-1-30-1; Hooper 10-1-44-1; Richards 8-0-37-0.
Innings time: 211 minutes. Overs 50.

WEST INDIES

	Runs	Mins	4s/6s	Balls
D. Haynes c Healy b McDermott	17	47	3	28
G. Greenidge b S. Waugh	19	76	2	75
R. Richardson c Jones b McDermott	64	129	5*	66
C. Hooper lbw S. Waugh	6	18	-	12
V. Richards b P. Taylor	18	13	3	18
G. Logie c S. Waugh b M. Waugh	65	57	7	67
M. Marshall run out (P. Taylor)	1	2	-	1
J. Dujon c Border b McDermott	1	8	-	3
A. Gray c Healy b McDermott	2	12	-	6
C. Ambrose lbw P. Taylor	0	5	-	5
C. Walsh not out	1	5	-	2
Extras (2 b, 6 lb, 4 nb, 3 w)	15			
Total	209			

Fall: 33, 48, 68, 95, 190, 191, 206, 206, 207, 209.
Bowling: McDermott 8.5-0-34-4; Reid 7-2-33-0; Whitney 7-1-16-0; S. Waugh 7-1-32-2; P. Taylor 9-1-48-2; M. Waugh 7-0-38-1.
Innings time: 190 minutes. Overs 45.4.
* Richardson hit a six.
Australia won by 35 runs.
Man of the match: D. Jones.

Second Match

9 March, Queens Park Oval, Port of Spain, Trinidad. West Indies won toss and sent Australia in. 12th man: M. Taylor (A) and G. Greenidge (WI). Umpires C. Cumberbatch and L. Barker.

AUSTRALIA

	Runs	Mins	4s/6s	Balls
D. Boon c Hooper b Moseley	5	12	1	9
G. Marsh c Hooper b Gray	23	84	1	41
D. Jones b Gray	64	113	9	76
A. Border c Dujon b Gray	0	1	-	1
M. Waugh b Simmons	16	21	1*	17
S. Waugh b Gray	26	29	3	30
I. Healy not out	13	33	1	18
P. Taylor c & b Gray	1	10	-	8
C. McDermott b Ambrose	1	2	-	2
M. Whitney c Hooper b Gray	0	9	-	7
Extras (2 b, 7 lb, 7 w, 7 nb)	23			
Nine wickets for	172			

Fall: 9, 84, 84, 106, 141, 161, 167, 168, 172.
Bowling: Ambrose 8-2-17-1; Moseley 5-0-22-1; Marshall 6-0-37-0; Gray 9-0-50-6; Hooper 3-0-18-0; Richards 1-0-4-0; Simmons 2-0-15-1.
Innings time: 161 minutes. Overs 34.
* M. Waugh hit a six.

WEST INDIES

	Runs	Mins	4s/6s	Balls
D. Haynes c Healy b Whitney	45	82	7	62
P. Simmons c Healy b Reid	13	11	1*	16
R. Richardson c S. Waugh b McDermott	5	29	1	17
C. Hooper c Healy b Whitney	3	11	-	9
V. Richards c Marsh b Whitney	27	58	1*	37
G. Logie run out (Boon/Whitney)	7	13	-	12
J. Dujon b McDermott	7	24	-	13
M. Marshall c Boon b McDermott	5	26	-	17
E. Moseley c P. Taylor b M. Waugh	2	6	-	4
C. Ambrose c P. Taylor b M. Waugh	7	9	-	6
A. Gray not out	0	3	-	2
Extras (2 lb, 4 nb)	6			
Total	127			

Fall: 14, 47, 52, 78, 90, 112, 113, 116, 126, 127.
Bowling: Reid 5-0-25-1; McDermott 7.1-0-29-3; Whitney 9-0-41-3; S. Waugh 8-0-24-0; M. Waugh 2-0-6-2.
Innings time: 143 minutes. Overs 31.1.
* P. Simmons and V. Richards both hit a six.
Australia won by 45 runs.
Man of the match: A. Gray.

Third Match
10 March, Queens Park Oval, Kingston, Jamaica. Australia won toss and batted.
12th man: G. Matthews (A) and M. Marshall (WI). Umpires C. Cumberbatch and L.
Barker.

AUSTRALIA

	Runs	Mins	4s/6s	Balls
G. Marsh b Gray	81	173	8	107
M. Taylor c Haynes b Ambrose	3	16	-	11
D. Jones c Richards b Gray	36	67	4*	49
M. Waugh b Simmons	17	24	-	23
A. Border c Dujon b Patterson	22	40	2	33
S. Waugh b Ambrose	23	47	-	30
I. Healy not out	33	42	3	23
P. Taylor b Ambrose	2	11	-	7
C. McDermott not out	3	3	-	3
Extras (2 b, 10 lb, 9 w, 4 nb)	25			
Seven wickets for	245			

Fall: 13, 82, 116, 165, 191, 225, 239.
Bowling: Ambrose 10-1-37-3; Patterson 9-0-52-1; Gray 10-0-59-2; Simmons 10-0-35-1; Hooper 10-0-50-0.
Innings time: 216 minutes. Overs 49.
* Jones hit a six.

WEST INDIES

	Runs	Mins	4s/6s	Balls
P. Simmons c Healy b Reid	0	3	-	3
D. Haynes b S. Waugh	16	65	1	38
R. Richardson c Border b M. Waugh	90	108	14	94
G. Greenidge not out	40	71	2*	50
G. Logie not out	24	24	5	21
Extras (1 b, 5 lb, 3 w, 2 nb)	11			
Three wickets for	181			

Fall: 3, 72, 132.
Bowling: Reid 7-0-28-1; McDermott 5-0-21-0; S. Waugh 7-0-39-1; P. Taylor 2-0-17-0; Whitney 7-0-38-0; M. Waugh 5.3-0-32-1.
Innings time: 137 minutes. Overs 33.3.
* Greenidge hit a six.
West Indies won on a superior run rate.
Man of the match: R. Richardson.

Fourth Match

13 March, Kensington Oval, Barbados. Australia won toss and batted. 12th man: G.
Matthews (A) and A. Gray (WI). Umpires: D. Archer and L. Barker.

AUSTRALIA

	Runs	Mins	4s/6s	Balls
M. Taylor c Dujon b Ambrose	5	30	-	25
G. Marsh b Ambrose	113	202	8*	140
D. Jones c Walsh b Marshall	7	14	-*	8
A. Border c Ambrose b Simmons	79	95	7*	87
M. Waugh run out (Ambrose)	49	53	1	31
S. Waugh lbw Ambrose	5	10	-	7
I. Healy not out	6	8	-	6
C. McDermott not out	1	4	-	1
Extras (2 b, 7 lb, 4 w, 5 nb)	18			
Six wickets for	283			

Fall: 19, 27, 173, 260, 271, 276.
Bowling: Ambrose 10-1-38-3; Marshall 10-1-67-1; Walsh 10-0-46-0; Simmons 6-
0-37-0; Richards 4-0-29-0; Hooper 10-0-57-1.
Innings time: 216 minutes. Overs 50.
* Marsh hit three sixes, Jones a six and Border two sixes and a five.

WEST INDIES

	Runs	Mins	4s/6s	Balls
P. Simmons b McDermott	23	34	2	24
D. Haynes b Reid	22	39	3	25
R. Richardson c McDermott b Whitney	25	42	3	23
G. Greenidge lbw S. Waugh	17	43	1*	25
V. Richards c & b S. Waugh	20	27	2	27
G. Logie c M. Taylor b M. Waugh	37	69	2	51
C. Hooper c M. Waugh b P. Taylor	18	29	-	23
J. Dujon c P. Taylor b M. Waugh	39	58	4	41
M. Marshall c Whitney b McDermott	19	28	2	28
C. Ambrose c & b M. Waugh	12	15	1	10
C. Walsh not out	4	6	-	5
Extras (3 nb, 6 lb, 1 w)	10			
Total	246			

Fall: 39, 49, 89, 95, 118, 158, 177, 226, 241, 246.
Bowling: Reid 7-0-52-1; McDermott 8-0-40-2; S. Waugh 7-0-25-2; Whitney 10-1-
39-1; P. Taylor 8-0-50-1; M. Waugh 7-0-34-3.
Innings time: 195 minutes. Overs 47.
* Greenidge hit a six.
Australia won by 37 runs.
Man of the match: G. Marsh.

Final Match

20 March, Bourda, Guyana. West Indies won toss and batted. 12th man: M. Taylor
(A) and C. Lambert (WI). Umpires: C. Cumberbatch and C. Duncan.

WEST INDIES

	Runs	Mins	4s/6s	Balls
P. Simmons c Hughes b P. Taylor	34	70	7	51
D. Haynes lbw P. Taylor	58	94	11	67
R. Richardson c Healy b Hughes	94	112	11*	88
G. Greenidge run out (M. Waugh)	6	24	-	13
V. Richards c Whitney b M. Waugh	10	9	1	12
G. Logie b McDermott	17	33	2	22
C. Hooper c P. Taylor b McDermott	10	24	1	15
J. Dujon b Hughes	2	11	1	6
A. Gray c Border by McDermott	6	10	1	6
C. Walsh b Hughes	2	11	-	6
P. Patterson not out	1	5	-	3
Extras (2 nb, 8 lb, 1 w)	11			
Total	251			

Fall: 85; 115, 136, 155, 217, 237, 239, 246, 248, 251.
Bowling: McDermott 10-0-29-3; Hughes 9.5-0-33-3; S. Waugh 3-0-33-0; Whitney
9-0-46-0; P. Taylor 10-0-45-2; M. Waugh 6-0-36-1; Border 2-0-21-0.
Innings time: 210 minutes. Overs 49.5.
* Richardson hit a six.

AUSTRALIA

	Runs	Mins	4s/6s	Balls
G. Marsh not out	106	216	8	158
D. Boon b Patterson	9	21	-	18
D. Jones run out (Gray)	11	21	1	15
A. Border c Dujon b Walsh	60	97	5*	61
M. Waugh stp Dujon b Hooper	7	19	-	13
S. Waugh not out	26	54	1	38
Extras (4 b, 4 lb, 11 w, 14 nb)	33			
Four wickets for	252			

Fall: 12, 37, 161, 181.
Bowling: Patterson 6.3-0-34-1; Gray 8-0-44-0; Walsh 10-0-54-1; Simmons 10-0-
53-0; Hooper 10-0-45-1; Richards 4-0-14-0.
Innings time: 216 minutes. Overs 48.3.
* Border hit two sixes.
Australia won by six wickets.
Man of the match: G. Marsh.
Australia won the series 4-1.

ONE-DAY INTERNATIONAL AVERAGES

Australian Batting

Player	M	I	NO	H/S	Runs	Ave
G. Marsh	5	5	-	113	349	87.25
D. Jones	5	5	1	88*	206	51.50
A. Border	5	5	-	79	169	33.80
M. Waugh	5	5	-	49	156	31.20
S. Waugh	5	5	2	26*	86	28.67
D. Boon	3	3	-	34	48	16.00
C. McDermott	5	3	2	3*	5	5.00
M. Taylor	2	2	-	5	8	4.00
P. Taylor	5	2	-	2	3	1.50
I. Healy	5	3	3	33*	52	—
M. Whitney	5	2	-	0	0	—
B. Reid	4	-	-	-	-	—
M. Hughes	1	-	-	-	-	—

Australian Bowling

Bowler	O	M	R	Wkts	Ave
M. Hughes	9.5	0	33	3	11.00
C. McDermott	39.0	0	153	12	12.75
M. Waugh	27.3	0	146	8	18.25
S. Waugh	32.0	1	153	5	30.60
P. Taylor	29.0	1	160	5	32.00
M. Whitney	42.0	2	180	4	45.00
B. Reid	26.0	2	138	3	46.00
A. Border	2.0	0	21	0	—

West Indies Batting

Player	M	I	NO	H/S	Runs	Ave
R. Richardson	5	5	-	94	278	55.60
G. Logie	5	5	1	65	150	37.50
D. Haynes	5	5	-	58	158	31.60
G. Greenidge	4	4	1	40*	82	27.33
V. Richards	5	4	-	27	75	18.75
P. Simmons	4	4	-	34	70	17.50
J. Dujon	5	4	-	39	49	12.25
C. Hooper	5	4	-	18	37	9.25
M. Marshall	3	3	-	19	25	8.33
C. Walsh	3	3	2	4*	7	7.00
C. Ambrose	4	3	-	12	19	6.33
A. Gray	4	3	1	6	8	4.00
E. Moseley	1	1	-	2	2	2.00
P. Patterson	2	1	1	1*	1	—

West Indies Bowling

Bowler	O	M	R	Wkts	Ave
C. Ambrose	37	5	138	8	17.25
E. Moseley	5	0	22	1	22.00
A. Gray	37	0	206	8	25.75
P. Patterson	15.3	0	86	2	43.00
C. Walsh	27	1	130	2	65.00
P. Simmons	28	0	140	2	70.00
C. Hooper	43	1	214	3	71.33
M. Marshall	22	1	131	1	131.00
V. Richards	17	0	82	0	—

FIRST TEST

1, 2, 3, 5, 6 March. Sabina Park, Kingston, Jamaica. West Indies won toss. 12th man: B. Reid (A), B. Lara (WI). Umpires: D. Archer and S. Bucknor.

West Indies First Innings

	Runs	Mins	4s/6s	Balls
G. Greenidge c & b McDermott	27	134	3	80
D. Haynes b McDermott	8	33	-	21
R. Richardson c Healy b Hughes	15	36	3	27
C. Hooper c Marsh b Hughes	0	10	-	6
V. Richards c Hughes b McDermott	11	25	2	21
G. Logie not out	77	167	12	110
J. Dujon c Marsh b Hughes	59	210	7	166
M. Marshall lbw McDermott	0	1	-	1
C. Ambrose c & b M. Waugh	33	72	6	47
C. Walsh lbw McDermott	10	26	-	14
P. Patterson b Hughes	4	33	-	20
Extras (6 lb, 1 w, 13 nb)	20			
Total	264			

Fall: 33, 37, 57, 68, 75, 75, 144, 166, 234, 264.
Bowling: McDermott 23-3-80-5; Whitney 21-4-58-0; Hughes 21.3-4-67-4; Matthews 11-2-28-0; M. Waugh 6-1-25-1.
Innings time: 379 minutes. Overs 82.3.

Australia First Innings

	Runs	Mins	4s/6s	Balls
G. Marsh c Dujon b Ambrose	69	198	10	117
M. Taylor c Hooper b Patterson	58	237	3	151
D. Boon not out	109	385	9	243
A. Border c Dujon b Ambrose	31	98	4	72
D. Jones c & b Hooper	0	3	-	2
M. Waugh lbw Marshall	39	146	3	90
G. Matthews c Dujon b Patterson	10	57	1	27
I. Healy lbw Walsh	0	6	-	4
C. McDermott b Patterson	1	17	-	16
M. Hughes c Hooper b Patterson	0	1	-	1
M. Whitney b Patterson	2	13	-	8
Extras (23 lb, 4 b, 4 w, 21 nb)	52			
Total	371			

Fall: 139, 159, 227, 228, 329, 357, 358, 365, 365, 371.
Bowling: Ambrose 30-3-94-2; Patterson 24-1-83-5: Marshall 22-3-57-1; Walsh 23-4-73-1; Hooper 21-7-37-1.
Innings time: 582 minutes. Overs 120.

West Indies Second Innings

	Runs	Mins	4s/6s	Balls
G. Greenidge c Healy b McDermott	35	136	5*	89
D. Haynes c Healy b McDermott	84	169	14	128
R. Richardson not out	104	318	15	233
C. Hooper b McDermott	31	102	3	80
V. Richards not out	52	183	5*	147
Extras (15 b, 6 lb, 6 nb, 1 w)	28			
Three wickets (dec) for	334			

Fall: 118, 134, 216.

Bowling: McDermott 24-10-48-3; Whitney 17-3-55-0; Hughes 22-5-79-0; Matthews 25-2-90-0; Border 10-3-21-0; M. Waugh 13-6-20-0.
Innings time: 455 minutes. Overs 111.
*Greenidge hit a six, Richards two sixes.
Man of the match: David Boon and Gus Logie.
Draw.

SECOND TEST

23, 24, 25, 27, 28 March. Bourda, Georgetown, Guyana. Australia won toss. 12th man: S. Waugh (A), B. Lara (WI). Umpires: C. Cumberbatch and C. Duncan.

Australia First Innings

	Runs	Mins	4s/6s	Balls
M. Taylor lbw Patterson	0	10	-	17
G. Marsh c Hooper b Patterson	94	325	12	201
D. Boon c Dujon b Marshall	7	56	1	31
A. Border b Marshall	47	148	4	88
D. Jones b Marshall	34	170	4	93
M. Waugh c Dujon b Patterson	71	231	7	145
G. Matthews c Dujon b Ambrose	1	6	-	4
I. Healy run out (sub Harper)	53	174	4	108
C. McDermott lbw Patterson	1	10	-	7
M. Hughes b Ambrose	0	18	-	11
M. Whitney not out	1	11	-	5
Extras (6 b, 8 lb, 2 w, 23 nb)	39			
Total	348			

Fall: 3, 24, 124, 188, 237, 238, 339, 346, 346, 348.
Bowling: Ambrose 31.4-9-64-2; Patterson 24-1-80-4; Walsh 24-2-81-0; Marshall 23-3-67-3; Hooper 13-3-37-0; Richards 1-0-5-0.
Innings time: 588 minutes. Overs 116.4.

West Indies First Innings

	Runs	Mins	4s/6s	Balls
D. Haynes c M. Waugh b Border	111	318	17	211
G. Greenidge lbw McDermott	2	12	-	9
R. Richardson lbw McDermott	182	344	26*	242
C. Hooper c M. Waugh b Matthews	62	149	8	114
V. Richards b Matthews	50	117	4*	68
G. Logie c Healy b Border	54	117	8	76
J. Dujon lbw Border	29	104	4	85
M. Marshall not out	22	72	2	48
C. Ambrose b Border	0	1	-	1
C. Walsh b Border	1	8	-	5
P. Patterson lbw Matthews	15	54	3	57
Extras (5 b, 13 lb, 23 nb)	41			
Total	569			

Fall: 10, 307, 353, 443, 444, 529, 530, 530, 532, 569.
Bowling: McDermott 36-3-114-2; Whitney 28-4-103-0; Matthews 37.5-6-155-3; Hughes 20-4-93-0; M. Waugh 2-0-18-0; Border 30-11-68-5.
Innings time: 654 minutes. Overs 153.5.
*Richardson hit two sixes, Richards three sixes.

Australia Second Innings

	Runs	Mins	4s/6s	Balls
G. Marsh b Walsh	22	125	3	61
M. Taylor lbw Ambrose	15	52	1	45
D. Boon c Dujon b Marshall	2	24	-	17
A. Border c Dujon b Marshall	34	209	3	131
D. Jones run out (sub Harper)	3	10	-	7
M. Waugh c Richards b Ambrose	31	92	4	75
G. Matthews c Dujon b Ambrose	16	63	1	47
I. Healy run out (Greenidge/Dujon)	47	150	4	120
C. McDermott c Dujon b Patterson	4	41	-	22
M. Hughes c Patterson b Walsh	21	115	4	65
M. Whitney not out	0	14	-	12
Extras (17 b, 6 lb, 2 w, 28 nb)	53			
Total	248			

Fall: 32, 43, 67, 73, 130, 161, 172, 187, 241, 248.
Bowling: Ambrose 24-5-45-2; Patterson 14-5-46-1; Walsh 23-4-55-2; Marshall 15-2-31-3; Hooper 18-6-35-0; Richards 4-2-13-0.
Innings time: 457 minutes. Overs 98.

West Indies Second Innings

	Runs	Mins	4s/6s	Balls
G. Greenidge not out	5	37	1	21
D. Haynes not out	23	37	4	27
Extras (1 b, 2 nb)	3			
No wicket for	31			

Bowling: McDermott 4-1-10-0; Hughes 3.5-0-19-0.
Innings time 37 minutes. Overs 7.5.
Man of the match: Richie Richardson.
West Indies won by 10 wickets.

THIRD TEST

5, 6, 8, 9, 10 April. Queens Park Oval, Port of Spain, Trinidad. West Indies won toss. 12th man: P. Taylor (A), B. Lara (WI). Umpires: D. Archer and L. Barker.

Australia First Innings

	Runs	Mins	4s/6s	Balls
G. Marsh c Hooper b Ambrose	10	38	1	27
M. Taylor c Walsh b Marshall	61	241	9	147
D. Boon c Logie b Patterson	27	173	3	111
A. Border run out (Hooper)	43	222	-	145
D. Jones lbw Patterson	21	123	3	75
M. Waugh lbw Marshall	64	201	3	178
S. Waugh c Dujon b Walsh	26	90	2	54
I. Healy c Dujon b Marshall	9	61	1	31
C. McDermott c Richardson b Patterson	1	5	-	3
M. Hughes lbw Patterson	0	2	-	3
B. Reid not out	0	2	-	0
Extras (6 b, 14 lb 13 nb)	33			
Total	294			

Fall: 24, 93, 116, 174, 210, 268, 293, 294, 294, 294.
Bowling: Ambrose 29-7-51-1; Patterson 26-2-50-4; Marshall 18.1-3-55-3; Walsh 30-9-45-1; Hooper 25-5-73-0.
Innings time: 530 minutes. Overs 128.1.

West Indies First Innings

	Runs	Mins	4s/6s	Balls
G. Greenidge c M. Waugh b Reid	12	25	2	15
D. Haynes b McDermott	1	19	-	15
R. Richardson c Taylor b Hughes	30	92	5	63
C. Hooper lbw Hughes	12	38	2	32
G. Logie c M. Waugh b Hughes	1	14	-	10
V. Richards c S. Waugh b Hughes	2	8	-	6
J. Dujon lbw McDermott	70	250	6	179
M. Marshall c McDermott b Border	12	34	2	28
C. Ambrose c Border b M. Waugh	53	124	6	110
C. Walsh not out	12	76	-	53
P. Patterson b McDermott	0	10	-	5
Extras (6 b, 7 lb, 9 nb)	22			
Total	227			

Fall: 16, 18, 46, 52, 56, 86, 110, 197, 225, 227.
Bowling: McDermott 14.2-2-36-3; Reid 22-0-79-1; Border 19-5-28-1; Hughes 17-5-48-4; S. Waugh 5-0-10-0; M. Waugh 6-2-9-1; Jones 1-0-4-0.
Innings time: 355 minutes. Overs 84.2.

Australia Second Innings

	Runs	Mins	4s/6s	Balls
M. Taylor b Patterson	2	7	-	9
G. Marsh lbw Marshall	12	85	1	49
D. Boon b Walsh	29	97	4	68
D. Jones not out	39	145	3	118
A. Border not out	27	125	3	78
Extras (1 b, 9 lb, 4 nb)	14			
Three wickets (dec) for	123			

Fall: 3, 49, 53.
Bowling: Ambrose 10-4-11-0; Patterson 7-0-27-1; Marshall 10-3-24-1; Walsh 12-6-11-1; Hooper 13-3-38-0; Richardson 1-0-2-0.
Innings time: 232 minutes. Overs 53.
Man of the match: Jeff Dujon.
Draw.

FOURTH TEST

19, 20, 21, 23, 24 April. Kensington Oval, Bridgetown, Barbados. Australia won toss. 12th man: T. Alderman (A), B. Lara (WI). Umpires: D. Archer and L. Barker.

West Indies First Innings

	Runs	Mins	4s/6s	Balls
G. Greenidge c Reid b McDermott	10	42	2	31
D. Haynes c M. Waugh b Hughes	28	212	3	134
R. Richardson c Boon b McDermott	1	10	-	9
C. Hooper c Jones b Hughes	0	7	-	6
V. Richards c Hughes b McDermott	32	93	6	64
G. Logie c M. Taylor b Reid	11	42	1	34
J. Dujon c Healy b Hughes	10	26	1	17
M. Marshall c Marsh b Reid	17	39	3	33
C. Ambrose not out	19	56	3	28
C. Walsh c M. Waugh b McDermott	10	23	1	20
P. Patterson c M. Waugh b Hughes	1	2	-	2
Extras (3 lb, 7 nb)	10			
Total	149			

Fall: 17, 21, 22, 72, 89, 96, 108, 125, 148, 149.
Bowling: McDermott 22-7-49-4; Reid 21-8-50-2; Hughes 16.1-2-44-4; S. Waugh 2-0-3-0.
Innings time: 279 minutes. Overs 61.1

Australia First Innings

	Runs	Mins	4s/6s	Balls
M. Taylor lbw Ambrose	26	122	2	82
G. Marsh c Logie b Ambrose	12	55	1	31
D. Boon c Hooper b Marshall	0	4	-	2
A. Border b Marshall	29	119	4	68
D. Jones lbw Marshall	22	71	3	51
M. Waugh not out	20	81	3	33
S. Waugh c Dujon b Patterson	2	5	-	5
I. Healy c Dujon b Walsh	2	17	-	10
M. Hughes c Logie b Walsh	3	22	-	15
C. McDermott b Walsh	2	11	-	10
B. Reid b Walsh	0	9	-	4
Extras (2 lb, 14 nb)	16			
Total	134			

Fall: 24, 27, 59, 95, 97, 100, 106, 121, 127, 134.
Bowling: Ambrose 16-5-36-2; Patterson 13-6-22-1; Marshall 16-1-60-3; Walsh 5.1-1-14-4.
Innings time: 266 minutes. Overs 50.1.

West Indies Second Innings

	Runs	Mins	4s/6s	Balls
G. Greenidge lbw Hughes	226	677	32	480
D. Haynes c Healy b M. Waugh	40	201	3	116
M. Marshall c Healy b McDermott	15	60	2	32
R. Richardson lbw M. Waugh	99	243	15	156
C. Hooper c Healy b M. Waugh	57	184	6*	111
V. Richards lbw M. Waugh	25	45	4	21
G. Logie not out	33	74	5	50
J. Dujon c M. Waugh b McDermott	4	15	-	13
C. Ambrose b Reid	2	6	-	5
C. Walsh c Marsh b Reid	0	1	-	1
P. Patterson not out	4	15	1	5
Extras (19 lb, 12 nb)	31			
Nine wickets (dec) for	536			

Fall: 129, 153, 352, 452, 470, 512, 522, 525, 525.
Bowling: McDermott 37.3-8-130-2; Reid 30-4-100-2; Hughes 36-6-125-1; S. Waugh 28-6-77-0; M. Waugh 28-6-80-4; Jones 3-1-3-0.
Innings time: 766 minutes. Overs 162.3.
*Hooper hit one six.

Australia Second Innings

	Runs	Mins	4s/6s	Balls
G. Marsh lbw Ambrose	0	1	-	1
M. Taylor lbw Marshall	76	368	7	243
D. Boon b Ambrose	57	186	7	135
A. Border c Dujon b Ambrose	0	8	-	5
M. Hughes c Dujon b Marshall	3	32	-	28
D. Jones b Hooper	37	104	6	66
M. Waugh b Hooper	3	26	-	27
S. Waugh not out	4	21	-	11
I. Healy lbw Marshall	0	4	-	3
C. McDermott c Sub (R. Holder) b Walsh	2	10	-	9
B. Reid b Walsh	0	3	-	1
Extras (3 b, 5 lb, 18 nb)	26			
Total	208			

Fall: 0, 111, 111, 122, 190, 200, 200, 200, 208, 208.
Bowling: Ambrose 19-7-36-3; Patterson 15-3-56-0; Walsh 14.2-3-37-2; Marshall 17-6-35-3; Hooper 19-4-28-2; Richards 3-0-5-0.
Innings time: 388 minutes. Overs 87.2.
Man of the match: Gordon Greenidge.
West Indies won by 343 runs.

FIFTH TEST

27, 28, 29 April, 1 May.Recreation Ground, St John's, Antigua. Australia won toss.
12th man: S. Waugh (A), B. Lara (WI). Umpires: L. Barker and S. Bucknor.

Australia First Innings

	Runs	Mins	4s/6s	Balls
M. Taylor c Dujon b Hooper	59	202	7	123
G. Marsh c Richards b Patterson	6	17	1	8
D. Boon c Greenidge b Ambrose	0	17	-	15
A. Border c Dujon b Hooper	59	192	8	112
D. Jones lbw Marshall	81	188	8*	120
M. Waugh not out	139	307	11*	188
I. Healy c Dujon b Marshall	12	51	1	41
P. Taylor c Dujon b Ambrose	2	21	-	18
M. Hughes b Ambrose	1	13	-	11
C. McDermott c Dujon b Walsh	7	31	1	28
T. Alderman b Walsh	0	2	-	4
Extras (1 b, 12 lb, 6 w, 18 nb)	37			
Total	403			

Fall: 10, 13, 129, 158, 342, 371, 381, 385, 403, 403.
Bowling: Ambrose 30-6-92-3; Patterson 12-1-44-1; Walsh 22-1-54-2; Marshall 22-1-72-2; Hooper 15-2-82-2; Richards 7-0-46-0.
Innings time: 522 minutes. Overs 108.
*Jones hit one six, M. Waugh hit three sixes.

West Indies First Innings

	Runs	Mins	4s/6s	Balls
G. Greenidge lbw McDermott	6	13	-	12
D. Haynes lbw McDermott	84	172	15	119
R. Richardson b McDermott	3	6	-	4
C. Hooper lbw Hughes	2	21	-	11
V. Richards lbw McDermott	0	16	-	7
G. Logie c Jones b P. Taylor	24	78	3	49
J. Dujon c Jones b Hughes	33	81	2*	58
M. Marshall c Healy b M.Waugh	28	69	5	45
C. Ambrose c M. Taylor b Hughes	8	31	1	21
C. Walsh not out	11	25	-	15
P. Patterson b Hughes	2	9	-	6
Extras (2 lb, 11 nb)	13			
Total	214			

Fall: 10, 22, 35, 46, 114, 136, 186, 195, 206, 214.
Bowling: McDermott 15-4-42-4; Alderman 7-0-42-0; Hughes 17-2-65-4; P. Taylor 11-2-40-1; M. Waugh 5-0-23-1.
Innings time: 272 minutes. Overs 55.
*Dujon hit two sixes.

Australia Second Innings

	Runs	Mins	4s/6s	Balls
G. Marsh c Dujon b Ambrose	1	9	-	6
P. Taylor c & b Ambrose	144	361	12	277
I. Healy c Logie b Patterson	32	62	3	43
D. Boon b Walsh	35	143	2	107
A. Border b Walsh	5	36	-	30
D. Jones b Walsh	8	18	1	15
M. Waugh lbw Walsh	0	1	-	1
P. Taylor lbw Marshall	4	66	-	44
M. Hughes c Walsh b Ambrose	13	33	2	16
C. McDermott c Dujon b Marshall	1	13	-	11
T. Alderman not out	0	2	-	2
Extras (11 lb, 7 lb, 4 nb)	22			
Total	265			

Fall: 4, 49, 142, 168, 184, 184, 237, 258, 265, 265.
Bowling: Ambrose 16-1-64-3; Walsh 26-2-56-4; Hooper 27-6-61-0; Patterson 1-0-1-1; Marshall 13.1-3-36-2; Richards 8-0-29-0.
Innings time: 386 minutes. Overs 91.1.

West Indies Second Innings

	Runs	Mins	4s/6s	Balls
G. Greenidge run out (Boon/Healy)	43	115	6*	73
D. Haynes run out (Hughes)	33	94	4	69
R. Richardson c Jones b M. Waugh	41	79	5*	70
C. Hooper c M. Waugh b P. Taylor	35	103	2*	74
V. Richards c Alderman b Border	2	10	-	8
G. Logie lbw Alderman	61	176	10	113
J. Dujon lbw McDermott	4	26	-	20
M. Marshall lbw Hughes	51	65	5*	63
C. Ambrose run out (Jones/Healy)	0	2	-	2
C. Walsh c Healy b Hughes	0	2	-	2
P. Patterson not out	7	21	1	6
Extras (5 b, 7 lb, 8 nb)	20			
Total	297			

Fall: 76, 92, 142, 145, 182, 193, 271, 271, 271, 297.
Bowling: McDermott 17-2-55-1; Alderman 15.4-4-63-1; Hughes 19-5-49-2; P. Taylor 10-0-39-1; Border 15-2-71-1; M. Waugh 5-3-8-1.
Innings time: 365 minutes. Overs 81.4.
*Greenidge, Richardson and Hooper hit one six and Marshall two.
Man of the match: M. Taylor.
Man of the series: R. Richardson.
Australia won by 157 runs.
West Indies won the series 2-1.

AUSTRALIAN TOUR AVERAGES

Batting

Batsman	M	I	NO	HS	Runs	Ave	100	50	Ct/St
M. Taylor	10	14	-	144	777	55.50	3	5	6
M. Waugh	9	12	2	139*	522	52.20	2	2	13
S. Waugh	6	7	2	96*	229	45.80	-	2	1
G. Matthews	4	4	1	95*	122	40.67	-	1	1
A. Border	8	13	2	59	386	35.09	-	1	1
D. Boon	10	14	1	109*	456	35.08	2	2	6
D. Jones	9	12	1	81	358	32.55	-	2	7
G. Marsh	8	13	-	94	264	20.31	-	2	6
P. Taylor	5	6	1	33	89	17.80	-	-	4
I. Healy	7	10	-	53	177	17.70	-	1	15/-
M. Veletta	4	4	-	14	28	7.00	-	-	9/1
M. Hughes	10	13	1	21	77	6.42	-	-	5
C. McDermott	6	9	1	17*	35	4.38	-	-	2
M. Whitney	4	5	2	6	11	3.67	-	-	0
T. Alderman	5	4	2	2	2	1.00	-	-	5
B. Reid	5	5	1	2	3	0.75	-	-	1

Bowling

Bowler	O	M	R	Wkts	Ave	5wi	Best
C. McDermott	209.5	42	608	28	21.71	1	5/80
M. Waugh	93.2	21	271	12	22.58	-	4/80
P. Taylor	158.0	45	382	15	25.47	1	5/37
A. Border	84.0	24	214	8	26.75	1	5/68
M. Hughes	304.5	53	1052	37	28.43	1	5/36
M. Whitney	150.0	28	445	14	31.79	2	6/42
B. Reid	160.1	28	527	16	32.94	-	4/76
T. Alderman	117.4	22	346	9	38.44	1	5/40
G. Matthews	106.5	20	370	8	46.25	-	4/57
S. Waugh	78.0	16	234	3	78.00	-	3/76
D. Jones	4.0	1	9	0	—	-	—

AUSTRALIAN TEST AVERAGES

Batting

Batsman	M	I	NO	HS	Runs	Ave	100	50	Ct/St
M. Waugh	5	8	2	139*	367	61.17	1	2	10
M. Taylor	5	9	-	144	441	49.00	1	4	3
A. Border	5	9	1	59	275	34.38	-	1	1
D. Boon	5	9	1	109*	266	33.25	1	1	1
D. Jones	5	9	1	81	245	30.63	-	1	4
G. Marsh	5	9	-	94	226	25.11	-	2	4
I. Healy	5	8	-	53	155	19.38	-	1	10/-

S. Waugh	2	3	1	26	32	16.00	-	-	1
G. Matthews	2	3	-	16	27	9.00	-	-	-
M. Hughes	5	8	-	21	41	5.13	-	-	2
P. Taylor	1	2	-	4	6	3.00	-	-	-
M. Whitney	2	3	2	2	3	3.00	-	-	-
C. McDermott	5	8	-	7	18	2.25	-	-	2
T. Alderman	1	2	1	0*	0	0.00	-	-	1
B. Reid	2	3	1	0*	0	0.00	-	-	-

Bowling

Bowler	O	M	R	Wkts	Ave	5wi	Best
M. Waugh	65.0	18	183	8	22.88	-	4/80
C. McDermott	192.5	40	564	24	23.50	1	5/80
A. Border	54.0	21	188	8	26.86	1	5/68
M. Hughes	172.3	32	589	19	31.00	-	4/44
P. Taylor	21.0	2	79	2	39.50	-	1/39
B. Reid	73.0	12	229	5	45.80	-	2/50
G. Matthews	73.5	10	273	3	91.00	-	3/155
T. Alderman	22.4	4	105	1	105.00	-	1/63
M. Whitney	66.0	11	216	0	—	-	—
S. Waugh	35.0	6	90	0	—	-	—
D. Jones	4.0	1	9	0	—	-	—

WEST INDIES TEST AVERAGES

Batting

Batsman	M	I	NO	HS	Runs	Ave	100	50	Ct/St
R. Richardson	5	8	1	182	475	67.86	2	1	1
G. Logie	5	7	2	77*	261	52.20	-	3	4
D. Haynes	5	9	1	111	412	51.50	1	2	-
G. Greenidge	5	9	1	226	366	45.75	1	-	1
J. Dujon	5	7	-	70	209	29.86	-	2	23/-
C. Hooper	5	8	-	62	199	24.88	-	2	7
V. Richards	5	8	1	52*	174	24.86	-	2	1
M. Marshall	5	7	1	51	145	24.17	-	1	-
C. Ambrose	5	7	1	53	115	19.17	-	1	1
C. Walsh	5	7	2	12*	44	8.80	-	-	2
P. Patterson	5	7	2	15	33	6.60	-	-	1

Bowling

Bowler	O	M	Runs	Wkts	Ave	5wi	Best
M. Marshall	156.2	25	437	21	20.81	-	3/31
P. Patterson	136.0	19	409	18	22.72	1	5/83
C. Walsh	179.3	32	426	17	25.06	-	4/14
C. Ambrose	205.4	47	493	18	27.39	-	3/36
C. Hooper	151.0	37	391	5	78.20	-	2/28
V. Richards	23.0	2	101	0	—	-	—
R. Richardson	1.0	-	2	0	—	-	—